Flipping Houses For Dummies

A Wiley Brand

2nd Edition

by Ralph R. Roberts with Joe Kraynak

For Dummies
A Wiley Brand

Flipping Houses For Dummies®, 2nd Edition

Published by: **John Wiley & Sons, Inc.,** 111 River Street, Hoboken, NJ 07030-5774, www.wiley.com

For general information on our other products and services, please contact our Customer Care Department within the U.S. at 877-762-2974, outside the U.S. at 317-572-3993, or fax 317-572-4002. For technical support, please visit www.wiley.com/techsupport.

Wiley publishes in a variety of print and electronic formats and by print-on-demand. Some material included with standard print versions of this book may not be included in e-books or in print-on-demand. If this book refers to media such as a CD or DVD that is not included in the version you purchased, you may download this material at http://booksupport.wiley.com. For more information about Wiley products, visit www.wiley.com.

Library of Congress Control Number: 2013954206

ISBN 978-1-118-80163-5 (pbk); ISBN 978-1-118-80159-8 (ebk); ISBN 978-1-80160-4 (ebk)

Manufactured in the United States of America

10 9 8 7 6 5 4

Contents at a Glance

Table of Contents

Introduction

Maybe you know somebody who buys and sells houses and makes as much money on a single transaction as you make in a year. Or perhaps you caught an episode of one of those house-flipping TV shows that demonstrate just how easy it is to buy a house for $250,000, fix it up for another $75,000, and sell it for a half million bucks in a matter of days. Now, you want in on the action. You want your slice of that capitalistic cannoli.

But where do you start? You can't imagine where you'd be able to get your mitts on the cash you'd need to finance a flip. You have no idea where to start looking for undervalued properties, and even if you could find a suitable house to flip, the only experience you have fixing houses is plunging the toilet. Surely you're not qualified to invest in the complicated world of real estate.

Well, it's time to stop all the negative self-talk and start reading *Flipping Houses For Dummies.* I started out with $900 that my grandmother gave me in the early 1970s. From the ripe old age of 19 to the present day, I've flipped one house after another and earned millions of dollars along the way. It wasn't easy. Some of my flips flopped. I didn't profit from every transaction. I did, however, have a plan in place and the sticktoitism (pronounced stick-*to*-it-ism) to successfully execute it. By following through, I was able to succeed, and so can you. (By the way, *sticktoitism* describes the determination and dogged perseverance required to build wealth in real estate. I could use *stick-to-itiveness*, which actually appears in the dictionary, but I like my word better.)

About This Book

Unlike other books, TV shows, and late-night-TV gurus, this book doesn't promise an easy, risk-free way to score quick cash by flipping houses. Instead, it takes an honest look at the practice of flipping houses.

In this book, I reveal what I've learned in more than 40 years of flipping houses and working with buyers, sellers, and other real estate investors and professionals. I show you how to do everything from building a team and securing the cash you need to finance your venture to finding undervalued homes and negotiating the price and terms that improve your chances of selling at a profit. I guide you through making renovation decisions that promise to deliver the most bang for your buck, and I show you how to spruce up a home to draw in more potential buyers.

I don't want to see you get in over your head or blow your entire life savings on a failed real estate investment, so throughout this book I provide plenty of time- and money-saving tips, cautions to help you avoid catastrophe, and sanity checks to keep your projects within budget and on schedule. I steer you clear of risky, unethical, and illegal ventures and encourage you to wade out slowly and remain well within your comfort zone. After you successfully flip a few easy properties, you quickly become aware of when you're ready to take on bigger projects, and by that time, you no longer need my advice.

My goal is to help you decide whether house flipping is for you, and, if it is, I provide you with the tools you need to succeed. Flipping houses can be one of the most rewarding and profitable ways to invest your time and money. This book shows you how to do it right, minimize risks, and maximize your potential profit.

Foolish Assumptions

If you're reading this book, I assume you're a homeowner. I wouldn't buy a car from a car salesman who didn't drive, and I wouldn't buy a house from someone who rents an apartment. When you own your own place, you pick up some street smarts about the value of a home, its emotional effect on people, its value as an investment, and the work required to properly maintain it. If you're not a homeowner, sell this book and put the proceeds toward a down payment on a house. Come back in a couple of years. I'll be waiting for you.

Other foolish assumptions I've made include the following:

- **You're of sound mind and body.** You can be a little kooky and out of shape, but if you can't make rational decisions or talk coherently on the phone, house flipping may not be for you.
- **You're interested in residential, not commercial, property.** Assuming you're new to this house-flipping thing, focus on the type of property you would buy as a homeowner. Later, when you're more experienced, you can venture into the world of commercial real estate.
- **You're prepared to learn from your mistakes (and mine).** I can't guarantee that you'll profit on your first flip, but I can guarantee that you'll make mistakes. Consider them an essential part of your education.

Renovating outside the box

A friend of mine, who's also a real estate agent, encountered some serious code restrictions when he decided to expand his lakefront property. He wanted to level the house and build a new three-story house on the property. Unfortunately, the building codes in the area prohibited the building of any new structures above a certain height. To work around this limitation, my friend decided to keep his old house intact. He raised it up, built two floors below it, and succeeded in creating his three-story home.

By retaining the existing structure and building below it, he created a house that's three times larger than current code allows. When the code was written, this scenario was never even considered.

up or out. Depending on your budget, the size of the yard, and building code restrictions (which you can find out about from your contractor), you may be able to add a dormer or even a second story atop the existing structure or build on to the front, back, or side of the house.

TIP: Older neighborhoods that are currently in the process of a generational shift (younger families moving in) are laboratories for studying ways to expand living quarters. Remain observant, and you can gather a host of ideas on how to build onto an existing structure.

When building onto a house, you have two options — you can build up or you can build out. If the yard is the size of a postage stamp, you have little room to build out. You need to allow sufficient space for the homeowners to walk their pet, hang out, and enjoy a bit of nature. Another option is to build up, either by expanding the attic space with a dormer or raising the roof and adding a second story.

TIP: If your budget allows it and your market demands it, adding a second story can add considerable value to a house. A small ranch house is the perfect candidate. By adding a second story, you essentially double the living space. You can even add a balcony.

Adding a Deck or Patio

Builders often erect houses on beautiful, spacious lots and leave the back or side yard completely undeveloped. Without a deck or patio and a wide door to enable the dwellers easy access to the great outdoors, the yard becomes a wasteland begging for development.

Like attached garages, however, porches are poorly insulated and rarely heated. If you convert a porch into a room, insulate it well, install thermal windows, and add ductwork or baseboard heat to make the room livable year round. For a porch conversion to qualify as a bona fide bedroom, the room must have a closet and its own private access.

Creating a room in the attic

Builders of older homes often built spacious attics for additional storage or to enable the homeowner to add bedrooms later as the family grew. By running electricity up to the attic, installing a staircase, and finishing the walls, you may be able to add a bedroom or two. The most challenging part of the project may be finding a way to add a stairway up to the attic — that vintage pull-down staircase has to go.

If the house has plenty of bedrooms and few other storage areas (like a basement, for instance), think twice about converting the attic into living space. You may be able to clean it up, add lighting, and perhaps even add a floor, but most house hunters like the additional storage space that an attic offers. Base your renovation decisions on the specific property and on market demands.

Deciding whether to finish a basement

A basement that's in pretty good condition is often the perfect prospect for a conversion job, especially if you're starting with a *walkout basement* — a basement that has a door directly to the outside world. By installing drywall or siding, laying carpeting or vinyl flooring, and installing a drop ceiling, you may be able to convert the basement into living space that adds to the square footage of the home and significantly boosts the home's value.

Keep in mind, however, that your municipality may have certain requirements for a basement to be considered living space; for example, the area may need to be heated and have a certain number of outlets per square foot and an emergency exit. Check with your municipality for its requirements. Also keep in mind that having a basement officially designated as living space is likely to increase property taxes. You may be better off simply painting the walls and laying some flooring to enable any buyers to use the space however they want.

Building New Rooms from Scratch

Your options for converting unused areas into living spaces inside a house are limited by its four exterior walls, but that doesn't prohibit you from building

This book was made possible by all the mistakes I've made. Without those mistakes, I'd have little wisdom to impart. The more you take away from the mistakes I made, the fewer mistakes you have to make yourself.

- **You want to flip properties legitimately.** Con artists often flip properties to scam buyers and lenders. I'm not a con artist, and I denounce this type of flipping. By flipping legitimately, you stand to earn much more than a low-life con artist ever will, and you keep your reputation and integrity intact.

Icons Used in This Book

Throughout this book, icons in the margins highlight different types of information that call out for your attention. Here are the icons you'll see and a brief description of each.

I want you to remember everything you read in this book, but if you can't quite do that, then remember the important points flagged with this icon.

When you're buying and fixing up a house, it's easy to get a little carried away and blow your entire budget on garden gnomes. Before you get too carried away, read the text marked with this icon to rein yourself in.

Tips provide insider insight. When you're looking for a better, faster way to do something, check out these tips.

"Whoa!" This icon appears when you need to be extra vigilant or seek professional help before moving forward.

Beyond the Book

In addition to the abundance of information and guidance on flipping houses that I provide in this book, you also get access to even more help and information at dummies.com. Go to `www.dummies.com/cheatsheet/flippinghouses` for a free cheat sheet that accompanies this book. It includes checklists for revamping a quick-flip property and for staging a home and offers tips for minimizing financial risks.

You can also head to `www.dummies.com/extras/flippinghouses` for some free supplemental articles and worksheets that you'll find helpful as you begin your journey flipping houses.

Where to Go from Here

Think of this book as an all-you-can-eat buffet. You can grab a plate, start at the beginning, and read one chapter right after another, or you can dip into any chapter and pile your plate high with the information it contains.

If you're looking for a quick overview of house flipping, check out Chapter 1. Before you even start house hunting, check out Chapter 4 to discover how to build a strong support network and Chapter 5 to find out how to finance your flip — you need cash and plenty of it to flip a house. Chapter 12 helps you determine how much you can afford to pay for a property to increase your odds of walking away with a profit. And the chapters in Part III are indispensable in helping you track down potentially profitable properties and negotiate the purchase. Wherever you choose to start, you'll find plenty of useful information and guidance.

Part I

Laying the Foundation for Successful Flipping

Visit www.dummies.com for free content that helps you learn more and do more.

In this part…

- Get up to speed in a hurry on the process of flipping houses.
- Flip houses the right way and avoid fraudulent flipping schemes.
- Find out whether you have what it takes to flip houses in terms of time, money, and mindset.
- Explore a variety of house-flipping strategies ranging from buy-fix-and-sell to buy-hold-and-lease.
- Devise a plan B to survive a flip that flops.
- Build a dream team of real estate professionals, lenders, and contractors to expedite your flips and cover your back.
- Get your mitts on some cash to finance your flips by using your own and other people's money (OPM).

Chapter 1

Wrapping Your Brain Around the Idea of House Flipping

In This Chapter

- Understanding the concept and challenges of flipping
- Flipping the right way — legally and ethically
- Developing a winning strategy and the right connections
- Surveying money matters and savvy renovations
- Marketing and staging a house properly to maximize your profit

Flipping sounds easy. You can flip a pancake. You can flip a coin. Without too much effort, you can even flip out. Flipping a house, on the other hand, requires a level of knowledge, expertise, and sticktoitism unrivaled by any of these mindless tasks. It requires access to cash, and lots of it. It demands time, energy, vision, attention to detail, and the ability and desire to network with everyone from buyers and sellers to real estate professionals, contractors, and lenders.

In this chapter, I offer a broad overview of what flipping houses is all about. I introduce the overall strategy of flipping houses — buy low, renovate, and sell a property at fair market value to earn a fair market profit. I reveal the difference between flipping the right way — legally and ethically — and flipping the wrong way — ripping off buyers, sellers, and lenders for a quick wad of cash.

REMEMBER

Throughout this chapter, I recommend a strategy that's worked for me during my over-30-year stint as a real estate professional and investor. I've built my approach on a strong foundation of honesty, integrity, dedication, and hard work, and I recommend that you do the same. With a positive mindset, a strong commitment, and the right approach, you stand a much better chance that your first flip won't flop.

Grasping the Concept of Flipping and Its Challenges

In investment circles, the secret to success is cliché — buy low, sell high. This same principle applies to flipping houses. To succeed, you buy a house at 20 percent to 50 percent below market value, repair and renovate the property to make it a more attractive purchase, and then turn around and sell it at market value. That three-step process — buy, fix, and sell — certainly sounds easy enough, but each step carries with it a host of unique challenges, as I point out in the following sections.

TIP

To buy low, you have to be in a position to buy quickly. The trick is to have your financial ducks in a row before you go house hunting. Chapter 5 reveals various ways to finance your flips.

Spotting distressed property . . . and property owners

Homeowners don't exactly line up around the block waiting to sell their homes for less than they're worth. As a house flipper, your job is to hunt for the homes in your area that are *dontwanners,* as in "the owners don't want 'er." These orphan homes usually appear bedraggled. The yard looks like a weedy wasteland, the gutters are hanging off like a pair of old false eyelashes, the paint's peeling, and the interior is completely trashed. These properties are often referred to as *distressed,* and their appearance indicates that their owners are distressed, as well. Their dream home has become a nightmare.

When the homeowners need to shed the burden of home ownership, they may not have the time and resources to make repairs and renovations, place the home on the market, and wait for months or even a year for a buyer to make a reasonable offer. In such cases, they're often willing to sell at a greatly reduced price to a serious investor who has the financial resources to close the deal. How do you discover opportunities like this? In Part II, I point out several techniques for scoping out distressed properties and their distressed owners.

REMEMBER

The average house hunter wants a nice house. When you're flipping houses, you want the ugliest house on the block. To succeed in finding potentially profitable homes, you may need to change your perspective so you can see the beauty in a beast.

Doing your homework

Flipping houses is a risky venture, but you can minimize risk and maximize profit by doing your homework:

- **Research the property.** If you're buying a property in foreclosure, probate, bankruptcy, or a similar situation, you need to research the property carefully to make sure you know what you're about to buy. Research includes a visit to the property and to the register of deeds office to research the title and other key documents. See Chapter 10 for details.
- **Estimate costs of repairs and renovations.** Knowing how much you're probably going to need to spend to make the property market-ready is key to knowing how much you can afford to pay for the property and still earn a profit. In Chapter 11, I explain how to inspect a property with an eye for repairs and renovations and estimate your rehab costs.
- **Calculate and stick to your maximum purchase price.** Before you bid on a property or make an offer, you need to know the most you can pay for the property in order to earn a 20 percent to 30 percent profit. When calculating your maximum purchase price, you need to figure in your desired profit and then subtract costs, including closing costs, renovation expenses, holding costs, agent commissions, and so forth. In Chapter 12, I walk you through the calculations.
- **Negotiate the price and terms in your favor.** At this point, you know the most you can pay for the property to earn a decent profit, but that's probably not what you *want* to pay for the property; you want to pay the least you can to get it. In Chapter 13, you discover various strategies and techniques to negotiate a better price and terms.

Making a few minor (or major) alterations

When you buy a house at a bargain-basement price, it usually requires some tender loving care to make it marketable. In some cases, a thorough cleaning along with a fresh coat of paint (inside and out) and new wall-to-wall carpeting does the trick. In a matter of days or a couple of weeks, and with a small investment, you can often boost the value of a home just by making it *look* brand-new again.

Other houses require more extensive renovations to make them marketable and boost your bottom line. You can transform a two-bedroom house into a three-bedroom house by converting unused attic or porch space into a bedroom; knock out a wall or two to combine the kitchen, dining room, and living room into a great room; install all new windows; or even build a second story. The chapters in Part IV cover everything from quick-flip cosmetic jobs to extensive renovations and provide plenty of tips and cautions to prevent you from sinking money into home improvements that offer little payback.

SANITY CHECK

Avoid the temptation to over-improve a house. You may be able to convert a $100,000 house into a $1 million mansion, but if a buyer wants a $1 million mansion, she buys a house in a neighborhood with $1 million homes. Shoot for making the house you buy competitive with other houses in its price range. Don't go overboard.

Reselling your rehabbed property for big bucks

The old adage of house flipping is that "You make your money when you buy." But you realize your profit only after selling the house. Assuming you purchase the property at the right price, you don't overspend on repairs and renovations, and the housing market remains relatively stable, you should have no trouble selling the house at a profit simply by selling it at or near market value.

TIP

Holding costs (insurance, property taxes, and utilities) can chip away at your profit. I estimate daily holding costs at $100, so for every month that your house lingers on the market, you're out about $3,000. To sell the house quickly at a fair price, set a price that's competitive with the prices of comparable houses in the same neighborhood. If your asking price is too high, it'll cost you.

The chapters in Part V show you how to set an asking price, market the property, and ultimately close the deal.

Flipping Ethically: The Good, the Bad, and the Illegal

In real estate circles, the word *flip* is often construed as just another four-letter word. Utter the "F word" at a real estate conference or seminar and you're likely to spend your lunch break at a cozy table for one. The reason for this cold shoulder from the real estate community is that way back in September 2001, the U.S. Department of Housing and Urban Development (HUD) released FR (Final Rule)-4615 Prohibition of Property Flipping, which made flipping illegal.

So, why am I writing a book that promotes this illegal activity? Because the word *flip* has a double meaning, a split personality, a sunny and a sinister side, as the following sections reveal.

Flipping illegally: Real estate fraud and other scams

Criminal minds have invented countless ways of milking the real estate industry, and one way is to flip houses. This sinister type of house flipping typically relies on some form of fraud — lying or misrepresenting information. In some cases, the con artists hook up with crooked appraisers who artificially inflate home values and then sell overpriced homes to ill-informed buyers.

Another way con artists scam the system through flipping is to build a team of buyers, none of whom intends to own the property for any length of time. They buy homes from one another, increasing the price with each sale. False appraisals or crooked appraisers make the price hikes look legitimate, and corrupt loan officers often expedite the loan-approval process. As the value of the property increases on paper, the amount of equity in the property increases. The final buyer takes out a whopping loan to pay the previous owner and then defaults on the loan. The team splits the proceeds, sticking the lender with the bill and leaving a legacy of foreclosures and vacancies.

WARNING!

The dark side of flipping destroys credit ratings, raises interest rates, and ruins neighborhoods. Over the long haul, it threatens to squash the American dream of home ownership. It's unethical, immoral, and illegal.

Flipping legally: Buy, fix, and sell

Flipping the right way is a perfectly legitimate strategy for making money in real estate. You buy a property below market value, fix it up, and sell it for more than you invested in it. Do it well and you can earn a handsome profit. Make a serious blunder and you suffer a loss. This fix-it-and-flip-it approach has a positive effect on the real estate market. It increases property values, improves neighborhoods, and provides quality housing for those who need it. It's the American way — capitalism at work.

REMEMBER

Throughout this book, I encourage you to flip the right way, and I caution you to avoid the gray areas that can get you into trouble. Flipping the right way enables you to legitimately profit from the system without having to tiptoe through legal minefields. It ensures that you establish the solid reputation you need to flip profitably for however long you want.

Determining Whether You're Ready for Flipping

Although anyone can profit from flipping houses, it's not quite as easy as it looks on TV. Buying a house that's brimming with potential for 20 percent to 50 percent less than you know you can sell it for is a huge challenge in itself, but after you take possession of the property, the real fun begins. Your contractor disappears after collecting your deposit. The landscapers hack through a buried cable. You find out that the septic system needs to be replaced. And the neighborhood association rejects every single one of your planned improvements.

To successfully deal with the unexpected twists and turns you're sure to encounter, you need to have the right stuff, including the following:

- **Time and energy:** Flipping houses requires considerable time and energy for house shopping, lining up financing, scheduling and overseeing repairs and renovations, and more. If you have a day job, plan on working nights and weekends on flipping. If you already feel overwhelmed and overworked, maybe this flipping thing isn't for you.
- **Focus:** Distractions can quickly derail a flip, so you'd better be able to focus in the midst of chaos, especially if you have a full-time job, a spouse, children, and a host of other factors that complicate your days. Without focus, you won't have the attention to detail required for success.
- **Ability to follow instructions:** You don't need to know everything about flipping houses to get started, but you do need to know how to follow instructions, including the instructions I provide in this book.
- **Ability to perform basic math:** Basic math skills (addition, subtraction, multiplication, and division) are essential when you're comparing financing options and crunching numbers to gauge how much profit you can wring out of a house. If you're not good with math, you at least need to know how to use a calculator.
- **Organizational skills:** A large part of flipping houses is about organization. When you're renovating a property, you need to be able to coordinate contractors and material so the work gets done as efficiently as possible. Remember, time is money.
- **People skills:** Being able to work with people and resolve any differences is key in many aspects of flipping, including convincing people to loan you money, negotiating lower prices for property, and managing contractors and work crews. If you prefer working alone to working with others, flipping probably isn't your thing.

- **Sticktoitism:** Flipping houses involves a great deal of failure and disappointment. Those who succeed at it don't give up. If you have sticktoitism, you probably have the perseverance to overcome any limitations you have related to other items on this list.

See Chapter 2 for additional guidance in deciding whether you have what it takes to flip houses.

Devising Your Own Surefire Flipping Strategy

No two investors follow the same flipping strategy. Some investors choose to live in the house they flip, while others find that too stressful. Some flip a house every two years to maximize their tax savings, while others flip a house once every month or two for quick profits. Some fly solo, while others team up with real estate agents. Many investors focus on a niche market, such as foreclosure properties, HUD properties, or For Sale By Owner (FSBO) homes.

REMEMBER

The strategy you ultimately settle on is yours to invent. What's important is that you have a strategy and the system and resources in place to execute it. Before you make an offer on your first house, you should already have the essentials in place:

- Financing not only to purchase the house but also to cover holding costs and the cost of repairs and renovations
- A plan for repairing and renovating the property (such as buying low, applying makeup, and selling high, or living in your flip while you renovate it)
- A realistic estimate of the costs of repairs and renovations and the monthly expenses for holding the property
- A schedule for completing the project
- Reliable contractors who are available to begin working on the property immediately
- A date on which you plan to put the house back on the market

REMEMBER

Flipping a house is like taking a vacation. You have to know your destination before you book your flight. Before you buy a house, know exactly what you're going to do to improve the property, how much the improvements are going to cost, how much you can sell the house for, and an estimate of your net profit. Chapters 3 to 5 help you lay the foundation for a successful flip.

Assembling a Team of Advisors and Experts

You probably won't find a course on flipping houses at your community college. The only school that offers such a course is the college of hard knocks. You learn by doing. But when you're gambling with more than $100,000 of your own or someone else's money, learning by trial and error can be catastrophic.

A safer way to develop the skills and foresight needed to reduce costly mistakes is to learn from the mistakes of others. Develop your own house-flipping team and rely on the following professionals to guide and educate you:

- Real estate agent
- Financier/lender
- Accountant
- Title company
- Appraiser
- Home inspector
- Real estate lawyer
- Contractors

In Chapter 4, I describe the role that each of these valuable individuals plays on your team, and I provide some criteria to show you how to select the best of the bunch.

Time is money, and your time is valuable. If you can make more money doing your day job than you'd pay a contractor, you're usually better off hiring a contractor. In addition, if one contractor charges a little more but can complete the job on schedule, you may save money on holding costs by hiring a slightly more expensive contractor. Overlooking the clock is easy when you're staring at dollar signs, but in flipping, time really is money.

Finding and Buying a Property Ripe for Flipping

The most critical stage of flipping a house is finding and buying the right house to flip. Buy a lousy house in a lousy neighborhood for more than it's worth, and you've already lost the game. Finding a house that's dripping with potential for 20 percent to 50 percent less than you can sell it for is quite a challenge, but as a flipper, that's the fun part. Flipping is an adventure, a treasure hunt, and a poker game all rolled into one. Finding and buying a property is a four-step process:

1. **Scope out a fertile neighborhood — often an area with homes that are at least 20 years old and are ripe for rehabbing and reselling.**

   See Chapter 6 for details.

2. **Zoom in on a dontwanner — a distressed property that the owner obviously doesn't want or can't afford to keep.**

   A distressed house usually has a distressed owner. See Chapters 7 to 9 for various ways to find distressed properties.

3. **Research the property carefully and calculate the most you can pay for it and still earn a decent profit.**

   Before you make an offer on a property, you should be fairly certain that you'll earn at least 20 percent for your trouble. See Part III for more about researching and evaluating properties and calculating a maximum purchase price.

4. **Haggle with the seller to purchase the house at a price that virtually ensures that you'll profit from the flip, as I explain in Chapter 13.**

   In some cases, you won't be haggling with sellers but bidding at an auction; see Chapters 8 and 9 for details on finding and buying properties in foreclosure and other special markets.

Rehabbing Your Fixer-Upper to Maximize Your Profit

When you buy a house to flip, it's like buying a beat-up antique at a garage sale. You got the house for a bargain because it needs work that the seller isn't motivated or hasn't the time or money to do. By cleaning up the joint, fixing whatever's broken, and perhaps doing a few renovations, you can bring the property up to market standards and sell it for its full market value. In the following sections, I walk you through the types of renovations you can make.

Putting your repairs and renovations in order

Repairs and renovations require careful planning and execution to keep them on schedule and within budget. Before you begin, prioritize your repairs and renovations so you know what's most important; I give you all the tools and tips you need in Chapter 14. Invest your time and money in the repairs and renovations that promise the most bang for your buck, and then if you need to trim costs, you can skimp on the less-important stuff.

Schedule the work so that it proceeds logically. If you install new tile and carpeting before painting the walls and ceiling, you risk ruining the new tile and carpeting. A good rule of thumb is to work on the infrastructure first — the foundation, electricity, plumbing, heating, and air conditioning. Then, work from the top down, finishing with the floors. Don't paint yourself into a corner.

Applying a little makeup

The ideal house for a first-time flipper is one that requires only cosmetic work. Cosmetic work, which I cover in Chapter 15, includes the following low-cost repairs and renovations:

- A fresh coat of paint throughout the house
- New wall-to-wall carpeting in any rooms that need it
- New light fixtures
- New outlet and light-switch covers
- A thorough cleaning inside and out
- Window washing
- Storm window and door repair or replacement
- Lawn mowing, weeding, trimming trees and shrubs, and other basic landscaping

Cosmetic repairs don't add as much real value to a house as, say, a new kitchen may add, but they attract buyers. Often a house is undervalued simply because prospective buyers can't stand looking at it.

Tidying up the exterior

Curb appeal is everything when you're trying to sell a house. If prospective buyers pull up in front of a house that looks disheveled, they're likely to pull away before you have time to open the front door. To sell your house for top dollar, the house has to make a good first impression. It must have *curb appeal* — a fresh, well-manicured appearance that draws people into the home.

Chapter 16 shows you how to landscape and prepare the exterior of the house to make it draw passersby inside for a closer look.

Focusing on kitchens and bathrooms

Depending on their condition, kitchens and bathrooms sell houses or sink deals. A spacious kitchen with plenty of counter space and all the essential amenities — a clean range, refrigerator, microwave oven, and dishwasher — creates an impression that the kitchen is a great place to prepare meals and hang out with friends and family members. A sparkling-clean, well-lit bathroom with plenty of storage space creates a sense of comfort and cleanliness that permeates the house.

REMEMBER

Although you should never over-improve a property, renovations that bring the kitchen and bath up to market standards in your area always pay for themselves by adding real value to the property and making it more attractive to buyers. See Chapter 17 for the full scoop on renovating kitchens and bathrooms.

Making moderate changes

Somewhere between painting a room and building a room addition are moderate changes that you can make to a house to improve its value and draw more buyers. These improvements include installing replacement windows, replacing the screen doors or entry doors, and refinishing wood floors or installing tile or vinyl flooring. Chapter 18 lays out your options.

TIP

According to the National Association of Realtors' 2013 Cost versus Value Report, you get the most bang for your buck on renovations by replacing the front door.

Overhauling the structure

Some houses are begging for a few major overhauls. Maybe the house has an unfinished attic that's perfect for an additional bedroom, or maybe it has a beautifully landscaped backyard that has no easy access and no deck or patio. In some cases, you may discover a dinky house surrounded by mansions. By raising the roof and building a second story, you can double the living space and boost the house into a higher bracket. Chapter 19 takes on some of these major renovations, stimulating your own creative visions.

Profiting from Your Venture

Although this book focuses on the buy-fix-sell approach to flipping houses, you can profit from a flip in numerous ways, including the following:

- Sell the property.
- Sell to an investor who's better equipped and more motivated to flip the property (you're essentially earning a finder's fee, also known as the bird-dog fee).
- Refinance to cash out the equity in the property, usually to help finance repairs and renovations or use the money for other investment properties.
- Sell the property on a lease option, essentially collecting rent with the hope that your tenants will eventually purchase the property.
- Lease the property — become a landlord!
- Sell property on a contract — you become the bank and collect the interest.

See Chapter 20 for details on the various approaches to profit from a flip. In Chapters 21 and 22, I explain how to market and sell your home for top dollar. And in Chapter 23, I explain certain tax considerations that may help you keep more of your profit, instead of turning it over to your rich Uncle Sam.

TIP

Your options for profiting from a house flip basically fall into two categories depending on your goals: cash or cash flow. In other words, do you want to receive your money all at once by selling the property or keep the property and use it to generate a steady cash flow (by leasing the property or selling it on contract, for example)?

Chapter 2

Do You Have the Right Stuff for Flipping?

In This Chapter

- Squeezing a house flip into your already hectic schedule
- Taking inventory of your financial readiness
- Checking your gut for the daring and determination to succeed

Anyone can do it.

If I had a nickel for every time I heard someone say that about flipping houses, I could retire on my own private island in the Pacific. When a real estate investment guru says "Anyone can do it," what she really means is "Anyone *like me* can do it."

I prefer presenting house flipping in a more realistic light by saying, "Anyone who has sufficient desire, energy, and sticktoitism can do it." By following the advice in this book, you can acquire the necessary knowledge, gather investment capital, and find plenty of properties to flip, but if you don't have sufficient gusto and grit, your flips will most assuredly flop.

This chapter leads you on a journey of self-examination to determine whether you have the right stuff to flip real estate — time, energy, a strong financial position (with your own or other people's money — OPM), organizational expertise, people skills, tenacity, decisiveness, imagination, endurance, a healthy sense of humor, and a good support system.

Tabulating Your Time Budget

Most casual house flippers are weekend warriors. They hold down a day job of 40 or so hours a week and then work nights, weekends, holidays, and vacations on flipping houses. These part-time flippers typically invest anywhere from 20 to 40 hours a week, depending on how dilapidated the houses are, how ambitious they are to turn a profit, and how much of the work they want or need to do themselves.

Full-time flippers have no day job, so they can work 24/7 flipping houses, assuming they have enough cash on hand to finance their flips and cover their living expenses. These full-timers typically invest 40 to 80 hours a week. Again, this amount varies depending on how much money they need or want to make, how hard they're willing to work, and how much of the work they do themselves.

TIP

If your spouse works full time and earns enough to cover the bills, and if you have plenty of time on your hands, consider flipping houses full time. Of course, you need to make sure your spouse is 100 percent behind you or the decision can have some negative consequences for your relationship.

Although you may be able to delegate most of the work that goes into flipping a house, several tasks demand your uninterrupted time and focus:

- House hunting
- Networking to develop relationships that expand opportunities and flip houses in less time and for less money
- Negotiating and closing the deal
- Securing financing for purchases and renovations
- Budgeting and other accounting tasks
- Planning, executing, and supervising rehab projects
- Marketing and selling the property

REMEMBER

The amount of time required for these tasks varies greatly depending on how you choose to have them done. For example, if you hire an agent to help you find houses to flip, you may spend only a few hours checking out prospects, but if you choose to cruise the neighborhood for distressed properties, you may spend several days or even weeks finding a good prospect. I suggest consulting a real estate broker who has expertise in residential real estate.

In the following sections, I explain the advantages and disadvantages of part-time flipping, tell you when you can safely start flipping full time, and list the tasks that you should (and shouldn't) delegate to save time.

For the time-strapped: Part-time flipping

When you're just starting to flip properties, keep your day job. Moonlight as a house flipper until you establish yourself. Part-time flipping offers a host of benefits that you shouldn't just toss in the dumpster:

- Your day job provides steady income and security.
- Steady income enables you to secure traditional financing with lower interest rates.
- Your paycheck helps you cover the mortgage payments, finance renovations, cover your quarterly income-tax payments, and stay afloat when the housing market cools.
- A full-time job typically provides you with health and dental insurance, retirement funds, and other benefits you don't get from flipping houses.

You never have to become a full-time flipper. Most house flippers, even when they're well established, keep their day jobs.

Although a day job provides part-time flippers with the income and security required to fuel this venture, it has its drawbacks:

- Flipping part time dilutes your focus. You may be in the middle of a complex renovation project late Sunday night and then have to show up for work bright and early Monday morning.
- Working overtime on flipping projects can sap the time and energy you have for your family and your day job. Keep in mind that part-time flipping is like having a second job.
- When you work a full-time job, you're less available for fielding calls and dealing with problems that arise when you're buying, renovating, and selling a property.

To compensate for some of the drawbacks, consider the following solutions for integrating part-time flipping into your life:

- Work the second or third shift so you can focus on flipping during the day.
- Schedule vacations around your rehab schedule.
- Ask your spouse for help with paperwork and fielding phone calls while you're at work — a perfect job for the work-at-home parent.
- Become a weekend warrior, performing cleanup, yard work, and other chores on your days off. If you're married with children, make the project a family affair.
- Partner with a trustworthy friend or relative who has more free time or a more flexible schedule.

All the time in the world: Full-time flipping

Full-time flipping requires a big time commitment and a cash reserve to back it up. You need enough cash on hand not only to fuel your flip but also to cover several months of living expenses, including your current house payment, property taxes, utilities, groceries, and car loan. Most flippers choose to become full-time flippers only after they successfully flip several properties, have a proven system in place, and have the financial resources to live without another source of income for at least one full year.

SANITY CHECK

Consider quitting your day job and flipping full time only if you suddenly become independently wealthy or you're absolutely certain you can *double* your income by flipping houses. You know you're ready to flip full time after you complete all the items on the following checklist:

- Spend five years successfully buying, fixing, and flipping real estate on a part-time basis.
- Sock away at least one year's income in reserves.
- Secure health, dental, disability, and life insurance and have sufficient funds to cover the premiums.
- Obtain a blanket insurance policy that covers liability.
- Set up a line of credit that enables you to carry out two projects at the same time.
- Develop a solid business plan. For professional guidance with a touch of humor, get *Business Plans For Dummies,* by Steven D. Peterson, Peter E. Jaret, and Barbara Findlay (Wiley).
- Assemble a team of experienced advisors with varied backgrounds — financial, legal, construction, and so on. (See Chapter 4.)

Without these essentials — a strong work ethic, determination, sufficient cash reserves, a well-defined goal, and a solid plan to achieve that goal — failure is almost guaranteed.

Delegating time-consuming tasks

You can get more done in less time by making use of other people's time — delegating tasks. But be careful when choosing tasks to delegate. You can safely farm out any of the following jobs:

- Lawn mowing and snow shoveling to any day laborer, even your own or someone else's kid in the neighborhood who has direct access to the home and can keep an eye on it for you, unless you find these activities therapeutic
- Heating, plumbing, gas, and electrical repairs to licensed and insured contractors
- Sale of the home to a qualified and trusted real estate agent, who can list the home, handle the mundane details, and call you when qualified buyers show up
- Setting up appointments to look at houses to your agent, your spouse, or another family member or friend (but don't delegate actually looking at the houses — that's your job)
- Cosmetic repairs, such as painting and carpeting, to qualified painters and carpet installers
- Minor repairs and small projects, such as repairing a leaky faucet, to a local handyman or woman
- Marketing the rehabbed home, including distribution of signs and flyers, to a real estate agent, family member, or friend
- Showing the rehabbed home to prospective buyers to a real estate agent, family member, or friend

Think of tasks in terms of time and money. If you earn $25 an hour, hire someone to do the $10-an-hour jobs, and do the $50-an-hour jobs yourself.

Some tasks are way too important to delegate, unless you trust the person nearly as much as you trust yourself. Avoid outsourcing any of the following jobs:

- Securing financing for purchases and renovations.
- Anything that requires the handling of money, including making monthly mortgage payments and paying property tax and quarterly estimated taxes (if applicable). You can hire an accountant to manage the record-keeping, but handle the money yourself.
- Meeting city inspectors.
- Accompanying home inspectors.
- Managing your files and data systems. (When you hit the big time and can afford it, you can hire a licensed and insured professional to perform these tasks.)

- Visiting properties prior to purchase. (Never buy a property you haven't inspected yourself or, as I like to say, "Your eyes or no buys.")
- Negotiating and closing the deal. (Your agent can advise you and present your offers for you, but call the shots yourself.)
- Planning and supervising rehab projects. (You can hire people to do the work, but you need to visit the worksite regularly to ensure quality and control costs.)

Shaking Your Piggy Bank

You don't need a lot of your own money to finance your first flip. You can beg, borrow, or partner up with an investor (see Chapter 5 for details on these options). Before setting out to flip your first property, however, tally the costs and your financial health, have a solid plan for obtaining financing, and know your debt tolerance, as I explain in the following sections.

Figuring out how much you need to get started

When you flip a house, you want your expenses (the cost of the house, repairs, renovations, and expenses to hold and sell the property) to be less than 80 percent of the amount you expect to get out of the house when you sell it. In other words, plan on netting at least a 20 percent profit.

REMEMBER

How much money you need to finance a flip depends on the grand total of all the costs for purchasing the property, fixing it up, holding it (taxes, utilities, and so forth), and selling it. You never know the actual costs until you resell the property, but you can do some ballpark estimates to determine how much money you need. See Chapter 11 for details on how to estimate the costs of repairs and renovations. In Chapter 12, I lead you through the process of estimating your total costs and the maximum amount you can afford to pay for a property in order to profit from flipping it.

The nomadic flipper

I'm currently living in house number 23, where my family has lived since 1990. I moved 19 times before getting married. Marriage kind of slowed me down. Before moving into a house, I'd fix up the bathroom, kitchen, and one bedroom. Then I'd live there for a few months to a year, fixing up the rest of the house. When the house was in pretty good shape, I'd either convert it into a rental or sell it for quick cash. I drew up a mini business plan for each property. Each plan was contingent on the current economic climate, my cash-flow needs, and the estimated long-term appreciation of the property.

Not all my deals were blockbusters, but from 1976 to 1990, I amassed property and cash worth millions of dollars. You can do the same, but don't expect it to happen overnight. Draw up a successful long-term plan, start slow, and stick to it.

Finding cash to fuel your flip

Coming up with a cool hundred grand, two hundred grand, or three hundred grand to flip a house may seem a little out of reach at first, but several financing options are available, including the following:

- Flip the house you live in.
- Borrow against the equity in your current home.
- Borrow from relatives or friends.
- Partner with someone who has money to invest but lacks the time, expertise, or motivation to flip properties.
- Borrow hard money from an investor. (*Hard money* is a loan from a private lender that typically costs money upfront, requires lump-sum payments on specific dates, and charges a higher-than-standard interest rate.)

Chapter 5 explores these and other financing options in greater depth.

TIP

Many lending institutions refuse to loan money for the purpose of flipping properties, but hard money is usually available through private investors. Expect steep interest rates — double or even triple the current rates for standard loans. The lender may also require as much as 6 percent upfront in discount points and large monthly payments in the form of *cash calls* (lump-sum payments on scheduled dates). This may sound like a lousy deal, but it's a common way to finance a flip, as long as you have a solid plan in place that accounts for the costs of borrowing the money and having funds available to cover the cash calls. To find a hard-money lender, search the web for "hard-money lender" followed by your city and state — these lenders are everywhere.

Taking stock of your financial health

To borrow money at a reasonable interest rate, you have a better chance if you can prove that you have money (or at least some valuable stuff), are currently making money, and generally pay your bills on time.

Having a strong financial position is a big plus because it gives you access to cheaper loans, but it isn't essential. If you have a great plan in place and can convince someone to lend you sufficient funds to fuel a flip, you can succeed.

To take stock of your financial position, formulate a financial statement that includes the following figures:

- Everything you own — cash, investments, house, car, boats, coins, jewelry, retirement accounts, and so on
- Everything you owe — mortgage, second mortgage, auto loan, student loans, credit-card balances, back taxes, and so on
- Your net worth (the value of what you own minus what you owe)
- Gross monthly income
- Total monthly bills

REMEMBER

Treat your financial statement like a report card and update it every six months to grade your progress. An A+ financial statement gives you the power to borrow money at lower interest rates. See Chapter 5 for more information about figuring out your financial health and using that information to secure funds for flipping. This is true for credit reports, too. The higher your score, the more access you have to other funds. Yes, it's ironic — if you need money and try to get a credit line, lenders turn you down, and if you *don't* need the money, they're eager to lend it to you.

WARNING!

CYA: Cover Your Assets. In general, the more you risk, the more you stand to gain, but don't overreach and put your current financial health at risk. To protect your assets, don't finance a house flip with your retirement money . . . at least until you've flipped several properties successfully and are confident that you know what you're doing. If you're married, put real estate investments in your name or your spouse's name, not both, so only one of you is legally liable in the event of a lawsuit involving the property. Establish a home-equity account for financial emergencies and use it only for emergencies.

Honestly evaluating your debt tolerance

Flipping properties requires a moderate tolerance for debt, especially early in your career. You have to owe money for extended periods of time before you reap a profit from that debt. Some people just can't handle debt. What about you? You may be debt intolerant if you:

- Pay cash for a vehicle even when you're offered 0 percent financing
- Pick up the tab every time you eat out so you won't owe somebody lunch
- Prepay your utility bills several months in advance
- Own only one credit card and use it only for emergencies

REMEMBER

Debt can be good or bad. Debt used to finance investments that have a higher rate of return than the interest you pay on the debt is good debt. Bad debt is any debt racked up on spending sprees for stuff that's worth less now than when you bought it. When flipping houses, loans and their costs can be fairly steep, but if you account for those costs in your budget and still turn a profit of 20 percent or more, the loan and related costs are worth it. (See Chapter 5 for the lowdown on good versus bad debt.)

Taking Your Personality Pulse

Not everyone has what it takes to flip houses. Some people are too nice, too nervous, too timid, or too lazy to pull off a successful flip. Others may get so emotionally attached to a house that they pay too much for it. And some people can't handle the math and extra paperwork. Those who excel are thick-skinned, high-energy, multi-tasking, task-delegating dynamos . . . but that's pretty much true for anything in life that's worth pursuing.

The following list highlights and describes the qualities required to succeed at flipping houses:

- **Energetic:** Flipping houses is stimulating, but the work involved can sap your energy faster than an overdue tax notice. Couch potatoes don't survive.
- **Function well under pressure:** Few crises are more stressful than real estate deals gone bad. Imagine that your financing falls through, or you discover that the house you just bought is infested with termites, or you put the house up for sale and it lingers on the market for more than a year. When your life savings are on the line and you find yourself in a situation that's completely outside your control, how well do you think you'll function?

- **Organized:** Flipping requires strong organizational skills, attention to detail, and the ability to schedule work for maximum efficiency. If you have these skills, you have an edge over less-organized flippers, but if these skills are lacking or completely absent, don't give up. Get organized, perhaps with the help of a computer; hire a top-notch assistant; or team up with someone who has the requisite organizational skills.
- **Good with people:** The most successful property flippers are approachable motivators with good people skills . . . or they partner up with someone who fits the bill. Being good with people means you can:
    - Knock on a stranger's door without fear of being shot
    - Calmly motivate others involved in the deal to move quickly
    - Empathize with the needs of others and meet those needs in a way that's encouraging and motivational
    - Be flexible enough to deal with ever-changing situations and quickly develop workable alternatives
    - Build solid relationships with agents, contractors, financial institutions, and others on whom you rely for help
    - Let everyone know how valuable they are
- **Assertive without being bossy:** You need to know what you want, ask for it, and don't settle for anything that's outside your comfort zone.

  While negotiating the purchase or sale of a property or trying to convince someone to do something for you, remember that "no" doesn't necessarily mean "no." Often it means "know," as in, "I don't *know* enough yet to say 'yes.'" Being assertive often means finding out what's holding the person back and addressing that issue.
- **Good with numbers (or a calculator):** Flipping for profit requires rudimentary math skills — addition and subtraction with a little multiplication and division thrown in for good measure. To keep your bottom line black rather than red, you simply have to make sure that you sell the home for more than you invest in it. Loan calculators and other useful tools are readily available in personal-finance programs, such as Quicken, and on the web. (Visit `bankrate.com`, for example, and click Calculators.)
- **The ability to handle rejection, failure, and success:** Flipping houses has its ups and downs. You need to be able to ride the waves:
    - **Rejection:** Rejection can come in the form of denial for a loan, a buyer or seller backing out of a deal, investors or partners abandoning you, or nobody showing up at your open house.
    - **Failure:** Even the most experienced and successful flippers encounter setbacks. They may underestimate the costs of repairs and renovations, underestimate the time required to sell the house, or even have to sell a property at a loss.

Don't get discouraged if your first flip flops. Flip at least three properties before you make the decision to skedaddle. Some of the most successful real estate investors have failed their way to fortune.

- **Success:** Success comes with its own set of problems. You may find a great deal, assume it's too good to be true (which is usually the case), and talk yourself out of it. You may put the house on the market, receive a good offer the first day, turn it down waiting for a better offer, and never get that better offer; I know how hard that is to handle. Or success may lead to overconfidence that results in failure.

Don't let success get you down. If your first flip is a grand slam and you're not careful with the next flip, the loss can soak up the profits you made with your grand slam.

How bad can a house flip be?

We (Ralph Roberts and company) discovered a fantastic foreclosure property — a $2 million beauty we could get for a cool $900,000! Although the owners, whom we refer to as Mr. and Mrs. Rose, were going through a divorce, they seemed willing to work with us at first. They even convinced us to let them stay in the house while we were rehabbing it. (Letting people stay in the house is always a bad idea. We agreed to this to get the deal done, but when you're flipping a house, you want to close on it only when it's vacant and "broom clean.") Mr. Rose lived in one half of the house, and the Missus resided in the other half.

As soon as the contractors showed up, the War of the Roses commenced. Mrs. Rose declared certain areas of the house to be no-work zones, and these zones changed daily. She tried to seduce the contractors, and when real estate agents arrived to show the house, she called the police. During the rehab, the Roses' son was caught doing drugs in the house.

Mrs. Rose moved out, only to be replaced by Mr. Rose's girlfriend. When the contractors returned to work, they found the girlfriend at the top of the stairs, dressed only in her nightie, drunk and in a jealous rage. She proceeded to fall down the stairs, shedding her wig along the way. By the time the Roses cleared out, the place was completely trashed.

We finally managed to take possession of the house, complete the rehab, and place the property back on the market. We were willing to sell for $1.8 million, and when we got our first offer for $2.2 million, we were ecstatic, but we weren't out of the rose bushes yet.

During negotiations we found out that the instrument the buyer was using to pay for the property qualified as an illegal use of treasury bonds. We informed the FBI, which set up a sting operation to nab the bad guys. The fraudsters showed up three hours early, discovered the sting, and split town.

We eventually sold the house for $2 million and netted a $250,000 profit for about a year's effort. Not bad for a year's effort, but it wasn't the quick and easy money we had expected.

Gathering the Essential Tools of the Trade

Every job requires a collection of specialized tools. For flipping houses, make sure you have the following bare essentials:

- **Flashlight**. You never know who or what is just around the corner or in the crawlspace — it could be someone in a nightie or pajamas, or it could be an animal.
- **Digital camera** for taking photos of properties and before-and-after pictures of repairs and renovations.
- **Calculator** for crunching numbers.
- **Day planner or tablet** for jotting down names, addresses, phone numbers, and appointment times and locations.
- **Smartphone** with plenty of useful apps, including GPS, a general-purpose calculator, a loan calculator, and a calendar. Realtor.com has an excellent app for iPhone, iPad, and Android (visit `www.realtor.com/mobile`). The Google Maps app is useful for scoping out a property, and Zillow has an app for doing a quick price check on a property (although Zillow property values aren't the most reliable).
- **Reliable transportation.**
- **For Sale signs** (if you're planning on selling the home yourself).
- **Business cards** to hand out to everyone you meet, so if someone needs to sell a home in a hurry, they can contact you.

Of course, if you're planning to do some or all of the repairs and renovations yourself, you also need a garage full of hand tools, power tools, and lawn and garden equipment.

Chapter 3

Devising an Effective Flipping Strategy

In This Chapter

- Exploring a variety of flipping strategies
- Plotting your course well in advance
- Formulating a back-up plan

When most people think of flipping houses, they immediately envision a process of buying a ramshackle house on the cheap, fixing it up, and then reselling it for more than they've invested in it. That's certainly the underlying theme, but the actual process of flipping houses spawns a shed full of choices and questions, including the following:

- Are you going to live in the house while fixing it up?
- How long can you afford to hold the house before selling it?
- How extensive are the renovations you're willing and able to perform?

Before you even consider making an offer on a house, know how you're going to profit from it. Are you going to buy it at a bargain and resell it immediately at market value or wholesale (discounting the property to sell it faster), do a quick makeup job and resell it, perform some major renovations, or fix it up and use it as a rental? Each of these strategies has benefits and drawbacks, but each strategy is a perfectly legitimate way to flip property for a profit.

This chapter explores several house-flipping strategies and encourages you to develop your own strategy based on your personality, your neighborhood, and the resources you have at your disposal.

Surveying Different Strategies

When developing a game plan, you want to maximize your strengths, minimize your weaknesses, and fully exploit the opportunities that surround you. Many flippers have already developed their own strategies that achieve those three goals. By becoming more aware of these existing strategies, you can choose the one that fits you best and perhaps even improvise to invent your own strategy.

In the following sections I reveal the top house-flipping strategies that many flippers practice with varying levels of success.

Always buy low. If you can't get a house for at least 20 percent less than what you estimate it will cost to repair and sell (including holding costs), keep looking. Chapter 12 shows you how to calculate your maximum purchase price to improve your chances of earning a decent profit.

Buy into a hot market

In a sizzling real estate market, you can turn a profit fairly quickly by buying a house, moving in, and then sitting back and watching the real estate values soar. This approach works only if you have time on your hands, are speculative by nature, and have a knack for purchasing houses in a hot market at just the right time. This strategy offers several benefits:

- If the market remains strong, your property value rises without your having to lift a finger.
- Your equity in the property rises, boosting your borrowing power for other investments.
- By living in the home for two years or more, up to $250,000 of your profit ($500,000 for a couple) is tax free, at least according to the tax laws in place when I was writing this book. See Chapter 23 for more tax-saving tips.

Buying into a hot market also carries some significant risks:

- In areas where property values are soaring, the housing bubble may burst, leaving you with a home that's worth less than what you paid for it.
- Stuff happens. You can have a great house at a great price in a hot market with the top agent working to sell it, and the house still may not sell. Prepare yourself for all contingencies.

REMEMBER

What goes up sometimes comes down — sometimes very quickly — but every market has profit potential as long as you recognize and account for the conditions and opportunities.

Chapter 6 has more details on taking the temperature of the real estate market in any neighborhood you're scoping out.

Buy low, do nothing, and sell quick

Occasionally, you stumble on a house that's priced significantly below market value and requires few or no repairs. The property may be in foreclosure or perhaps is part of an estate that's being liquidated, making the owner very motivated to sell. By being at the right place at the right time with ready cash and a solid plan in place, you can pounce on the deal and then put the house back on the market the very same day!

Sounds great, huh? Well, getting a house that's way below market value is great when it happens, but being in the right place at the right time takes time and effort. You need to build a solid team (see Chapter 4 for details), do plenty of research, secure some solid investment capital (see Chapter 5 for tips on financing your flip), and be properly equipped to execute this strategy. If you haven't done your homework and you're ill prepared, you're more likely to make costly mistakes. With the proper preparation and persistence, you're more likely to put yourself in the right place at the right time.

WARNING!

Beware of deals that are too sweet. If a stranger approaches you at an investment seminar with a hot tip on a piece of real estate, for example, he may just be looking for a sucker to buy a property he got stuck with. Unless you know the market values in the area, see the house with your own eyes, and research the title (as I explain in Chapter 10), don't take the bait.

Buy low, apply makeup, and sell quick

You can learn a lot from used-car salesmen. The first thing they do when they take possession of a vehicle is clean and polish it and vacuum the interior. The car may still be a clunker, but with the right cosmetics and an air freshener hanging from the rearview mirror, the vehicle becomes an attractive clunker that can sell for a handsome profit.

Even a good home, if not clean and well maintained, can look disheveled. Many homeowners place their homes on the market without properly *staging* (showcasing) their homes. They don't mow the lawn, trim the bushes, touch up the paint, or even tidy up the house during showings. Unknowingly, they turn away prospective buyers, and the house lingers on the market until even their agents lose interest. The homeowner may then lower the price to generate interest.

This kind of home gives you a perfect opportunity to swoop in and get a great deal. You buy the home for significantly less than market value, add elbow grease, and then resell the home for thousands of dollars more than you invested in it. In Chapter 21, I show you how to properly market and stage a home to get top dollar.

REMEMBER

Buying low, applying makeup, and selling quick is an excellent strategy for the first-time flipper. By purchasing a property that's an easy rehab job, you can focus on the process of flipping instead of on the complexities of rehabbing. After you master this strategy, you're better prepared to move up to more distressed properties.

Buy low, renovate, and sell high

Some homes are undervalued because they're missing an essential feature — a livable living room, a third bedroom, a deck, or a laundry room on the main floor. (Heaven forbid the previous owner rips out his kitchen in frustration over losing a house in foreclosure.) Other homes may have major eyesores, such as an outdated kitchen or bathroom. In either case, moderate to major renovations may improve the marketability of the house and its profit potential in two ways:

- **Increase the home's actual value.** Wear and tear depreciate a home over time. Updates restore value, while added living space can boost the house into a higher price bracket.
- **Expand the pool of interested house hunters.** A two-bedroom house, for example, appeals only to people who are looking for a one- to two-bedroom house. Adding a third bedroom attracts anyone looking for a one- to three-bedroom house or a house with office space.

Adding to the real value of a home is a great way to maximize your profit, but don't take on more than you can handle or build a mansion among bungalows. If you're a weekend warrior or you have contractors on your team (see Chapter 4 for details), consider this strategy. If not, you may want to hold off until you get to know some local contractors.

Buy low, move in, renovate, and sell high

To maximize your profit, reduce expenses, and take a more hands-on role in rehabbing a home, consider moving into the home you purchase and renovating it at your own pace. If you and your family don't mind living in the chronic chaos of a construction zone, this approach is appealing for several reasons:

- By living in the home you're flipping, you avoid a second mortgage payment, tax bill, and utility costs.
- Because you're living in the home, you get a better feel for the types of renovations that can make the house more attractive to future buyers.
- If you live in the home for at least two years, up to $250,000 of your profit ($500,000 for a couple) is tax free, at least according to the tax laws that were in place when I was writing this book.
- You're onsite for any repairs or renovations you have to hire out. And you're around more often to prevent thieves from walking off with your tools and materials.

If you're single or married with no kids, this strategy is an excellent choice. However, if you have children in school, I recommend that you avoid this approach, unless you intend to remain in the same school system. Your children begin to make relationships, and big moves disrupt their lives.

If you're planning major renovations like gutting the house or completely rehabbing the kitchen, consider performing that renovation before you move in or plan on residing elsewhere during the renovation, especially if you have kids and pets. The persistent noise, dust, and inconvenience can rattle nerves and strain relationships.

Buy, hold, and lease

You don't have to sell a house to profit from it. Many real estate investors opt to buy a house and lease it out for at least enough to cover the monthly expenses of holding it — mortgage, taxes, maintenance, utilities, and so on. Here's a rundown of how this strategy works:

- You buy the house at less than market value, so you earn equity at the time of purchase. In other words, if you buy a $100,000 house for $80,000, you immediately earn $20,000 in equity. You don't realize your profit until you sell the house, but you can borrow against the equity.
- Assuming the rent you charge covers your mortgage and other expenses, the rent pays down the principal of the loan, so your equity in the home gradually rises. (Your renters are paying off your debt.)
- As real estate values rise, your equity in the home rises accordingly, so the house is worth more when you sell it — assuming, of course, that your tenants don't trash it.

In short, you're making money three ways: when you buy the house, when you hold the house, and when you sell the house. If you perform some value-add renovations while you own the property, you may even boost your profit when you sell. Of course, with this strategy you won't see the immediate influx of cash that accompanies a quick flip, but your net worth (the value of your assets minus what you owe on those assets) gradually rises until you cash out your chips at the end of the game.

See Chapter 20 to find out more about the various approaches for profiting from real estate investments.

Invest in new construction

A home doesn't have to be old and beat up for you to flip it. Many real estate investors profit from flipping new homes or condos. Unless you're focusing on a niche market that rules out new construction (see the next section for more about niche markets), don't overlook newly constructed homes.

The best time to hit newly constructed homes is at the very beginning, when the builder first starts to sell units. After 60 months of construction, the cost to build may have risen by $50,000, so if you bought at the beginning, five years later you have that extra equity built up in the property compared to the other homes in the division.

When a new subdivision is starting, ask if you can buy the model from the builder. The builder can then rent it from you for a few years. It'll be very well taken care of because it's for showing to prospective purchasers.

When purchasing a newly constructed home or condo, read the purchase agreement very carefully and check the following:

- The purchase agreement should have a clause stating that the purchase is conditional upon the satisfactory completion of the building and on your ability to secure financing for the purchase. If you sign a purchase agreement and then are denied financing, the builder may keep your earnest money and perhaps even sue you for breach of contract.
- Watch out for clauses that give the builder a percentage of the profit when you resell the unit. In a strong market, builders often insert wording that if you sell the unit within a specified time period, you must pay the builder all or a significant portion of the profit.
- Beware of inflated profit estimates. Developers who are trying to get their projects off the ground often make unrealistic estimates, sometimes claiming that their properties will double in value over a short period of time. You've probably heard stories of people who invested in a development and made $100,000 in short order. What you don't hear are the stories of people who *lose* money, and those stories are much more common.
- If, after doing your research, you're convinced of the benefits, then at least make sure you're among the first 10 percent of buyers. These buyers make the lion's share of the profit because as construction proceeds, building costs rise.

Focus on a niche market

When you're looking for properties to flip, the first impulse is to cast a wide net in your search for the best deals, but sometimes you can find better deals by fishing deeper in one spot, such as one of the following:

- **Foreclosures:** You can find more homes in foreclosure than you can possibly flip, and by focusing your efforts on these properties, you quickly discover the ins and outs of locating them and effectively negotiating the price and terms you want. See Chapter 8 for details about foreclosures.
- **VA foreclosures:** To narrow your scope even further, consider focusing on VA (Veterans Affairs) foreclosures.
- **Probate:** You can get leads from probate lawyers and the neighborhood grapevine to locate families who need to unload a house in order to settle an estate.
- **Divorces:** When couples divorce, they're often stuck with a home that neither of them can afford. By keeping your ears open and letting people know that you buy houses, you can often get first dibs on these houses.
- **HUD homes:** Working with an agent who specializes in HUD (Department of Housing and Urban Development) homes, you can build a career purchasing these homes at a discount and rehabbing them for quick, profitable sales.
- **FSBO (For Sale By Owner):** When everyone else is searching the MLS for great deals, you may prefer driving around the neighborhood looking for homes with a For Sale or For Sale By Owner sign on the front lawn or searching for the ugly duckling on the street and then visiting your county's Register of Deeds to see who owns it. (MLS stands for Multiple Listing Service — an organization that maintains a database of houses and other real estate for sale or rent. They're all over the country.)
- **Seized homes:** Law-enforcement agencies commonly seize property and then have to unload it. By focusing your energy in this area, you can corner the market on seized homes.
- **Teardowns:** Homes that are beyond hope may still hold opportunities if the price and location are right. Some investors earn a great return by tearing down old homes and building new ones in their place.

WARNING!

Don't try to be a high roller and master everything all at once. Select a niche (foreclosures, probate, divorce, whatever) and work that niche until you achieve success. After you establish yourself in that area, you can add another to expand your operation. Chapter 9 provides more guidance on niche markets. Your niche market can also be a specific area that you farm by becoming an expert in the area and establishing a strong network. Chapter 6 offers additional details on how to effectively farm a neighborhood.

Flip contracts (or do it all on paper)

Technically, you don't even have to lift a hammer to flip a house. If you can scribble with a pen and dial a phone (and if you're Internet savvy), you have all the skills you need to flip contracts. *Flipping contracts* (also known as *pass-throughs*) consists of locating a distressed property and then contracting with the homeowner to sell it to an investor. In other words, you earn a finder's fee by serving as an investor's bird dog.

Chances are good that you've already heard a little about flipping contracts. Here's how it works: You pay the homeowner a deposit, typically $1,000 or 5 percent to 10 percent of the purchase price. In return, you get a purchase contract giving you the right to sell the property to an investor. You then find an investor who's willing to purchase the property and pay you a fee in excess of the amount you have tied up in the property.

WARNING! This strategy may sound rosy, but I strongly discourage you from flipping contracts. I include the strategy here only because you're going to hear about it elsewhere, and you should be aware of the high risk. If someone ties up a $100,000 house and wants to sell you her purchase agreement for $5,000, you're purchasing the house for $100,000 *and* paying a fee of $5,000. You're taking all the risk and giving that person $5,000. If it's such a good deal, you need to analyze it and ask yourself why she's not flipping the house herself.

Cook up your own strategy

Successful investors, whether they invest in real estate or stocks, devise unique strategies based on their personalities, their abilities, and the resources they have at their disposal. If you like to help people and you're good at dealing with uncomfortable situations, for example, you may want to focus on foreclosures or divorces. If you're good at primping a house but not so good at rehabbing, consider focusing on homes that require only a little makeup.

You can even mix and match strategies to develop a custom strategy of your very own. You may, for example, choose to buy a quick flip in a hot market or buy only duplexes that need a lot of work, move into one half, and rent out the other half while renovating the half you're living in. The variations are truly limited only by your imagination.

REMEMBER Re-evaluate your situation and be ready to shift your strategy as your skills, knowledge, resources, and market change. At this point, you may not feel confident taking on major renovations, but in a year or two, it could well become your area of expertise.

Drawing Up a Detailed Plan in Advance

Every day you own a property, holding costs chip away at your profit, unless of course the property is a rental. *Holding costs* are the daily expenses — mortgage interest, property taxes, utility bills, and maintenance costs. The trick to reducing these costs is to flip the property as quickly as possible, and that means planning well in advance. Make sure that your plan covers all five stages of the flipping process:

- **Secure financing:** Secure financing before you go house hunting. This tip may seem counterintuitive, but with financing in hand, you can move on the deal much more quickly than other buyers and negotiate from a position of power if other prospective buyers don't have cash. Know how much you can afford to pay and still have sufficient funds for renovations before you make your offer. See Chapter 5 for more about financing your flips and Chapter 12 to determine how much you can pay for a property to earn a decent profit from it.
- **Search and research:** The fun, exciting step in the process of flipping houses is searching for and finding diamonds in the rough. To limit your exposure to risk, however, you need to follow up your search with research, particularly if you're buying a home in foreclosure. See the chapters in Part II for more about finding properties to flip and Chapter 10 for guidance on how to research distressed properties.
- **Purchase:** Buying the property is probably the easiest step in the process, but you want to be sure to negotiate (or bid) a price that's at least 25 percent to 30 percent less than the cost of buying, renovating, holding, and selling the property. You also need to negotiate other terms, including the closing date and the date on which the previous owners move out.
- **Rehab:** Jot down a list of improvements you want to make to the property when you first see the house, and schedule the work before you close on the purchase. Ideally, you should start renovating the property the same day or the day after closing. Chapter 11 walks you through the process of inspecting a property for the first time; Part IV is devoted to fixing up your fixer-upper.
- **Sell or lease:** As soon as you know your closing date for purchasing the property, determine the date on which you want to put the house back on the market or have it available for tenants. If you're selling the house, you must also decide whether you want to sell it yourself or work with an agent. You don't have to wait to market the house until renovations are complete — the activity that surrounds the house during renovations can be an excellent marketing tool. It gets the neighbors talking. See Chapter 20 for various ways to realize a profit from your investment and Chapters 21 and 22 for more about selling your rehabbed property.

Plan B: Surviving a Flip That Flops

Throughout this book, I provide tips, tricks, and warnings to enable you to maximize your profit and minimize your risks, but that doesn't guarantee a successful flip every time. Flips sometimes flop, even for experienced investors. You may buy a house that has costly unforeseen problems, buy into a market that tanks soon after you close on a property, or encounter a host of unexpected problems that can derail your dreams. Know the risks before you roll the dice, and always have a plan B in place. The following tips can help you avoid some of the more serious situations and recover your composure when something goes wrong:

- If your flip flops because of a dip in the housing market, skip to Chapter 20 to explore other ways to profit from your investment.
- As soon as you see that a property is a money pit, cut your losses. Don't throw good money after bad. You may need to sell the house now at a small loss instead of later at a bigger loss.
- Keep in touch with your team, especially your financial backers and agent, when a situation sours. Communication is key, especially when times are bad. Good team members can help you out of a jam and assist you in your recovery.

TIP

Don't give up just because one flip doesn't turn out as well as you expected it to. Failure is one of the best educators, and if you can work through it, it can be a real confidence builder. If I gave up every time I failed, I would never have achieved my current level of success. Flip three or four houses before throwing in the towel. I know that the possibility of a flop isn't something you want to hear about. Certainly the late-night TV gurus don't teach or talk about this possibility. Your plan, however, must include an exit strategy for all contingencies; otherwise, your flop will take you by total surprise, and you won't know what to do.

Chapter 4

Building Your Dream Team

In This Chapter

- Picking a real estate agent with flipping know-how
- Acquiring sound financial advice
- Covering your back with a title company, appraiser, inspector, and attorney
- Hiring contractors and subcontractors to handle the heavy lifting

Most people who talk themselves out of investing in real estate are defeated by a false assumption — that they have to do it alone. The truth is that you don't have to do it alone. In fact, attempting to fly solo is one of the most common and serious blunders you can make when you're getting started. Investors who excel at flipping houses are team builders, capable of selecting talented players, coordinating their efforts, and harnessing their skills.

By surrounding yourself with a team of experienced and talented people, all you really need to succeed is a long list of qualified individuals with diverse talents, along with a phone, a pad of paper, a pencil, and some people skills. You don't know what a house is really worth? Consult a qualified real estate agent. You're not good with money? Hire an accountant. Can't hammer a nail? Call a carpenter.

Sure, hiring these additional people costs extra, but as long as you can accurately estimate the total costs, calculate them into your budget, and still profit from the flip, you win. (See Chapter 12 for details on calculating costs.)

I don't have all the essential qualities to successfully flip houses. What I do have is the ability to admit that I lack certain qualities and a knack for finding people who complement my skills. In this chapter, I show you how to build your own house-flipping dream team.

REMEMBER

A dream team is more than just a skilled workforce. It's a combination of people who have your best interests at heart. They want you to succeed. Money alone can't buy a dream team. You have to nurture these relationships by rewarding the people who reward you through their expertise and hard work. Fair payment on time, sincere compliments and thanks, positive referrals, and free food go a long way.

Hooking Up with a House Hunter — A Quality Real Estate Agent

A real estate agent (or house hunter) who knows the ropes and has the right contacts can assist you in managing the two transactions that are critical to your success — purchasing a house at less than market value and selling the rehabbed house quickly at a profit. In the following sections, I explain the beneficial services that agents can provide and give you guidance on finding the best agent for your flipping needs.

WARNING!

Although you may be able to handle one or both transactions (selling and buying) on your own in an attempt to trim costs and boost your bottom line, I strongly discourage it, especially when you're flipping your first property. You're about to invest tens or perhaps hundreds of thousands of dollars. A qualified agent can help you navigate the process and avoid common pitfalls that can turn a plump profit into a big, fat loss.

Recognizing the value of agents

A good real estate agent is more than just a clerk who pushes paperwork through the system and juggles numbers. He's more like the concierge at an upscale hotel. He's dedicated to serving your real estate needs, whatever they may be. And if he can't personally attend to those needs, he knows someone who can.

Sure, a qualified real estate agent costs money, typically a 6 percent to 8 percent commission, but when you consider the amount of money you're investing, a single mistake can cost you thousands more. A real estate agent who has plenty of experience working with investors can assist you with the following:

- Determining how much money you can borrow and which types of loans are best and helping you obtain pre-approval for a loan. (See Chapter 5 for more about financing your flips.)

- Finding houses that meet your search criteria, even when those houses aren't actively advertised as being on the market. (See Part II for more about finding properties to flip.)
- Assisting in evaluating properties that you may want to purchase so you don't pay more for a property than it's worth. (See Chapters 10 and 11 for tips on evaluating specific properties for purchase.)
- Ensuring that your offer has appropriate conditions in place to protect you. For example, you may want to make your offer contingent upon the sale of another property you own, your ability to acquire financing, the property passing inspection, and the title company's assurance that the title work is in order. (See Chapter 13 for details on offers and negotiations for buying a home.)
- Negotiating price, financing, terms, date of possession, and other sticky areas of a purchase agreement.
- Expediting the closings (whenever you buy or sell a property) to ensure that nothing goes wrong at the last minute and offering solutions when everything goes wrong at the last minute.
- Assisting you in estimating the cost of repairs and renovations.
- Referring you to contractors, subcontractors, and other professionals who have a good track record (see "Contacting Contractors and Subcontractors" later in this chapter).
- Broadcasting your rehabbed home to every real estate agent in the neighborhood via the Multiple Listing Service (MLS) — a listing of homes for sale that goes out to all the real estate agents in your area — and helping you sell it in half the time it would take you to sell it yourself. (See Chapter 21 for more about marketing your rehabbed home.)
- Evaluating offers on the rehabbed home in a way that doesn't compromise your position in the market. Some offers, for example, can tie up your home and leave you little compensation if the buyer backs out. (See Chapter 22 for info on negotiating and closing the sale of your rehabbed home.)
- Advising you on how much rent you can charge for a property if you want to hold onto it for awhile and you need some cash flow.

WARNING!

A talented agent can help you locate excellent investment properties in a fraction of the time it would take you to do so and help you purchase properties for thousands of dollars less than you would pay if you negotiated the purchase yourself. On average, you take twice as long selling a property yourself than you do when you work with a real estate agent, and every day your home sits on the market costs you money.

Real estate agent or Realtor: What's the difference?

A real estate agent is anyone who has a state license to negotiate the sale or purchase of a property and works for a real estate broker or brokerage company. A Realtor is a real estate agent who's also a member of the National Association of Realtors. The United States has more than 2 million real estate agents, but only 1.2 million are Realtors.

So, what's the difference? Because the qualifications for obtaining a real estate license vary from state to state, the quality of real estate agents varies much more than the quality of Realtors. The National Association of Realtors requires its members to complete additional training and testing to improve their knowledge and abilities and encourages members to follow a strict code of ethics. The association also provides its members with additional resources and tools to assist in finding and marketing properties effectively.

Of course this association membership doesn't mean that a particular Realtor is more qualified than a given real estate agent, but the odds are pretty good that you'll receive superior advice and service from a Realtor. To find a bona fide Realtor, look for the Realtor logo on business cards and stationery. Almost all Realtors make a point of proudly displaying this logo. You also can search for a Realtor in your area at `www.realtor.com`.

Picking an agent with the right stuff

Any licensed real estate agent can help you find, purchase, and sell a house, but you want someone whose experience and training are rooted in the business of flipping properties. The qualities to look for include

- **Specialty in your target area.** The agent should know the market in which you want to invest and be well-versed on property values, market conditions, and neighborhood news that may affect future property values.
- **Experience in other methods of finding homes to purchase.** Shop for a real estate agent who specializes in your area of interest, such as FSBOs (For Sale By Owners), foreclosures, HUD (Housing and Urban Development) homes, probates, or bankruptcies. The best-case scenario is finding someone who specializes in all of these collectively. A real estate agent who checks only the MLS listings may overlook the best deals.
- **Proactive approach.** The agent shouldn't wait for you to call but should call you with any leads for properties in your target area. If calling isn't your preference, your agent should be able to set you up to receive automated e-mail messages that notify you of new listings immediately. If agents are dinosaurs and their phones are hooked to strings, consider looking for someone who's more tech savvy.

- **Eagerness to show houses.** The agent should be willing to show many houses before arriving at the right house.
- **Availability on short notice.** If you see a For Sale sign in someone's yard and want to see the house, you should be able to quickly contact your agent to set an appointment for viewing the house at a convenient time for you. The agent should have a cellphone number, home number, and e-mail address; check for messages regularly; and promptly return phone calls. If your agent is going to be out of town, she should notify you of the dates and line up someone to handle your affairs.
- **Comfort with presenting low-ball offers.** If an agent cringes at offering a price well below market value, he's not the agent for you. He should be willing and able to pitch one or more low-ball offers with a poker face.
- **Top-seller status.** An ideal candidate is skilled not only in finding good deals but also at marketing and selling properties for top dollar and in a reasonable amount of time.

  As you search the classifieds and notice For Sale signs and brochures in the neighborhood, note which companies and agents do a better job of marketing their properties.
- **Internet savvy.** The tools and information available on the Internet can give you a significant edge.
- **Personal experience flipping properties.** Personal experience is a big plus, because the person knows what flippers require to turn a profit and typically has a strong network of affordable contractors to perform repairs and renovations. Preferably, the person is no longer in the business of flipping properties; otherwise, she may take the best deals for herself.

  Don't use experience in flipping houses as your sole criteria for choosing one agent over another. You want a quality agent — experience in flipping is a bonus.

The best way to find an agent is through referrals from other homeowners (buyers and sellers), preferably your friends, relatives, or neighbors. When you have a list of 10 to 15 names, start calling around and interviewing your candidates to compare their experience, education, and certification as described in the preceding list.

Many books on buying and selling houses recommend that you try to convince the agent to accept a lower percentage in commissions or a flat fee for helping you buy or sell a property, but this tactic can backfire. I suggest that you find the best agent and then pay the agent the going rate or a little more. Your agent is going to work harder for clients who pay more, and no card-carrying capitalist can blame her.

Recruiting Moneymen (and Women)

Flipping properties for a profit is all about money — getting it, spending it, paying taxes on it, and using it for your next flip. To succeed, you need someone who's good at managing the finances while you're busy buying, rehabbing, and selling. Actually, you may need three people who are good with money — one to loan you money, a second to help you manage it and save on taxes, and a third to recommend the best way to invest it. The following sections describe the types of financial assistance you need.

Finding financiers

Unless you're independently wealthy, you need a source of cash to get started. You may be able to tap into your savings account and max out your credit card, but strong financial backing from investors can provide you with the capital you need to leverage your personal investment. The big question is: Who can you ask for investment capital? Here's a list to get you started:

- Start with friends, family, and your attorney. They already know you, and charity begins at home.
- Tell everyone you come in contact with that you flip houses. An investor may hear about it and contact you, but be careful — an investor may be looking for a newbie to snooker into a raw deal. Question any deal that requires you to take on an inordinate share of the risk.
- Contact doctors, lawyers, dentists, and other highly paid professionals you know who may be looking for a better return on their investments than they're currently getting.

WARNING!

Whoever lends you money is going to want a mortgage in the first position that protects her investment. If you're investing in foreclosure properties, make sure that you purchase a first mortgage — not a second mortgage or a junior lien. In Chapter 10, I explain how to do your homework so you know exactly what you're buying. Even if lenders choose to forgo security, insist on it. The most important thing as a flipper is that you protect your investors' assets.

If you contact everyone you know and you're still short on cash, consider approaching a *hard-money* lender. Hard money is typically a short-term, high-interest loan. In Chapter 5, I discuss various types of loans, including hard money.

REMEMBER

Finding investors can initially be a frustrating chore, but your future success will draw investors to you who are willing to share the risk and eager to work with an experienced and knowledgeable flipper. See Chapter 5 for more ways to finance your flip.

Hiring an accountant

Most of the accounting that applies to house flipping consists of simple addition and subtraction. Add up the costs of buying, renovating, and selling the house and subtract that from the amount you receive when you sell the house, and if you come up with a positive number, you made money.

Unfortunately, reality is a little more complex, and having a professional accountant on call can help you avoid unnecessary expenses and legal woes. Your accountant can take all your money and receipts out of your shoe box, sort through them, figure out whether you made any money, and if you did make money, he can calculate the amount of tax you owe. An experienced accountant also delivers the following services:

- Saves you money on income tax while remaining in compliance with complex IRS tax laws. (See Chapter 23 for more about tax issues.)
- Reminds you to pay your property taxes on time.
- Evaluates your house-flipping activity to determine whether you're considered an investor or a self-employed dealer.
- Makes sure you pay your quarterly estimated taxes if you're considered a self-employed dealer.
- Ensures you pay your quarterly estimated taxes on your capital gains if you're considered an investor.
- Offers a sanity check to make sure that your grand vision for the house doesn't blow your budget.

TIP

Ask your family and friends for referrals to qualified accountants who have experience with real estate. If you already have an accountant who has little experience in real estate, ask her whether she knows of someone. Interview at least three candidates and be sure to ask about their experience in real estate.

Obtaining sound investment advice

When the money starts rolling in, your first impulse may be to roll your profits into your next flip, but that's not always the savviest approach. You may want to sock away some money in tax-deferred accounts to save on taxes and protect your gains. A knowledgeable financial advisor can provide the advice you need to make the best use of your profits.

REMEMBER

People who flip houses are often short-sighted. They focus three to six months into the future but can't see 20 to 30 years down the road. A financial advisor trains her vision on your long-term financial future and can help you take appropriate action now to build wealth for your retirement years. For details about long-term financial planning, check out the latest edition of *Personal Finance For Dummies,* by Eric Tyson, MBA (Wiley).

Consulting a Title Company and Insurance Agent to Cover Your Back

When you sign on the dotted line to purchase a property, you own not only the property but also all the problems associated with it. Buy a property from someone who's facing foreclosure, and you may just own a property that has one or more *liens* against it — legal claims against the property to secure a debt. (See Chapter 8 for more information about foreclosures and Chapter 10 for guidance on how to research a property.)

To avoid unforeseen problems associated with the title of a property you're about to purchase, hire a title company to search the title history. A title search ensures that:

- The property you think you're buying is the property you're actually buying.
- The person selling the property is the person who owns it.
- You're aware of any liens against the property or taxes due.
- Any rights, such as mineral rights, are transferred to you.
- Your deed or title is in recordable form.
- You're aware of any restrictions on the property; for example, if you're buying a home in a historical area, the renovations may have restrictions.

Reputation and location are the two main considerations in choosing a title company. Pick a company that's nearby and has the best reputation for smooth closings. Your real estate agent can recommend a title company that has a solid reputation in the area.

At the closing, obtain a copy of the final title insurance policy, which the seller typically pays for. This policy is your guarantee that the title is clear. If any hidden issues arise later, the title insurance company is accountable. Always get title insurance when buying a house.

Speaking of insurance, you should always obtain a homeowner's insurance policy for any property you purchase. In fact, you should consult an insurance agent prior to purchasing a property to make sure the policy is in effect as soon as possible after you close on the property. I know of a case involving raccoons that got into the attic of a home and did about $15,000 worth of damage. The good news was that the investor had the right insurance on the house and was covered for the damage.

Make sure you have an insurance agent on your team who can help you insure not only the properties you purchase but also anyone who does work for you and doesn't carry insurance for himself or herself. The added cost for insurance is well worth the price. If someone gets hurt on the job, that can cost you big time.

Locating a Valuable Appraiser

When someone buys a home, the person typically borrows money from a lender and uses the property as collateral for the loan. The bank or other lending institution orders an appraisal of the property to make sure it's worth enough to cover the loan in the event that the buyer defaults on the loan. The buyer typically pays for the appraisal as part of the closing costs.

As a flipper, you don't need an appraisal unless you're borrowing money from a lender who requires an appraisal to approve the loan. However, if you're unsure of the value of a particular piece of property, an appraiser can help you confirm the potential profitability of a property or perhaps present you with some figures that make you think twice about pitching an offer. You can ask the appraiser to provide you with two estimates: property value before repairs and renovations (as-is value) and property value after repairs and renovations (after-repair value). An appraisal may cost a little extra, but the additional information may help you make a better decision, especially when you're just getting started.

If you're in the market for an appraiser, ask your real estate agent, title company, or attorney for a recommendation.

TIP

To determine whether a property is worth buying, check out the recent sale prices of comparable properties in the same neighborhood and consult your real estate agent or another experienced investor for a second opinion. An appraisal may do you little good when you're buying distressed properties at a deep discount.

WARNING!

Whether you're buying or selling a home, beware of inflated appraisals. Some real estate scams rely on inflated appraisals to sucker mortgage companies into lending more than the home is actually worth. If the seller is willing to take $185,000 for the house, but it appraises at $225,000, paying the seller $225,000 with the intent of receiving cash back from the seller is fraudulent. Nefarious appraisers may also jack up the value of a home to inflate the homeowner's equity so the owner can qualify for a loan. Don't rely solely on an appraisal to determine the true value of a property. By specializing in properties in a certain price range, you can become an expert on property values in that range.

Adding a Real Estate Lawyer to the Roster

All lawyers are not created equal. You can find attorneys who specialize in divorce, disability, criminal law, personal injury, corporate law, and so on. When you're flipping properties, you want a real estate lawyer. An experienced real estate lawyer can offer valuable assistance in the following areas:

- **Purchase agreement:** Purchase agreements are complex documents that cover not only the sale price but also the terms of sale — tax prorations, occupancy issues, water bills, personal property in the house, and so on. Unless it's in writing, a purchase agreement is subject to dispute. Inexperienced real estate agents often introduce errors, costing their clients hundreds or thousands of dollars.
- **Title:** Your lawyer can advise you on the best way to take title in your situation. For example, you may want only your name on the title or your name and your spouse's name if you're married. A lawyer can also inspect the title work to ensure your protection. (See the earlier section "Consulting a Title Company and Insurance Agent to Cover Your Back" for more details.)
- **Complex transactions:** Some transactions may include an assumption of the mortgage or enable the seller to finance the purchase. When complexities arise, having a lawyer on call is always a plus.

TIP

To find a qualified real estate lawyer, ask your real estate agent, friends, and family for referrals or contact your local bar association. Don't resort to merely picking a name out of a phone book unless you really have to. The ideal candidate possesses the following qualities:

- **Efficient and affordable:** Attorneys often charge by the minute, so beware of long talkers.
- **Supportive:** Someone who second-guesses all of your investment decisions can paralyze you with doubt.
- **Unobtrusive:** Your lawyer should protect you from unseen risk without sinking the deal. Some lawyers justify their fee by becoming too technical with the documents, and that's just plain irritating.
- **Available:** A good lawyer is available when you need her.
- **Experienced:** A real estate attorney who owns real estate and rentals is better than one who doesn't.
- **Generous:** A lawyer who shares his leads can help you find properties that you couldn't find on your own.

WARNING!

Lawyer fees can range from a hundred to a couple thousand dollars. Compare rates and services closely and make sure that you consult a lawyer who specializes in real estate.

Lining Up a Home Inspector

Whenever you make an offer on a house, make the offer contingent upon the house passing inspection. Then, have the home professionally inspected. This contingency ensures that you don't get stuck holding the bag on any of the following big-ticket items:

- Damaged foundation or other structural anomalies
- Electrical wiring problems
- Poor plumbing or aging septic systems, especially if the house has been vacant for some time
- Leaking, nonfunctioning, or nonexistent gas lines
- Poorly functioning furnace or central air-conditioning units
- Leaking or ramshackle roof
- Termite or other critter damage
- Health hazards, such as lead-based paint, toxic mold, radon gas, asbestos, and hazardous insulation
- Neighboring structures built on your property. Always check the survey to make sure that the homeowner didn't allow the neighbor to build his new garage ten feet over on your property.

TIP

Although most buyers hire private home inspectors, I prefer using city inspectors because they tend to be more thorough and they're well versed on local building codes. The city inspectors in our area show up as a team that typically includes a plumber, an electrician, a heating and air-conditioning specialist, a builder, and someone who specializes in zoning. You get a thorough inspection and a complete write-up for about the same price you pay a private inspector. If the inspection uncovers problems, you can sign off on the recommendations, agreeing to make the necessary repairs after you take possession. However, not all towns and cities offer inspections, and some offer them only for new homes, so this option may not be available to you.

If you decide to hire an inspector, you can crack open the phone book and find listings for dozens of home inspectors in just about any area of the country. Finding a qualified home inspector, however, is a challenge. Begin by asking your real estate agent or other real estate professionals you know for references.

TIP

The National Association of Certified Home Inspectors (NACHI) is a nonprofit agency that works toward educating and ensuring the quality of home inspectors. Its website at www.nachi.org features an online referral service that you can search to find certified home inspectors in your area.

When you have a few leads, contact your candidates and ask them the following questions:

- **Are you certified, licensed, and insured?** Certification and licensing ensure that the inspector has the basic qualifications for the job. Insurance covers any serious defects he may overlook.
- **How long have you been a home inspector?** Length of service is often, but not always, a good indication of experience and expertise.
- **How many homes have you inspected?** "One or two" isn't the answer you're looking for. A busy home inspector is usually busy because she's good.
- **What did you do before becoming a home inspector?** Someone who's a retired carpenter or home builder is probably a better candidate than, say, a burned-out dance instructor.
- **Do you have references I can call?** If the inspector has a good track record, people don't hesitate to provide positive references.
- **Do you recommend remedies or simply identify problems?** Look for an inspector who's had experience in construction. The builder who constructed my home made an excellent home inspector and actually moved into this field full time. His approach was to not only point out problems but also recommend repairs and renovations.

WARNING!

You don't want a home inspector who makes mountains out of mole hills. He can deflate your balloon of enthusiasm with a thousand pin holes. Don't nitpick a great deal. A homeowner who's selling a property at a clearance price often does so to avoid the costs and headaches of making repairs. Nitpicking can ruin your chances of acquiring a great piece of property. Also, don't hire your inspector as your contractor — such a move only tempts your inspector/contractor to find more problems with the property.

Also, never hire a family member or friend as a home inspector even if they're qualified, because they'll become the expert and tell you what you're doing right and wrong. The problem is they may not completely understand the project and what you're trying to accomplish.

TIP

Make sure all utilities (electricity, gas, water) are turned on prior to the scheduled inspection, so the inspector can check the furnace, plumbing, and electrical system. In vacant homes, the previous owner or the bank may have the utilities turned off. Be at the property when the gas and water are turned on, just in case something's leaking or a faucet is turned on.

Contacting Contractors and Subcontractors

When flipping a house, you can do as much of the fixing up as you're qualified, comfortable, and willing to do (see Chapter 14 for details on determining do-it-yourself projects). For everything else, hire a professional — contractor or subcontractor.

- A *contractor* (or general contractor) is the boss. He or she manages the budget and workflow, hires subcontractors, coordinates the work from start to finish, and hands you the bill.
- *Subcontractors* perform specific tasks, such as wiring, plumbing, installing ductwork, and so on.

REMEMBER

On isolated jobs — jobs that require only one subcontractor — you can often do the contracting yourself. For more extensive projects that require the coordination of multiple workers, a general contractor may be better suited. To me, a general contractor represents additional overhead I don't need to pay for. By working closely with the subcontractors to coordinate the work, you should be able to handle the general contracting yourself, but if you have any doubts about your own abilities in managing the project, hire a qualified contractor. Chapter 14 can help you plan and manage your renovations so that the subcontractors aren't tripping over each other.

In the following sections, I explain how to find and hire contractors and subcontractors. I also tell you when a handyman may be better suited for your needs.

WARNING!

If you decide to play the contractor role, obtain a permit before starting work on any project that requires a permit, such as building a room addition, a deck, or a garage or installing a pool. If you don't obtain a required permit, authorities may show up and issue a stop work order. You may have to pay a fine. If you've already completed the project and the work doesn't adhere to local building codes, you may need to redo or undo the work at your own expense.

Tracking down top-notch contractors and subcontractors

Good help shows up on time, performs quality work, charges reasonable fees, and completes the job on time or ahead of schedule. Finding good help is one of the main challenges of successfully flipping properties. Fortunately, you can network your way to the best help in your area by doing the following:

- Ask for referrals at your local hardware store. Word-of-mouth is better than advertisements or a name on a grocery store bulletin board.
- Ask real estate agents, investors, and other real estate professionals for references. When they're not working, real estate people talk . . . a lot. Good contractors and subcontractors have a solid reputation.

  If your real estate agent volunteers to act as your general contractor, think twice about hiring him; good agents typically make horrible contractors. If your agent is good, he's serving his clients well and has neither the time nor the desire to get involved in construction. Besides, agents don't like to get their hands dirty; contractors do.
- Contact your insurance company. Most insurance companies have a database of contractors who do everything from installing carpet to cleaning up after floods and are happy to steer you toward the right person, especially if they're footing the bill.
- Talk to friends, relatives, and neighbors who live in the area and find out who they hire for specific jobs.
- Contact a referral service such as Angie's List, `www.angieslist.com`, which provides ratings and comments from homeowners.

Contracting with contractors and subcontractors

When you're hiring a contractor or subcontractor, you have three goals. You want the job completed to your satisfaction, on budget, and on schedule. To achieve these goals, here's what you do:

- Draw up a one-page agreement stating when the contractor is to start and finish, with a built-in fee of $50 for every day beyond the scheduled completion date. When you get the contractor's estimate and proposal, attach your agreement to it. The contract should specify a start and end date and contain language stating that the contractor must consult with you before performing any additional work not mentioned in the contract. Your agent or lawyer can help you draft a suitable contract.
- Let them know when the For Sale sign is going up.
- Give them what they need to succeed, including deposits and supplies.
- Have them furnish you with receipts of their purchases.
- Show up unannounced at the worksite to see whether they're working.
- If the workers are doing a good job, tell them so, and do it often.
- Don't strive for perfection. If the work is 90 percent satisfactory, shut up about the 10 percent that's not quite perfect.

WARNING!

Beware of the following issues when contracting workers:

- When hiring a contractor or subcontractor, make sure that the person is insured against both property damage and personal injury. An average hospital bill can wipe out your profit.
- Be careful about deposits, especially when you're dealing with a contractor you don't know. Contractors have been known to take the deposit and disappear. A 25 to 50 percent deposit is normal — generally, the smaller the contractor, the larger the deposit. You can pay most handymen weekly.

TIP

To lessen the risk of getting ripped off, do your due diligence: Check references, workmanship, and the amount of time the contractor has been in business; ask the contractor whether he's licensed and insured; and check with the state or your local Better Business Bureau to see whether anyone has filed complaints against the contractor. Also consider searching the web for the contractor by name to determine whether any positive or negative reviews have been posted online.

WARNING!

Your contractor should supply you with a separate *proof of insurance* form, attached to the bid, that verifies that the contractor and his workers are insured for this particular job. If you're hiring a subcontractor who's moonlighting from his day job, he may be covered under his company's insurance policy, but he may *not* be covered during his stint as a moonlighter. When hiring a contractor or handyman who can't provide you with proof of insurance, contact your insurance company and take out a separate workman's comp policy (or add coverage to your current policy on the house you're flipping) that covers anyone who's working on your house. Added insurance takes a little extra time and costs a few hundred dollars, but if you're not covered and a worker is injured on the job, he may sue you, and you may lose your entire profit and even some of your own personal savings. I estimate that only about 5 percent of the people who flip houses follow this advice — but those who don't are vulnerable to suffering a big loss.

When I hire contractors to do work for me and they don't have insurance, I get insurance for them. It's affordable, and you don't want to be responsible for injuries.

Finding a handyman and other helpers

You don't necessarily need a licensed subcontractor to do odd jobs around the house. A *handyman* (someone who's handy with power tools and hand tools) can often complete small jobs for a fraction of the cost a subcontractor charges. If the house needs all new wiring or plumbing or has structural damage, pay a little extra for a licensed expert. For smaller jobs, such as leaky faucets, clogged drains, drywall repairs, and new window dressings, a good handyman is usually the more affordable choice. I say "usually" because sometimes a specialty service, such as a replacement window company or Grout Doctor, can provide quality workmanship for less.

Word-of-mouth is still the best way to find a handyman, but your neighborhood newspaper provides additional leads in the classifieds. (The local paper is also a good source for finding general laborers and trash haulers — perfect for cleaning out that cluttered basement, attic, or garage.) Craigslist is fine for finding a candidate, but make sure the person has positive reviews or testimonials or can provide names of people in your area who will vouch for her work. The handyman with the fanciest truck and flashiest ad isn't always the best or most affordable. Look for a worker with paint-stained pants and worn hands. Performance and reputation carry more weight than marketing glitz.

In the summer, consider hiring neighborhood high-school and college students who are off for the summer. Many of these kids work hard, especially with the lighter stuff like painting, cleaning, and doing yard work. Just be sure you're there to supervise and make sure that your eager students are following safety precautions.

Chapter 5

Securing the Funds to Fuel Your Flips

In This Chapter

- Understanding the concept of leverage
- Unlocking the equity in your current home
- Locating lenders and comparing their rates and terms
- Discovering other creative financing options

Flipping houses is an expensive habit. You need money — *investment capital* — to finance the purchase of a house, perform renovations, pay the utilities and taxes, sell the home, and cover your living expenses while you're hard at work. The good news is that it doesn't all have to be *your* money. You can borrow against the equity in your home, hunt for the best loan, finance the purchase of the house through the seller, and even find eager investors who are willing to finance your venture in exchange for your expertise and sweat.

Lining up financial resources in advance of your house hunting enables you to pounce on a bargain and gives you leverage in negotiating the price you ultimately pay for a property. When you place an offer on a house and other bids come in, the seller may accept your offer of thousands of dollars less, simply because you have the cash on hand or financing in place to quickly close the deal. Ready cash also frees you to plan and begin rehabbing the property immediately rather than waiting around for sluggish credit checks and loan approvals.

Lining up financing can never be done too soon, and it's something you should continue to work on. Always be on the lookout for additional sources of investment capital — cheaper money that's more readily available.

If you're thinking that you can't possibly get your mitts on enough cash to finance your house-flipping venture, this is the chapter for you. Here you find out what you're really worth — financially speaking, of course — and investigate the myriad sources of house-flipping investment capital.

Grasping the Power of Working with Borrowed Money

Some people have a natural aversion to debt for good reason — you pay more for stuff if you have to pay interest on the money you used to buy it. As a house flipper, however, you quickly discover that debt can be either good or bad. *Bad debt* is any money you borrow to purchase something that decreases in value over time, such as a boat or a pair of designer shoes. *Good debt* consists of money you borrow to acquire items that increase in value at a rate that exceeds the interest you pay on that debt.

As a real estate investor, good debt gives you *leverage.* It enables you to use other people's money to make money. Sure, borrowing money means you have to pay interest, and it carries some risks (if you don't turn a profit, you stand to lose money), but if you do everything right, you stand to earn considerably more than what the loan costs you in interest.

With house flipping, your goal is to move as much house as you can with as little of your own money as possible. If you invest $100,000 of your own money in a property, for example, and you flip it for a profit of $20,000, you make a 20 percent profit on your $100,000 investment. On the other hand, if you invest $20,000, borrow $80,000, and flip the property for a profit of $20,000 ($20,000 more than your investment), you earn a 100 percent profit.

To look at it another way, suppose you have $100,000 to invest. Many people assume that using that $100,000 to finance a single flip is the smart thing to do because you avoid paying interest on borrowed money. However, by leveraging that $100,000 with borrowed money, you stand to earn a bigger profit. For example, you can combine that $100,000 with borrowed money to flip a higher-priced property — perhaps a $500,000 house that you know you can sell in the $575,000 to $600,000 range.

Borrowing money is always risky, but you have to take some risk to earn the big bucks. Throughout this book, I show you ways to reduce risk, but unforeseen events can undermine the best-laid plans. As a flipper, you need to decide for yourself whether the potential benefits outweigh the risks.

The following sections show you how to gain leverage by using other people's money to finance your flips. And if you don't have money, I show you how to convince private lenders to put up some initial investment capital to get you started.

Unleashing the Equity of Your Current Home

Your home is more than just a place to live — it's an investment, perhaps the best-performing investment you have (or the worst, if property values in your area have dropped dramatically). As you pay down the principal on the mortgage, equity in the home grows (assuming the house appreciates). *Equity* is your home's net worth — if you sold the home today and paid off the mortgage, equity is the money you would stuff in your pocket.

You don't have to sell your home to pocket the equity. By refinancing the home or taking out a home equity loan, you can unleash the equity and use it (or a portion of it) as investment capital to finance your house-flipping venture. I cover both of these options, along with the risks of unleashing equity in your home, in the following sections. Further on in this chapter, I show you how to work with banks and other lending institutions to unlock the equity in your home.

REMEMBER

You don't have to tap into the equity in your home to flip houses. Tapping into your equity can place your primary residence at risk, and if you and your spouse both sign the loan documents, you're both at risk. If you're uncomfortable placing your home and other possessions at risk, consider borrowing *hard money* — high-interest loans that typically require an upfront payment and scheduled *balloon* (lump-sum) payments. Hard money loans often finance the purchase of the property along with the cash needed to repair and renovate it. The property and any future improvements function as collateral for the loan. Banks, mortgage companies, other lending institutions, and private lenders often offer hard-money loans. The drawback is that hard money isn't cheap — lenders may charge two to three times as much in interest as banks and other lending institutions, along with 3 percent to 10 percent in closing costs.

Recognizing the risks

In many ways, equity is funny money . . . or fuzzy money. Nobody really knows how much you can sell your home for until you actually sell it, so borrowing against equity is a bit risky. Before taking the leap, be well aware of the risks:

- If real estate values drop, you may owe more on your home than it's worth.
- Unlike other types of loans, mortgage and home equity loans use your home as collateral. If you can't afford the higher house payments on your new loan, you may lose your home.

- If interest rates rise, refinancing at a higher rate or for a longer term results in your paying more for your current home — potentially tens of thousands of dollars more.
- Frequent refinancing can cost you thousands in *closing costs* that may take you years to recoup.

Refinancing your mortgage

The easiest way to unlock a chunk of equity is to refinance your home, giving you a whole new mortgage, paying off the old mortgage, and leaving you the rest. (I cover the basics of mortgages in the later section "Winding your way through the mortgage maze.") Ideally, you refinance a mortgage not only to cash out equity for investment capital but also to snag a lower interest rate or shorter term, so you pay less interest over the life of the loan.

Suppose, for example, that you currently have a $200,000, 30-year mortgage at 8 percent with a monthly house payment of $1,467.53. You've owned the house for 10 years and still owe $175,000 on the mortgage. If you refinance for $250,000 (the home's current appraised value) and take out a 20-year mortgage at 6 percent, now you have a house payment of $1,791.08, and you walk away with the $75,000 equity that was locked up in the house (the refinanced amount of $250,000 minus the $175,000 to pay off the old mortgage) to use as investment capital.

Well, that certainly looks pretty rosy, but what have you lost in the transaction?

- You now owe $250,000 on your home and have no equity built up in it.
- Your new house payment is $323 more than your previous house payment.
- Over the life of the loan, you're scheduled to pay $77,651 more than you would have paid by sticking with your original mortgage.

In short, you're pretty much getting money now and paying it later. But think of it this way — by putting your equity to work for you in successful flips, you can eventually profit enough to pay off your mortgage in much less time. If you can make ten times what it cost you, you earn $750,000 by putting your equity to work for you.

Of course, you don't have to unleash all the equity in your home. To build on the previous example, you could take out a 20-year, $225,000 loan at 6 percent, with a monthly payment of $1,611.97, freeing up $50,000 in equity, or a 20-year, $200,000 loan at 6 percent with a monthly payment of $1,432.86, freeing up $25,000 in equity. Your choice depends primarily on your comfort level and risk and debt tolerance. The more equity you leave in the house, the greater your cushion, but the less investment capital you have to work with.

When refinancing, take the following precautions:

- Don't refinance into a loan that has a *prepayment penalty* — a provision in the loan agreement stating that if you pay off the balance of the loan early, you have to pay extra. The amount you're required to pay is usually a percentage of the balance at the time you pay off the loan or a certain number of months of interest. The purpose of a prepayment penalty is to ensure that the lender receives some compensation for its work.
- Don't refinance if you have to roll the closing costs into your new mortgage — thus increasing the principal.
- Don't refinance a fixed-rate mortgage into a new adjustable-rate mortgage. Adjustable-rate mortgages are unpredictable; you could get burned by a sudden increase in the interest rate and your monthly payments. See "Riding the waves with an adjustable-rate mortgage," later in this chapter, for details.

Taking out a second mortgage with home equity loans and lines of credit

Taking out a second mortgage, in the form of a home equity loan or line of credit, unlocks the equity in your home without affecting your current mortgage:

- A *home equity loan* provides you with a single chunk of money — a one-time payment to you. Lenders may not charge closing costs on home equity loans. Some banks even pay for the credit report and appraisal.
- A *home equity line of credit* enables you to borrow only what you need and pay interest on only what you borrow, making this option attractive for financing renovations. It's sort of like a credit card, often with a lower interest rate.

Home equity loans and lines of credit often come with adjustable interest rates, which carry additional risks, as I explain in the section "Riding the waves with an adjustable-rate mortgage."

Taking out a second mortgage may be a better financial choice than refinancing your current mortgage in the following situations:

- The interest rate on your first mortgage is low compared to current interest rates. Refinancing a home at 8 percent when you already have a loan at 4.5 percent is usually a poor choice.
- You've been paying on your first mortgage for several years. With every payment you make, you pay more on principal and less on interest, so if you've been paying 15 years on a 30-year mortgage, refinancing now may cost you in the long run.

- You can quickly flip the property you're investing in and pay off the second mortgage. Assuming the loan has no prepayment penalty, if you can unlock the equity in your home and then quickly pay back the money, you retain your home's equity.

TIP

Home-equity loans are almost always preferable to taking out a second mortgage, assuming you can get a low-cost, low-interest, fixed-rate loan, because they're reusable. That is, you can pay down the amount you owe on a home-equity loan and then start it up again. Second mortgages are fixed and can't be reused; after you pay it off, that credit is no longer available.

Making Yourself Look Good to Prospective Lenders

After you establish yourself as a successful house flipper, private investors will stuff your pockets with cash because you have a proven track record. Until then, you had better look good on paper. That means you must have money in the bank, investments, or assets you can sell. It means you pay your bills on time. It means you're not so heavily burdened by debt that one more loan is likely to push you into bankruptcy.

Before you begin flipping houses, examine your financial position as carefully as any lender would examine it. Pretend that you're the lender. Would you lend yourself the money? Lenders look at your five C's: collateral, character, credit, confidence, and cash flow:

- **Collateral** is the property you intend to purchase. When you're flipping houses and attempting to obtain loan approval before looking at houses, you're not in a position to describe the collateral, but you can put together a plan that shows the price ranges of the houses you intend to purchase, appreciation percentages for the area, and how you plan to renovate and sell the properties for a profit. See "Pitching your plan" later in this chapter.
- **Character** is the way you present yourself to the lender. You need to convince the lender that you have the knowledge and resources available to profit from your investments. A strong plan and presentation can convince the lender that you have the right stuff.
- **Credit** is your credit report, credit score, and credit-worthiness (how much you can afford). A clean credit report shows that you pay your bills and aren't over your head in debt. See "Checking and correcting your credit report" later in this chapter.

- **Confidence** is the confidence you and the lender have that you can deliver what you promise. Pitching a solid plan can build the lender's confidence. How you portray your project either gives the lender confidence in your abilities or sends the lender running to the hills.
- **Cash flow** is your current monthly income minus your monthly expenses — the amount of money you have free each month to take on your project.

The following sections take a snapshot of your financial picture and highlight the details that lenders commonly consider before approving a loan. By identifying areas of improvement, you can airbrush out any imperfections to make yourself look as good as possible to prospective lenders.

Determining what you're worth in dollars and cents

REMEMBER

Net worth is simply whatever money you would have if you sold all your stuff and then paid off all your debts, including your taxes. Officially, the equation goes like this:

Net Worth = Assets – Liabilities – Taxes

A strong positive net worth indicates that you:

- Own more than you owe
- Don't borrow more than you can pay for
- Can pay off a loan by liquidating assets, if necessary
- Pay your taxes on time
- Probably know more about net worth than you realize

To prove to a lender that you're net worthy, type up a page that lists your assets, liabilities, and the taxes you owe and presents your net worth. The following section shows you how to calculate your net worth. If you have a spreadsheet program or a personal finance program, such as Quicken, use the Reports feature to generate a net-worth report.

REMEMBER

A strong net worth can help you borrow money at competitive interest rates, but a low or even a negative net worth is not a death knell. If you have a solid investment strategy and the energy and commitment to implement it, you can secure the capital you need to get started. See "Pitching your plan" later in this chapter for tips on how to prove to a lender that you have a solid investment strategy.

The following sections explain how to calculate and boost your net worth.

Tabulating your net worth

Nobody has much trouble subtracting liabilities from assets to determine their net worth. The tough part is identifying assets and liabilities. First, jot down a list of everything you own, including cash, savings, investments, and possessions. The following list of items may stimulate your brain cells:

- **Home:** If you sold your home today, what could you get for it? If you recently had an appraisal, use that number, assuming the appraiser assigned it an honest value. (See Chapter 13 for more about appraisals.)
- **Car:** The Kelley Blue Book value (current value), not what you paid for it.
- **Savings account:** Whether you have $5 or $50,000, it counts.
- **Checking account:** The current balance as recorded in your check register. No cheating. If you just wrote five checks that haven't cleared yet, you don't really have that money.
- **Retirement savings:** 401(k), IRA, SEP, or other accounts that you don't dip into for your daily living expenses.
- **Investments:** Stocks, bonds, and mutual funds that aren't part of a retirement account.
- **Jewelry, antiques, and artwork:** If you're not sure what this stuff is worth, have it professionally appraised and insured. People often think that their stuff is worth much more than it really is.
- **Furniture:** If you sold all your furniture at an auction or garage sale, what could you get for it?
- **Cash value of life insurance:** If you have term life insurance, that would be $0. If you use a life-insurance policy as an investment, how much is it worth today?

WARNING! If you don't have it, don't count it. The money you stand to inherit when Aunt Millie kicks the bucket doesn't count.

Now for the painful part. Jot down a list of liabilities, such as the following:

- **Mortgage principal:** The amount you owe on your house today and on any other loans you've taken out on the house.
- **Car loan:** How much would it cost to pay off your car loan today? Write it down.
- **Student loans:** If you're paying off any student loans from your old college days or are named as a co-signer on any of your kids' student loans, record the amounts as liabilities.

- **Credit-card debt:** Dig out your credit-card bills and tally up the total you owe on them.
- **Personal loans:** Did you borrow $500 from your rich Uncle Louie to make a down payment on your car? Write it down.

You can get most of the liability information you need from your credit report, as I discuss later in this chapter in the section "Checking and correcting your credit report." However, if you know that you have a debt that doesn't appear on the credit report, be sure to include it in your calculations.

Now, add up your assets, subtract your liabilities, subtract any back taxes you owe, and the next time someone asks, "What's your net worth?" you're prepared to answer.

Boosting your net worth

As a general rule, net worth grows about as fast as an oak tree. Unless you score big in the lottery or inherit a couple hundred thousand dollars, you can do little to jack up your net worth in a hurry. By becoming fiscally responsible, living within your means, and paying down credit-card debt, however, you can improve your net worth over time.

Some companies can set you up with phony savings accounts and lease assets to make you look like Ritchie Rich, so you can qualify for loans you can't qualify for legitimately. Don't get sucked into asset rental scams. You can end up in jail. Boost your net worth the old-fashioned way — earn it.

Checking and correcting your credit report

Good credit is gold. Without it, you have access only to your own money. With it, you can put other people's money to work for you. Whenever you apply for a loan, the lending institution performs a *credit check* — sort of a background check to make sure that you're not up to your gills in debt, that your income covers expenses, and that you pay your bills on time.

To ensure success at obtaining loans, become proactive. Check your credit report every three months or so, correct any errors, and take steps to improve your credit rating, as instructed in the following sections. No irregularity is too small to correct.

The following sections show you how to obtain, review, and correct your credit report. I also explain how to improve your credit score.

Obtaining a credit report

Back in 2005, the Federal Trade Commission made it mandatory for the three major credit-reporting companies to provide you with a free credit report once every 12 months. To obtain your free credit report, do one of the following:

- Submit your request online at `www.annualcreditreport.com`.
- Phone in your request by calling toll-free 877-322-8228.
- Download the Annual Credit Report Request Form from `www.annualcreditreport.com/cra/requestformfinal.pdf`, fill it out, and mail it to Annual Credit Report Request Service, P.O. Box 105281, Atlanta, GA 30348-5281.

If you already obtained a free credit report this year and want something more recent, you can order a credit report from any or all of the following three credit-reporting agencies (prices and terms vary):

- **Equifax:** 800-685-1111 or online at `www.equifax.com`.
- **Experian:** 888-397-3742 or online at `www.experian.com`.
- **TransUnion:** 877-322-8228 or online at `www.transunion.com`.

Inspecting your credit report

When you receive your credit report, inspect it carefully for the following red flags:

- Addresses of places you've never lived.
- Aliases you've never used, which may indicate that someone else is using your Social Security number or that the credit-reporting agency has mixed someone else's data into yours.
- Two or more Social Security numbers, flagging the possibility that information for someone with the same name has made it into your credit report.
- Wrong date of birth (DOB).
- Credit cards you don't have.
- Loans you haven't taken out.
- Records of unpaid bills that you either know you paid or have good reason for not paying.
- Records of delinquent payments that you either know you paid on time or have a good excuse for not paying on time.
- Inquiries from companies with whom you've never done business. (When you apply for a loan, the lender typically runs an *inquiry* on your credit report, and that shows up on the report.)

An address of a place you've never lived or records of accounts, loans, and credit cards you never had may be a sign that somebody has stolen your identity. Yikes! Contact the credit-reporting company immediately and request that a fraud alert be placed on your credit report. For tips on protecting yourself against identity theft and recovering from it, check out *Identity Theft For Dummies*, by Michael J. Arata, Jr. (Wiley).

Last but certainly not least: Your credit report should contain your credit score. If it doesn't, contact the credit-reporting agency and request your score.

Understanding what your credit score means

To give your credit rating an air of objectivity, credit-reporting agencies often assign you a credit score that ranges roughly between 300 (you never paid a bill in your life) and 900 (you borrow often, always pay your bills on time, and don't carry any huge balances on your credit cards).

Your credit score determines not only whether you qualify for a loan but also how much you're qualified to borrow and at what interest rate. A high credit score lets you borrow more and pay less interest on it. A high score can also lower your home-insurance, auto-insurance, and life-insurance rates — just another reason why the rich get richer and the poor stay poor.

Credit score stats

Credit-reporting agencies rely on one or more statistical models to determine your credit score. One of the most popular models is the Fair Isaac Company (FICO) rating system. The credit company assigns numerical values to particular pieces of data in your credit history, such as the length of your credit history and the various types of interest you're paying. They then plug these numbers into the statistical model, which spits out your credit score. It's basically a numbers game that weighs the data on your credit report in the following manner:

- 35 percent of the score is based on payment history
- 30 percent is based on outstanding debt or how much you currently owe
- 15 percent is based on the length of your credit history or how long you've been borrowing
- 10 percent is based on recent inquiries on your report (whenever a lending institution requests a report)
- 10 percent is based on the types of credit, such as mortgage or credit-card interest

Cranking up your credit score

If you have a credit score of 700 or higher, pat yourself on the back. You're above average and certainly qualified to borrow big bucks at the lowest available rates. Anything below about 680 sounds the warning sirens. This number is the point at which lending institutions get out their magnifying glasses and begin raising rates and denying credit. If your credit rating dips below 700, take steps to improve it, such as the following:

- Dispute any erroneous items on your credit report. Disputing a claim doesn't always result in a correction, but you can request to have a paragraph explaining your side of the story added to your report.
- Apply for fewer loans and credit cards. When you apply for a loan or credit card, the lending institution typically orders an inquiry that shows up on your credit report. Evidence that you're applying for several loans or credit cards in a short period of time can make you appear financially desperate.
- Pay off your credit-card balances or at least pay off enough so the balance is 50 percent or below your available credit limit. If you have enough equity in your home, you can refinance to consolidate high-interest credit-card bills into your mortgage payment, but avoid the temptation to begin racking up more credit-card debt after refinancing. (I cover refinancing your mortgage earlier in this chapter.)

WARNING!

Avoid credit-enhancement companies on the web that claim to provide seasoned credit within 90 days. Law-enforcement authorities are shutting down these sites on a regular basis. Legitimate credit counselors can help you repair your damaged credit, but it takes some work and belt-tightening. Quick fixes are typically fraudulent fixes.

Avoiding mistakes that can sabotage your loan approval

After you apply for a loan, resist the urge to make any life-changing decisions that negatively affect your current financial status. Major changes can undermine your efforts to secure a loan. When you're applying for a loan, follow the advice of our friend and colleague, loan officer Marc Edelstein, with his Ten Commandments When Applying for a Mortgage Loan:

1. Thou shalt not change jobs, become self-employed, or quit your job.
2. Thou shalt not buy a car, truck, or van (or you may be living in it)!
3. Thou shalt not use charge cards excessively or let your accounts fall behind.

4. Thou shalt not spend money you have set aside for closing.
5. Thou shalt not omit debts or liabilities from your loan application.
6. Thou shalt not buy furniture.
7. Thou shalt not originate any inquiries into your credit (for example, by applying for a new credit card).
8. Thou shalt not make large deposits without first checking with your loan officer.
9. Thou shalt not change bank accounts.
10. Thou shalt not co-sign a loan for anyone.

To simplify the loan process, supply your lender with copies of your last three bank statements and last three federal tax returns.

If your financial situation changes between the application and the time of closing, you are legally obligated to inform the loan officer and lender of the change.

Bargain Hunting for Low-Interest Loans

When money is readily available and you have a credit score in the mid- to upper-700s or higher, lending institutions trip over themselves to win your business by offering bigger loans at lower interest rates. By shopping around and haggling, you can often convince a lending institution to loan you money at a rate lower than advertised.

Smart shoppers are well aware of the market and the factors that make one loan more attractive than another. The following sections bring you up to speed on mortgage-speak, show you where to look for the best deals, and help you compare loans that appear to be similar but can be drastically different. For the full scoop on mortgages, be sure to check out the latest edition of *Mortgages For Dummies*, by Eric Tyson and Ray Brown (Wiley).

Winding your way through the mortgage maze

Before you start loan hunting, brush up on the five main types of loans that I cover in the following sections: fixed-rate, adjustable, interest-only, balloon-payment, and minimum-payment. Although one loan type isn't necessarily better or worse, each has unique characteristics that make it better suited for a particular house-flipping strategy (I cover these strategies in Chapter 3).

When financing a flip, having access to cash is the most important consideration, followed closely by the cost of the money. Ask yourself:

- Can I afford the payment?
- Are the rates reasonable?
- Will I be able to make a profit in the end?

Holding steady with fixed-rate mortgages

A fixed-rate mortgage is a loan whose interest rate remains unchanged throughout the life of the loan. If you take out a 30-year loan at 6 percent today, you still pay 6 percent interest 25 years down the road. Fixed-rate mortgages are most attractive under the following conditions:

- Interest rates are low.
- Your house-flipping strategy hinges on holding the property for several years.
- You expect interest rates to rise suddenly in the next few years.

For quick flips of one year or less, the benefits of a fixed-rate mortgage are typically negligible. If you're a buy-and-hold-'er, fixed-rate is probably the way to go. If you're doing a quick flip and have the stomach for a bit more risk, an adjustable-rate, interest-only, or minimum-payment mortgage may be a better choice, as I describe in the following sections.

Riding the waves with an adjustable-rate mortgage

Adjustable-rate mortgages (ARMs) have interest rates that fluctuate. You may take out a loan for 5 percent and find yourself paying 9 percent the following year, which is why I discourage you from taking out an ARM. Stick with fixed-rate loans so you don't need to rely on a crystal ball to figure out what your monthly payments will be.

If you're determined to take out an ARM instead of a fixed-rate mortgage, examine the following factors to determine the worst-case scenario:

- **Initial interest rate:** The interest rate when you sign for the loan. This rate is usually lower than the rate for a fixed-rate mortgage (see the previous section).
- **Adjustment period:** The frequency at which the rate can go up or down. This period is typically one, three, or five years but can be in months rather than years. (You'd need a crystal ball to determine what's best. If rates decline in the future, a shorter adjustment period is better. If rates rise, a longer adjustment period is better.)
- **Index:** Adjustable-rate mortgages are tied to an index that typically rises or falls based on government lending rates. Ask which index the lender uses, how often it changes, and how it has performed in the past.

- **Margin:** The percentage above the index that the lender charges. Think of it as a markup. For example, if the index is at 3 percent and the margin is 2 percent, you pay 5 percent interest. If the index rises two percentage points to 5 percent, you pay 7 percent interest. Obviously, you want the loan with the lowest margin.
- **Cap:** The cap is the highest interest rate the lender charges, no matter how high the index rises. So, if the lender sets a lifetime cap at 9 percent, you never pay more than 9 percent interest. If the lender sets an adjustment-period cap of 2 percent and the adjustment period is one year, the interest can rise a maximum of 2 percent each year. ARMs typically specify an adjustment period and a lifetime cap; for example, for an ARM with a cap of 2 and 6, the rate can jump a maximum of 2 percent per period but no higher than 6 percent over the life of the loan. The lower these caps are, the better for you.

WARNING!

Don't bite when a bank dangles an unbelievably low-interest ARM in front of you — a *teaser rate* that may be as low as 1 percent. Lenders may use this marketing ploy to snag unwary borrowers and then hit them with huge interest rate increases a few months down the road; the fine print may say that the rate can be adjusted every three to six months and can go as high as 12 percent! Such loans were a major contributor to the 2008 mortgage meltdown because they made monthly payments unaffordable for many homeowners.

Paying later with interest-only loans

An interest-only loan is just what it sounds like: You pay interest only and never pay down the principal. If you take out an interest-only loan for $100,000, in two years you still owe $100,000. Sound like a bum deal? If you plan on living in your home for 15 years and the value of the home doesn't appreciate significantly, it may be a bum deal, but if you're using the loan for a quick flip, it may be perfect. You pay off the loan in full right after you sell the house. In the meantime, your monthly payments are lower, so you have more investment capital for buying properties and financing renovations.

When considering interest-only loans, be aware of the following:

- Most interest only loans are ARMs (see the previous section), so check the adjustment period, index, margin, and caps.
- Make sure the loan doesn't come with a prepayment penalty. You may be able to pay off the loan early by flipping quickly, but if you have a 3 percent early-payment penalty, a $100,000 loan can cost you an additional $3,000.
- Rarely is an interest-only loan interest-only for the life of the loan. Read the fine print to determine when and how you must pay the principal. Some loans require a lump-sum payment three to five years down the road. They suck you in with low monthly payments early and then sock you with huge bills later.

Interest-only loans are great for quick flips or for homeowners who have jobs with wildly fluctuating monthly incomes, such as CEOs who receive fat seasonal bonuses and can pay off the principal in huge chunks. For the average homeowner, however, interest-only loans can be quite risky, especially in an inflated housing market.

Reducing interest with balloon payments

You can often find loans with lower interest rates by committing to pay off the principal after a fixed period of time with a *balloon payment* — a lump-sum payment due at the end of the term. Balloon-payment loans are often acceptable for quick flips, especially if the balloon payment is scheduled to coincide with the sale of the house.

Don't commit to balloon payments if you have any doubts that you can make the payments — you may set yourself up for failure. If renovations take longer than scheduled and payment is due before you can sell the property, you may have to refinance or get another loan to cover the balloon payment. If you can't secure additional loans, you may lose the property.

Flexing your finances with minimum-payment loans

Minimum-payment or *reverse-amortization* loans specify the absolute least you can pay each month. When you're strapped for cash, you pay just enough to cover the interest, and the principal remains unchanged. When you have a cash surplus, you can increase the payment to reduce the principal. When you're buried in bills, you can make the minimum payment, which doesn't quite cover the interest and increases the principal.

Minimum-payment loans aren't the most financially sound for the average homeowner, but they're attractive to flippers who need more flexibility in their financing. If you're running short on cash because renovations are running a little high, you can make the minimum payment and have more money to pay for renovations.

Playing the numbers game when you compare loans

When considering any type of loan, carefully examine interest rates and other factors to determine what's best overall and which loan is most suitable for your situation. An interest-only loan may offer lower monthly payments, but it may not be the best choice. A fixed-rate loan at a slightly higher interest rate may be better.

The best way to compare loans is to determine the total cost of the loan over the life of the loan:

1. **Start with the amount the bank charges you upfront in loan origination fees, discount points (interest you pay upfront, typically a percentage of the loan, to lower the interest rate), and other fees.**
2. **Multiply the monthly payment times the number of months you plan to pay on the loan.**
3. **Add the two amounts to determine your total payment.**
4. **Total the amount of each payment that goes toward paying the principal of the loan. (Your lender can tell you how much of each payment goes toward principal.)**
5. **Subtract the total you determined in Step 4 from the total in Step 3.**

Suppose you're considering two loans, each for $100,000. You plan on using the loan to buy and renovate a home over two years and then sell it and pay off the remaining principal on the loan. You have a choice between a 30-year, traditional fixed-rate mortgage at 6 percent or a 30-year interest-only loan at 5 percent. Look at the 6 percent, fixed-rate mortgage first:

Loan origination fee and discount points:	$1,000.00
Plus monthly payment of $599.55 × 24 months:	$14,389.20
Equals total payment:	$15,389.20
Minus total paid toward principal:	$2,531.75
Equals total cost of loan:	$12,857.45

Here are the numbers for the 30-year, interest-only loan at 5 percent:

Loan origination fee and discount points:	$1,000.00
Plus monthly payment of $416.67 × 24 months:	$10,000.08
Equals total payment:	$11,000.08
Minus total paid toward principal:	$0.00
Equals total cost of loan:	$11,000.08

If you've ruled out interest-only loans because you think you'll save money by paying down the principal, the numbers compel you to reconsider. With the traditional mortgage, you're not only paying more than $180 more every month, but by the time you sell the house, you've paid $1,800 more for the privilege of borrowing the money!

TIP

As a general rule for quick flips, opt for loans with low (or no) closing costs, low (or no) discount points, and low interest rates. Avoid any loans that have prepayment penalties.

Finding eager lenders online and off

To secure investment capital for flipping properties, you need to know where to look. Obvious sources, such as banks, may be a little reluctant to loan money to a novice for investing in real estate, so you may need to poke around to find willing lenders and investors. The following sections show you where to start looking. Your agent can also help steer you toward lenders.

WARNING!

Don't request quotes from more than a couple of lending institutions. When several lending institutions query your credit report in a short period of time, it shows up on your credit report and can lower your credit score and jeopardize your ability to qualify for a loan. Shop around first and then apply for a loan with only one or two lenders who offer the best rates and services.

Sticking close to home with local institutions

Small, local banks and credit unions often run loan specials in an attempt to lure you into doing all your banking with them. They may offer low-rate loans regardless of whether you open a checking or savings account with them. Check your local newspaper for ads, call around to four or five banks in the area to check out their loan offerings, or check with your current bank or credit union, which may offer an even better deal because you already have an account there.

WARNING!

If you have the choice, obtain your loan from a lender that doesn't sell its loans. Some smaller banks and mortgage brokers sell to larger, out-of-state banks, which can foul up the handling of your *escrow account* (the account from which the lender pays your taxes and insurance), resulting in unpaid property taxes and insurance.

Expanding your search through the Internet

You've probably seen those commercials in which a couple goes online to submit a request for quotes from various lenders. The lenders descend on the house like a flock of fawning suitors and grovel to win the couple's favor. Funny, yes, but realistic? Not quite. You still have to perform due diligence by checking the numbers, as I explain previously in this chapter.

WARNING!

I recommend that you stay close to home when borrowing money to finance your flip, especially when you're first starting out. Local lenders are typically more motivated and capable of servicing your loan, and they can work with you more effectively if something goes wrong.

Exploring Other Creative Financing Options

You have a credit score pushing the 500 mark, you just got divorced and your spouse got the house, you hate your day job, and house flipping, as you see it, is your only hope. You have the time, skills, and pent-up angst to power a successful flip. You just need to get your mitts on some moola. What do you do?

With the right attitude and a strong work ethic, you can hop on that train out of town by tracking down alternative sources of investment capital. The following sections show you where to start looking for your pot of gold.

Passing the hat among friends and family

Charity should begin at home. If you have a rich Auntie Ellen who has a stash of cash she's willing to invest, and you don't mind calling in some favors, hit her up for the money. With family members, you may be able to get a short-term, no-interest loan, assuming you're not considered the black sheep of the family.

Borrowing from a private investor

Lots of people have money to invest and are disenchanted with returns on their stocks and bonds. Convince them of your ability to turn a profit flipping properties, and they just may provide you with the investment capital you need to get started. I show you what to do in the following sections.

TIP

Loans from private investors often come in the form of hard money, as discussed earlier in this chapter.

Finding private investors

You can often locate private investors (or private lenders) through the newspaper, real estate agents, and mortgage brokers; by attending landlord meetings or investment seminars; or by joining a real estate investment group (I cover these groups later in this chapter) and doing a little networking. Most private investors lend money through mortgage brokers because most states require that lenders be licensed.

Pitching your plan

Before approaching a private investor, do your homework and draw up a business plan showing that you know what you're doing. Here are a few ideas on how to proceed:

- Show the investor a sample of a property that someone else recently flipped in the area — for example, a property that the person bought for $80,000 on August 8 and sold for $146,000 on November 16. Convince the investor through your knowledge and enthusiasm that you can do the same.
- Present a property you would purchase now if you had the money and explain how you would fix it up and sell it.
- Tie up a property on paper (either through a purchase agreement or an option to buy) and present this property as an opportunity. It sounds risky, but it often works, and it definitely forces you to find the money to close on the deal! (Your agent or attorney can help you acquire the necessary paperwork.)

If you're not comfortable drawing up a plan yourself, ask your agent and attorney for help. Not only can they assist you in creating a plan, but they can also point you in the direction of private investors they know.

If at first you don't succeed, try, try again. If a lender rejects your proposal or gives you the cold shoulder, figure out why, change your package or presentation, and give it another shot. When I first started, a lender told me no and explained that I didn't have enough experience. I added my father, an experienced carpenter and builder, to my proposal and pitched it to the same lender, who eventually loaned me the money I needed. My perspective has always been that "no" means the person I'm dealing with doesn't "know" enough information to say "yes."

Calculating the splits

When you're just getting started and you have no money and no solid track record, your negotiating muscle is a little flabby. The person with the cash usually calls the shots. A 50/50 deal is about the most you can expect, but even that can be iffy at first. With each successful flip, you strengthen your position and eventually can offer investors slightly more than what they can make by investing their money elsewhere, so you keep most of the profit.

Remain cautious of experienced investors, landlords, or real estate gurus who try to sell you their dontwanners. As a house flipper, you typically look for properties that owners don't want, but properties that these guys don't want could be real lemons; otherwise, they would probably flip the properties themselves.

Establishing effective partnerships for the long haul

Partnering with one or more friends or family members may be an option, especially if you have rich friends whose house-flipping skills complement your own. With their financial backing and your combined knowledge and skills, you may be able to form a long-lasting and financially rewarding partnership. You may also consider taking on a partner in the following situations:

- Your credit is damaged, and you need someone who has a better credit rating to help you secure the loan.
- You can obtain a loan for purchasing the property, but you need a partner to provide funds for renovating it.

WARNING! Taking on a partner is like getting married, so if you don't trust a person as much as you trust your spouse, you probably shouldn't become partners. Great partnerships are rare, but when they work, they enable both parties to achieve more than they could achieve individually. All too often, however, a partner runs off with the cash, fails to pay the contractors, cashes checks made out to the water company or building supply store and pockets the money, files an insurance claim to collect for damages without your knowledge, or figures out some other way to pick your pocket.

REMEMBER If you partner with someone, have your attorney write up a contract that details the responsibilities of each party and how profits are to be divided. Need an attorney? Head to Chapter 4 for help in finding one.

Granny and me

My first partner was my grandmother. She put up the money for my investments. We made a deal — every time I sold a house, I had to take her out for lunch. When we started having lunch regularly, I was able to obtain traditional financing.

Partnering with friends or family members can be one of the most fulfilling experiences, but when it comes to money, friends and family can be more brutal than bankers, especially if your flip flops. In most cases, I discourage investors from taking on a partner, but with Granny and me, the partnership turned out to be a rewarding experience for both of us.

Investing your retirement savings in real estate

Newcomers are often attracted to real estate investments because they may result in a higher percentage return than stocks or bonds. In addition, real estate gives you more control over the performance of your investment. In the case of flipping houses, if you do it right and the housing bubble doesn't burst, you stand to earn 20 percent or more on each house you flip. You're not likely to see that sort of return on your IRA investments.

Because real estate is an investment opportunity that's as legitimate as stocks and bonds, some real estate investors are choosing to structure their IRAs (or at least a portion of them) around real estate investments. In other words, you can convert your IRA into a *self-directed IRA* and use the money in your retirement account to fuel your flips. Consult your accountant and your personal-finance specialist to determine whether this option is one you want to explore and to work out all the details if you choose to go this route. It's risky, but so is the stock market.

I use a company called Equity Trust (`www.trustetc.com`). It is helpful, offers webinars, and tries to educate you on how to use a self-directed IRA as a tool to buy and flip real estate.

Part II

House Hunting with an Eye for Flipping

Listing Information

Listing Date:	08/07/13	Off Mkt Date:	08/26/13	Pending Date:		Contingent Date:	
Road Frontage:	Paved			Possession:	0	BMK Date:	
Protect Period:	0						
Directions:	I-696 HWY TO 10 MILE RD EXIT TO JEFFERSON						

Features

Foundation:	Crawl						
Basement:	Unfinished						
Exterior Feat:	Fenced						
Exterior:	Brick			Construct Feat:			
Fireplc Fuel:				Fireplace Loc:	Living Room		
Interior Feat:	Cable Available						
Heating:	Gas, Forced Air			Cooling:	Central		
Wtr Htr Fuel:	Gas						
Water Source:	Municipal Water			Sewer:			
% Wooded:		% Tillable:		% Tiled:		Soil Type:	

Room Information

Room	Level	Dimensions	Room	Level	Dimensions
Bathroom	Entry		Bedroom	Entry	12 x 10
Bedroom	Entry	12 x 12	Breezeway		
Kitchen	Entry	16 x 9	Laundry	Entry	10 x 8
Living Room	Entry	20 x 13	Master Bedroom	Upper	19 x 13

Legal/Tax/Financial

web extras

One of the best sources for underpriced homes is the foreclosure market, and the earlier in the process you get involved, the better chance you have of getting the property at the right price. Check out www.dummies.com/extras/flippinghouses for a sample schedule of foreclosure-related activities that can keep you on track.

In this part…

- Find and cultivate your *farm area* — a great neighborhood with plenty of good opportunities for flipping houses.
- Discover *dontwanners* in your farm area — properties that are neglected because the owners don't want them and are probably eager to sell.
- Read foreclosure notices and notices of default (NODs) to find properties that you may be able to pick up at bargain prices.
- Pick your point of entry in the foreclosure process: pre-foreclosure, foreclosure auction, or post-foreclosure (properties the banks repossess).
- Avoid the most common and costly mistake novices make at foreclosure auctions. (This tip alone may save you more than $100,000!)
- Capitalize on bargains in special markets, including divorce, bankruptcy, and probate.

Chapter 6

Scoping Out a Fertile Neighborhood

In This Chapter

- Identifying the hot residential districts in your town or city
- Checking important indicators in a market
- Distinguishing the signs of good and bad neighborhoods
- Researching school performance, crime statistics, and the business climate

Inspiration for flipping properties often comes from real estate muses on late-night infomercials. Some guy posing in front of a private jet on the tarmac convinces you that you can become a multi-millionaire real estate investor simply by following his advice and making house flipping your weekend hobby. Of course, he fails to mention that the jet in the background really isn't his and that he makes most of his money from selling his books and CDs rather than from flipping real estate.

Probe the background of these real estate gurus and you often discover that, if they're legitimate, they hit pay dirt in very affluent areas with red-hot real estate markets. They're working their magic in the hottest markets in the country. All they have to do is buy, hold, and sell, and they make $100,000 snoozing in their recliners. In the meantime, you're trying to eke out a modest profit in an area where home prices top out at $150,000, and you're wondering what you're doing wrong.

You don't have to pack up and move to Phoenix to make money flipping houses, but farming a fertile market improves your chances of reaping bountiful profits. This chapter shows you how to dig up pertinent information so you can pinpoint potentially profitable real estate markets in your area.

TIP: As you begin researching neighborhoods, create a three-ring binder for each area, complete with all the information you dig up, including names and addresses of schools and school administrators, local politicians, local law-enforcement organizations, the names and phone numbers of the crime watch committee members, and so on. This information can come in handy later and even help you market the property when you're ready to sell. You can hand prospective out-of-town buyers a relocation package that contains all the information they need to successfully navigate the neighborhood.

Pinpointing House-Flipping Hot Spots

Whether you're an average home buyer or a seasoned real estate investor, every search for the right home begins with a search for the right neighborhood. After all, location is everything. In the following sections, I help you zone in on a neighborhood. First, I introduce you to a few basic traits that help you choose a range of neighborhoods. Then, I help you narrow the search to the top neighborhoods on your list. And finally, I help you scratch a few neighborhoods off your list that aren't quite in your price range. By the end of the process, you should have one to three top candidates.

Tagging neighborhoods with the right basic traits

You can make money in any real estate market, but some markets are more profitable than others. Trying to target flippable properties in an area where all the homes are immaculate and people tend to stay put is tough. Stable areas that have their fair share of ugly or unkempt homes provide enhanced opportunities. Look for areas with the following qualities:

- Steady or rising real estate values
- Great school systems
- Low crime rates
- Multiple offers on recently sold homes and homes currently for sale
- An influx of homeowners moving in from other areas
- A decrease in the number of homes for rent
- An increase in the number of homeowners in the neighborhood moving into bigger homes rather than moving out
- Older homes — homes built at least 20 years ago — and homes that generally require more rehab
- Areas with aging homeowners — homeowners who may be downsizing or retiring

- Visible updating in older neighborhoods — new roofs, aluminum replaced with vinyl siding, replacement windows, modern earth-tone trim paint
- City improvements, including street repaving, new street lights and street signs, and repaved sidewalks

Although agents in your area can steer you toward hot markets, an agent may try to steer you toward *her* market instead. Talk with several agents who work in different areas you're considering before selecting an agent so you have a better feel for which areas are most conducive for flipping houses. Then, pick one of the top agents who knows the area inside and out, as recommended in Chapter 4.

Don't dismiss a neighborhood simply because it has few homes for sale. Every neighborhood has property for sale and people who need to sell it. In a tight market, you may just have to look a little longer.

Recently, I bought a house for $17,000 in an area I normally wouldn't buy in. (We rarely look in neighborhoods with only a few houses for sale, because such neighborhoods are usually rental areas.) My agent said we could flip it for $55,000 after spending $15,000 to spruce up the home. It flipped for $50,000 cash. That's about a 50 percent return on investment.

Finding your focus

As you explore various neighborhoods in your town or city and evaluate their potential for flipping, you can save time by narrowing your focus to particular types of property or a specific area:

- **New construction:** When an area is growing rapidly, purchasing a newly built home where property values are rising provides an excellent opportunity to flip, especially if you can get a great deal on the property. (The people who stand to make the most money are the first 20 percent to buy into the area.)
- **Depressed area that's on the rebound:** An older neighborhood where homeowners are currently renovating their properties provides ample opportunities to buy, fix, and sell homes at a profit.
- **Farm area:** Pick a limited geographical area, often referred to as a *farm area.* This area can be your zip code, a school system (see "Grading local schools" later in this chapter for more about finding school information), your town or city, four major intersections that define your perimeter, or whatever else you want to use to set your boundary. Agents commonly use this technique to become experts in a particular area. As a flipper, you can take advantage of this same tactic. As an expert, you know the property values in your farm area and can spot a deal instantly.

In the following sections, I give you a few additional pointers on keeping your search focused and manageable.

Dissecting your city or town

Given about 30 seconds to mull it over, most residents of a town or city can name the upscale areas — neighborhoods where everyone would live if they could afford it. The selection of homes for sale may be slim pickings, but when you put the house back on the market, you have little trouble finding eager buyers.

Grab a map of your town or city and highlight the hot spots — areas where the rich people live, the artists hang out, or people gather for activities and entertainment. These are the happenin' places. Here you see a lot of new construction or older, well-kept homes. People walk or ride their bikes through the neighborhood and keep an eye out for any riffraff.

Run-down neighborhoods where the community center is the corner liquor store or a triple-X movie theater don't draw families and first-time home buyers.

WARNING!

You can resuscitate a dying neighborhood by investing heavily in it and changing its reputation over the long haul, but don't try to go it alone, and don't expect it to improve overnight. If you decide to rebuild a run-down area, work with other investors, town officials, local businesses, and neighborhood residents, and plan on sticking around for quite a while. This isn't something I recommend for newbies.

Sticking close to home . . . or not

Pinpointing the hottest real estate market across town doesn't mean that's where you should farm. Farming an area closer to home offers several advantages:

- You have a vested interest in the community.
- Getting up to speed on property values is less of a chore.
- Your neighbors can turn you on to great deals.
- Commuting distances are shorter.
- Neighborhood news and gossip are within earshot.

WARNING!

Farm your own neighborhood only if it makes financial sense to do so. If property values are falling without the hope of recovery, investing in your neighborhood can lead to your own financial demise and further deterioration of the neighborhood. If the neighborhood housing market is less than promising, you may need or want to cultivate more fertile areas, but try to stay within an hour's drive of your house.

Identifying areas in your price range

Your financing dictates where you can shop and how much house you can afford. Anyone who's played Monopoly knows that you need a wad of cash to build hotels on Boardwalk and Park Place. To score that kind of money, you may need to start out earning some investment capital on Tennessee Avenue.

When you spot an attractive area — a neighborhood you would consider farming — check real estate values in the area to make sure they're in your price range. Don't worry if you're eliminating neighborhoods that you thought were your best prospects. The process of elimination is necessary to establish a realistic focus.

Check the fringes of areas where homes are outside your price bracket. Adjacent areas often ride the coattails of their pricier neighbors. If you can time your purchase just right, you stand to earn a profit as the neighboring areas become more popular.

Refer to Chapter 6 to find sources of capital to fuel your flip. See Chapter 12 to determine how much you can afford to spend on a property and still earn a decent profit. You need enough cash on hand to purchase, renovate, hold, and sell the property while turning a profit of at least 20 percent in a healthy market. How much money you can gather dictates your price range.

Taking the Pulse of the Real Estate Market in a Neighborhood

You've identified two or three housing markets that look promising, but now you have to pick the area in which you want to buy a house. Your choice boils down to two questions:

- Which of the few areas I've selected has the best deals?
- Where can I resell the home for the highest profit?

The ideal real estate market is an area with rising property values, a few homes available at below-market prices, and a strong market or desire for homes in the area. With the help of your real estate agent — who can provide you with exact numbers on prices, homes for sale, and average time on the market — you can research various areas to identify signs of a healthy real estate market or warning signs of a market turning sour.

Research not only neighborhoods but also specific areas in those neighborhoods. You can discover two different real estate markets right across the street or across the tracks from each other. Just because two homes are within 100 yards of each other doesn't place them in the same market.

What's the annual appreciation percentage of the average home?

One key indicator of the health of any real estate market is the rate of appreciation — the percentage that properties increase in value from one year to the next. To determine the appreciation percentage, look at the prices of two comparable homes — one that sold recently and one that sold approximately one year ago. Use the following formula to determine the appreciation percentage:

(P2 – P1)/P1

In this equation, P2 (property 2) is the sale price of the home that recently sold and P1 (property 1) is the price of a comparable home that sold one year ago. For example, if a home recently sold for $175,000, and a comparable home sold for $160,000 one year ago, the annual appreciation percentage would be:

($175,000 – $160,000)/$160,000 = $15,000/$160,000 = .09375 = 9.375%

So, what's considered good? Anything in a range of 5 percent to 10 percent is good. Lower percentages may indicate a stagnant market or a market that's taking a downturn. Appreciation in the 15 percent to 20 percent range is bubble burst material — buying into this market is highly speculative.

Don't get too excited about a 10 percent appreciation rate. Just because your calculations show that a home sold for 10 percent more this year than a comparable home sold for last year doesn't mean that homes in the area are selling like hotcakes. Check the sale prices of several comparables and examine other statistics, as I explain in the following sections, to determine the overall health of the market.

How many homes are currently for sale?

The number of homes for sale can often help you size up a real estate market. Of course, the number is relative, so I can't give you a specific number of homes that indicate a healthy or unhealthy market. You have to define the geographical location of your market (for example, a zip code or an area that sits inside four major intersections) and then compare the number of homes currently for sale to past numbers. A change in the number of listings from one year to the next indicates a shift in the market. If, for instance, you see a 20 percent increase in homes for sale over the course of one year, the numbers indicate a shift from a seller's market to a buyer's market. You may be able to buy a house for less, but reselling the house in the near future may be more challenging.

TIP

By including sales volume in your calculations, you can determine whether a market is slowing, remaining steady, or growing in popularity. If plenty of houses are listed and plenty are selling, you have another sign that the market is shifting. Combine this data with the data you have on appreciation percentages (see the previous section), and you can determine whether the shift is positive or negative. If lots of homes are selling and prices are declining, you can readily see a flight pattern. If homes are selling briskly and property values are increasing, the neighborhood may be ripe for flipping.

How long is the average house on the market?

The time it takes to sell a house varies according to several factors, including the location and condition of the house, the asking price, and market conditions. A good house in a healthy market with the right asking price should sell within 30 days. If the average house sells within 60 days, the market is cruising along at a good pace. If most homes are lingering on the market for longer than 90 days, the market may be slowing. Price range also affects time on the market — higher-end properties typically take longer to sell.

Markets often appear slower than they really are. When the market begins to cool, agents and sellers take a while to pick up on the shift, and they continue to set asking prices that are higher than what the market can bear. Because the houses are overpriced for the current conditions, they remain on the market for much longer. When agents and sellers begin adjusting their list prices down, the market begins to pick up, and houses sell more quickly (assuming other factors, such as mortgage interest rates, remain steady).

TIP

Adjust your strategy as needed for the current market conditions, as I explain in Chapter 12. In a slow market, housing values can decrease while your holding costs increase (because your house may be on the market longer). To reduce your risk in a flat or declining market, you need to purchase homes for less than you'd pay in a strong market.

Evaluating the Good and Bad in a Neighborhood

The housing market in a particular area may look good on paper — property values are rising, demand is high, and home sales are brisk — but you should compare these indicators with what you observe on the ground. Is the neighborhood on the upswing or the downswing? Is the entire neighborhood turning into a dontwanner? (You want to buy dontwanners in good neighborhoods. You don't want to buy into entire neighborhoods that are dontwanners.)

The following sections help you distinguish a neighborhood that's an excellent target for flipping properties from a neighborhood that's not.

Spotting the signs of a good neighborhood

Good neighborhoods look nice. Residents mow their lawns, trim their trees, fix any cracks in the sidewalks, and keep their roofs and gutters in good repair. You can see the neighbors out working in their yards when the weather's nice. After work, you see neighbors strolling, jogging, and riding bikes. At sunset, the neighborhood quiets down, and by 10 p.m. or so, it slips into its knapsack and settles in for the night.

If you're driving down a street at dusk and neighbors are sitting on their front porches with guns across their laps, that's not a neighborhood you should consider flipping in.

To spot the signs of a good neighborhood, don't just drive around the area after work. Take a walking tour. Visit the neighborhood in the morning, afternoon, and evening. Check it out on weekends. If you happen to bump into a resident or two, introduce yourself and ask them why they moved to this neighborhood, how long they've lived here, and what they like and dislike about the area. The attitude of the residents often determines the future course of the neighborhood.

TIP

The perfect neighborhood is one in which almost all the homes are in excellent condition, you see few or no For Sale signs, and the block has one dontwanner — a run-down property that nobody wants. This is the grand slam of opportunities.

Seeing the warning signs of a declining neighborhood

Broken windows; dangling gutters; weedy, overgrown lawns; and wandering gangs of pimple-faced hoodlums are all signs of a neighborhood in decline. The residents gave up long ago. Maybe the major employer in the area moved out, leaving its workforce to deal with unpaid mortgages, or perhaps declining schools and increasing crime triggered a mass exodus. Here are some additional warning signs:

- A large number of For Sale or For Rent signs
- Eviction notices on doors with belongings and debris piled along the curb

- Broken-down cars in the streets or alleys or on lawns
- Security bars on many doors and windows
- Large animals chewing on the fence next door

Whatever the reason for the decline, don't buy into a declining market unless you have the scoop on some imminent change that promises to turn the neighborhood around. Perhaps a new company is planning on moving in or a state-of-the-art medical center is in the works.

Even if you do hear of a neighborhood improvement, approach with caution. Good news can take many years to impact an area, so if you're considering buying in, be prepared to hold onto the property for several years. An even better approach may be to wait until you see early signs that the neighborhood is on the rebound.

Taking Other Neighborhood Factors into Consideration

Local politicians obsess about three things — schools, crime, and business. If the schools are top notch, the crime is low, and the business climate is healthy, people like to live in the area, property values rise, the tax base grows, the town or city can afford to pay for improvements, and the citizens reelect the politicians or promote them to higher offices.

When you're scoping out an area to flip, you should obsess about these same three factors because they strongly influence the resale value of the property. The following sections show you how to research and evaluate school performance, crime rates, and the business climate. I also show you how to find the scoop on upcoming neighborhood improvements.

Having the neighborhood scope you out

While you're scoping out neighborhoods and deciding which area you want to farm, don't simply focus on your target. Make yourself a target. Increase your visibility so you won't have to work so hard at discovering leads. When people know who you are and what you do and you've established a solid reputation for sticking to your word, they begin coming up to you and providing you with additional leads and prospects.

Don't be the invisible man or woman. Let people know every day who you are and what you do — first by word of mouth, possibly by advertisement, and best of all by reputation.

Grading local schools

Great schools boost more than just test scores — they increase property values, sometimes by as much as 20 percent. Real estate agents have known this for years, but studies prove a direct correlation between student performance on standardized tests and the percentage that homes in the area appreciate. So when you're comparing housing prices, be aware of the dividing lines between school districts. The following sections show you how to research area schools.

Don't rely on the name of a housing addition to determine which school district it's in. Sly builders often name their additions after popular school districts in an attempt to confuse home buyers who are moving into the area.

Researching school systems online

Quantifying the quality of education is difficult, if not impossible, so standardized test scores, low student-to-teacher ratios, and other statistics are the only measures we have to compare schools. Fortunately, most state departments of education publish current and historic data on test scores, graduation rates, and so on for every school in the state. Contact your state department of education or visit its website to see what you can dig up.

If you hit a dead end with your state department of education, you may be able to find the information you're looking for on the web. Check out the following websites, where you can search for schools by name or location:

- GreatSchools at `www.greatschools.net`
- eSchoolprofile at `www.eschoolprofile.com`
- SchoolMatch at `www.schoolmatch.com`

You may also find the information you need posted on school websites, especially if the students did particularly well; administrators love to boast about student success. Word of mouth is another great way to find out about neighborhood schools. If you're flipping in your own backyard, you probably know a lot of what you need to know already.

Picking the brains of teachers and school administrators

Visiting local schools in person is often a better way to evaluate schools than researching online. In person, you can get a feel for the atmosphere of the school — how orderly and how well organized it is. Be sure to schedule your visit in advance and inform the secretary or principal about the purpose of your visit. Don't show up unannounced. Meet with the principal and find out how long she's been in the system. Ask the name and phone number of her predecessor, and then call him and find out whether he liked the school and why he left.

When you meet with the principal, be prepared to ask some probing questions, such as the following:

- What's the student-to-teacher ratio? A ratio of 30 to 1 is a little high; 25 to 1 is more in the average range, and 20 to 1 and lower ratios are good.
- How long does the average teacher remain on the job? If teachers stay five years or more, the system is fairly stable. If most of them move on after a year or two, you should be concerned.
- How do students perform overall on the standardized tests compared with students in nearby school systems? Are scores on the upswing or downswing?

Strike up a conversation with a teacher or one of the school's secretaries. Administrators are often optimistic PR people. Teachers and secretaries are typically more willing to offer an unbiased analysis, assuming they know you, of course. If you're a stranger to the area, they may be a little tight-lipped, too.

Gabbing with parents and students

Before you buy a home in a particular neighborhood, talk with parents and students, if their parents allow it. They usually know which elementary school in the area is considered the best, whether discipline is getting out of hand at the junior high or middle school, and how well the high school students fare after graduation.

Insider information from teachers, administrators, secretaries, parents, and students is often much more valuable and timely than the statistics you can obtain online. Don't expect your agent to provide this information — an agent can quote facts and statistics, but if he offers opinions, he may just get slapped with a "steering" lawsuit for steering you toward or away from a particular school system.

Digging up crime statistics

In addition to dragging down property values, high crime rates can directly slash your bottom line. If you're rehabbing a home, theft of tools and materials can significantly increase your expenses and cut into your profits. (Tools and building materials may disappear from houses in *any* area, so avoid leaving anything of value in or outside the property overnight.) To be safe, research crime statistics before you buy, using the resources I describe in the following sections.

Checking crime statistics online

Online research into crime statistics is somewhat limited. You can visit the following websites to compare crime rates in major cities, but the sites don't break the numbers down by neighborhood:

- Crime Comparison at `www.bestplaces.net/crime`
- Relocation Crime Lab at `www.homefair.com/real-estate/city-profile`

Some areas have 911 call maps that indicate the location of the calls and the type of emergency (for example, a shooting or a heart attack). These maps provide snapshots of crime in different neighborhoods. To track down a 911 call map (or find out if such a map exists for your town), search the web for your town or city and state followed by "911 call map."

You may also want to search the National Sex Offender Registry (`www.nsopw.gov`) to see whether any registered sex offenders live in the area. Prospective home buyers often perform the search and may not purchase a home near the residence of a registered sex offender. You can also download an app called Sex Offender for your smartphone, and local newspapers may also occasionally publish crime maps.

Grilling local law enforcement

Local law-enforcement officials can provide much more detailed information on crime than you can get online, and they're usually pretty willing to talk with concerned citizens. Call or visit the law-enforcement department that serves your farm area and ask the following questions:

- Is crime a problem in this area?
- What types of crimes are most prevalent — violent crimes, theft, vandalism?
- Are crime rates rising, falling, or remaining about the same?
- Does the community have active crime-watch programs?

TIP: If your farm area has a crime-watch program, contact one or more of the organizers and ask the same questions. Find out what the community is doing to fight crime and how successful they've been. Community activism can significantly lower crime rates.

Exploring the business climate

Just as the health of the national economy drives new home construction and development, local businesses drive local economies and influence population growth and eventually real estate values. Local employers provide income-producing jobs that draw families to the area, increasing the demand for housing.

When a large employer moves out of an area and nobody moves in to fill the gap, real estate values commonly plummet. By exploring the business climate and talking with business owners in the area, you can get a good feel for the health of the local economy and become aware of any impending developments — positive or negative. I give you a few helpful pointers on researching a neighborhood's business climate in the following sections.

TIP

The health of area businesses played a larger role in real estate values in the horse-and-buggy days. Nowadays, people think nothing of driving 30 minutes or an hour to work, one way. However, if you're buying and selling real estate in a small town that's a considerable distance from a major city, the business climate can have a strong influence over property values.

Contacting the local chamber of commerce

The local chamber of commerce can fill you in on the business environment and local resources available to residents. Don't go in expecting to hear anything negative, however; one of the organization's primary goals is to promote development in the area. Ask the following probing questions:

- How many new businesses have moved into the area in the past year?
- How many businesses have moved out of the area in the past year?
- How many new jobs have come to the area in the past year?
- How many jobs have disappeared over the past year?

Talking to business owners

When you want to know about the business climate, call around and talk to the business owners. To get the ball rolling, try opening with one or more of the following questions:

- How long have you owned a business in this area?
- Does business seem to be picking up or tapering off?
- What do you think of the mayor? (If the other questions don't generate some conversation, this one usually works, especially if businesses are suffering.)

Getting the lowdown on planned neighborhood improvements

Community centers, shopping malls, new schools, and other neighborhood improvements can boost property values, so if you're planning to flip houses in a particular neighborhood, keep abreast of the latest developments by using the tips in the following sections. If you know that the town is planning on building a new health and fitness center near the park, you're more prepared than other investors to capitalize on the plan.

Perusing the neighborhood newspaper

Read the neighborhood newspaper from front to back. Reporters in small towns and neighborhoods have little to report, so they usually broadcast every minor incident . . . DUIs, petty thefts, lovers' quarrels, and so on. When news leaks about something big like a city beautification plan, reporters splash it across the front page. Neighborhood newspapers also announce all the important meetings scheduled for the coming weeks.

If your neighborhood doesn't have a newspaper, look for a neighborhood blog or other online resource for information about the neighborhood. Some homeowners associations may maintain websites, as well.

Sitting in on town meetings

To listen to people gripe, hear the local gossip, and discover all the important and petty problems that set the community abuzz, sit in on town meetings. Here, you get the lowdown on everything from planned sewer projects and street repairs to complaints about inappropriate content on billboards.

Even if you find no enlightenment in the meeting itself, you can usually tune your ear into an errant discussion to pick up some interesting bits of news on property issues, such as abatements and plans to tear down houses. Town meetings are also a great forum for networking and finding leads on property for sale. I've attended several meetings in which I've picked up on leads that have turned into transactions.

TIP

If you have cable TV, you may have a local channel that airs the town hall meetings. The broadcast is usually delayed, but if you can't attend the meeting, you can still watch it. Certain towns have the technology to stream video of town meetings live on the web or post a delayed broadcast you can watch at your leisure. But keep in mind that by not attending the meeting in person, you stand to miss out on any networking opportunities.

Chatting it up with the locals

Chat it up with the locals to discover what's really going on in the community and establish a feel for the local sentiment. Are people pretty positive about where they live, or are they getting fed up with the conditions? Who's died recently? Who's moving out and why? Who's been laid off?

TIP

Donut shops, coffee houses, diners, and cafes are great places to pick up leads as well as general information. I often visit the local eateries in my farm area, and I usually walk out with at least one new lead or prospect. Of course, I tip a little high, hand my business card to the server, and leave a few additional cards at the counter. Pharmacists and butchers are often tuned in to the local gossip channel, as well.

Chapter 7

Hunting for Houses in Your Target Area

In This Chapter

- Staying focused on a certain price range
- Exploring key resources for information on bargain properties
- Focusing your search on for-sale-by-owner properties
- Spotting potential flips in special areas of the market

Buried in every neighborhood are hidden treasures offering real estate investors opportunities to turn a handsome profit. You just have to dig a little to discover these buried treasures. To figure out where to dig, you need a map. The real estate market offers an entire atlas full of treasure maps, ranging from the all-important Multiple Listing Service (MLS) to classified ads and real estate publications. You have to dig a little to find these valuable resources, and then you need to know how to read them to discover key words that identify the most promising properties.

In this chapter, I point the way to the plethora of publications, websites, and other resources that provide information on properties for sale, and I show you how to use the information they provide to hunt for buried real estate treasures in your target neighborhood. If you follow the suggestions in this chapter, you can create a list of at least ten promising prospects — and figure out how to select the most qualified candidate.

Focusing Your Search on Affordability

When you go hunting for a home you want to live in, you don't look at every house in the neighborhood that has a For Sale sign out front. You narrow your list of prospects by stipulating your selection criteria. You typically begin with a price range and style of home — say a ranch-style house between $120,000 and $150,000. You may not consider a home that has fewer than three bedrooms and two baths (or even three baths if you have more than one teenager). Or you may insist on an oversized garage with a tile floor, where you can safely park your massive new SUV. You narrow your focus in order to prevent becoming overwhelmed by the wide selection of homes on the market.

When you begin looking for investment properties, take a similar approach. Settle on a price range and style of home. Depending on the predominant features in your target neighborhood, you may focus further by considering only brick homes or only two-bedroom homes that have attic space you can convert into a third bedroom. You don't want to specialize to the extent that you limit yourself to only one or two properties, but try to limit your prospects to the number of houses you can realistically consider in your allotted timeframe and price range.

Specializing can help you master a narrow market, search more efficiently, and establish an edge over your competition. The fewer houses you have to look at, the more quickly you can inspect prospective properties, make your offer, and begin renovations.

You don't have to start counting your pennies yet, but before beginning a serious search for properties, you should have a ballpark figure in mind — how much you can afford to spend on a property. (Chapter 6 helps you zone in on affordable neighborhoods with promising prospects.) Several factors influence your price range, including the following:

- Amount of *financing,* or how much money you can get your hands on (see Chapter 5).
- Type of financing, such as cash, a bank loan, a personal loan from a relative, or *hard money* — a high-interest, short-term loan from a private investor. (See Chapter 5 to discover more about acquiring hard money.)
- Cost of renovations.
- *Holding costs* — the monthly costs of owning the property while you're renovating it.
- Cost of purchasing and selling the property.
- Additional (and often unforeseen) costs, such as unpaid back taxes or utility bills, major appliances that break down a day after closing, and residents who refuse to move out.

You're not purchasing the house yet. You're simply determining a realistic price bracket for the houses you want to consider. If you have the financing to make a $100,000 purchase (and an additional $20,000 on hand for renovations and other costs), you may consider looking at homes in the $90,000 to $130,000 range. Because you need enough to cover purchase costs, renovations, and holding costs, you probably don't want to pay more than $100,000 for a house in this case, but you should extend your range a little higher — you may stumble on a property that's way overpriced or a motivated seller who's willing to accept significantly less than the asking price or is willing to pay for some of the essential repairs.

Don't overextend yourself, especially on your first deal. Calculate the total amount of money you need with enough padding to cover the costs of buying, holding, renovating, and selling the property. You need enough money to cover:

- Your current living expenses
- The cost of buying, renovating, and selling the property
- Holding costs: a buffer of about six months' worth of payments on the new property, including taxes, insurance, and utilities
- The cost of cheeseburgers for you and your crew

See Chapter 12 for guidance on estimating the total cost of flipping a particular house and how much you can afford to pay for the property in order to earn a decent profit.

Digging Through Property Listings, Ads, and Publications

When homeowners decide to sell their property, they do what any good capitalist does — they market and advertise. It's all about supply and demand. They can't do much on the supply side, so they try to increase demand by getting the word out and catching the interest of as many buyers as possible.

The most comprehensive marketing blitz begins by listing the property with a real estate agent, who advertises the property through various publications online and off and markets it through a network of motivated real estate agents. When you're scoping out a neighborhood for properties to flip, start your search with the valuable and easily accessible resources presented in the following sections.

Searching MLS listings with the help of your real estate agent

The *Multiple Listing Service* (MLS) is like a dating service for home buyers and sellers. Through a real estate agent, a home seller can post a complete description of the property, including the asking price, total square footage of the house, room specifications, and a host of other details about the home's layout and construction. Prospective buyers can search the MLS (or, in some areas, multiple MLS listings) with the assistance of a real estate agent to find the ideal match for their needs.

TIP

Your agent should be able to set up a search with exactly what you're looking for and configure options to automatically send you an e-mail message as soon as a match comes on the market. If your agent can't do this, find one who's more tech savvy.

If an area has more than one local MLS board, more than one MLS may list homes for sale in the area. Choose a real estate agent who has access to all MLS listings for your target area, or use two or more agents. To access MLS listings, an agent needs to be on the local MLS board or be a member of the National Association of Realtors. In other words, for access to the most comprehensive database of homes for sale, you're going to need some real(tor) help. Chapter 4 has more information about selecting the right agent for your needs.

In the following sections, I show you how to navigate the MLS listings to locate and assess basic information, sniff out important clues, and weed out potential time wasters.

TIP

The National Association of Realtors (`www.realtor.com`) offers a searchable database of more than 2.5 million listings. Consider this database the CliffsNotes version of the MLS.

Checking out MLS basics

Ask your agent to supply you with the listing and listing history of all properties for sale that match your search criteria, including the following:

- Location
- School district (see Chapter 6 for the importance of school districts)
- Asking price
- Style of home
- Construction materials
- Total square footage
- Number of bedrooms
- Number of bathrooms
- Presence (or not) of a basement

The *listing history* indicates when, for how long, and for how much the home has been on the market. And it provides you with the following key information:

- All transactions on the property in the past few years.
- How much the seller paid for the property.
- Whether the seller listed the property with another agency in the past — and how long it was listed and for how much. (This information is helpful in determining actual time on the market. The current listing shows only the time that the seller listed the property with the current agent. Generally, the longer a home is on the market, the more eager the owner is to get rid of it.)
- The amount the property has appreciated from one sale to the next.
- Whether the seller has dropped the asking price and by how much.
- How much trouble the seller is having trying to unload the property.

Through the MLS, your agent can also look up the number of homes that have been on the market in the area and have sold in the past three years. By looking at sales over the most recent six-month period, the agent can clue you in to the health of the housing market. If ten homes are on the market and six sold in the past six months, that's a good sign. If 20 homes are on the market and only three have sold, that could mean trouble. Chapter 6 has more on taking the pulse of the real estate market in a particular neighborhood.

TIP

Keep an eye on sale-pending properties. Often, someone makes an offer that ties up the property but then fails to close on the sale. The property is typically placed back on the market at a reduced price. The law forbids your agent from disclosing the sale price of a pending sale, because if the transaction falls through, the seller will have a tough time negotiating the next offer, but you can compare the new asking price with the old one to determine whether the seller has become more motivated.

Ask your agent to print out five listings of homes that have recently sold in the same price range, so you can comparison-shop. Ask for five listings of homes that have sold in the next higher price bracket, so you can determine the types of modifications you need to make in order to sell the property at a higher price. With MLS materials in hand, you're ready to begin your search.

Sniffing out clues on a listing

TIP

Each MLS listing contains a deluge of details about the property, all of which can be very helpful in your search (see Figure 7-1 for a sample listing). Some of these details, however, are more useful than others. Focus your search on the following golden nuggets:

- **List price:** Now that you're looking at listings of only those homes in your price range, examine the list price and compare it to that of other comparable houses in the same area. An inordinately low price can signal a buying opportunity, or it can raise a red flag, making you (and others) wonder, "What's wrong with this one?"

- **List date or time on the market:** How long has the home been on the market? You typically find your best opportunities in homes that have recently been listed (in the past couple of days) or in homes that have been on the market for a couple of months. A home that's not selling may be overpriced for the current market. In many cases, the longer the seller holds out, the harder it is to sell, and the more desperate the seller becomes. This cycle can signal a buying opportunity now or in the near future. Your agent can tell you the average time a home is on the market in any given neighborhood so you can properly gauge what's considered "a long time."
- **Remarks:** Near the bottom of every MLS listing is a Remarks or Property Description section that offers additional bits of information. Look for key terms, such as "sold as is," "handyman's special," "in need of a little TLC," or "needs a little work." These phrases translate to "You'll get the house for less because the current owner doesn't want to clean, paint, or re-carpet."

22600 Manor Street, Saint Clair Shores 48081-2331

MLS#:	213079586	Area:	03151 - St.Clair Shores	Short Sale:	No	LP:	$99,900
P Type:	Residential	DOM:	Y/243/243	Trans Type:	Sale	OLP:	$109,900
Status:	Unconditionally Withdrawn				ERTS/FS		

Location Information		Parking		Lot Information	
County:	Macomb	Garage:	Yes	Acreage:	0.1
City:	Saint Clair Shores	Grg Sz:	2 Car	Lot Dim:	50X83
Mailing City:	Saint Clair Shores	Grg Dim:		Front Feet:	50
Map:	L-3	Grg Feat:	Detached, Side Entrance, Workshop		
School D:	Lakeview				
Location:	N, 10 Mile Rd E, Jefferson				
Square Footage		**Layout**		**Contact Information**	
Sqft Source:	Prd	Beds:	3	Name:	Showingtim
Est Tot Fin:	1,274	Baths:	1.0	Phone:	(586) 337-2600
Est Fin Abv Gr:	1,274	Style:	Bungalow		
Est Fin Lower:		Arch:	2 Story		
Est Tot Lower:		Site Desc:			
Waterfront Information				**General Information**	
Wtrfrnt Name:				Year Built:	1940
Wtrfrnt Desc:				Year Remod:	
Wtrfrnt Feat:				Homestead:	No
				Addl Docs:	No

Listing Information

Listing Date:	08/07/13	Off Mkt Date:	08/26/13	Pending Date:		Contingent Date:	
Road Frontage:	Paved			Possession:	0	BMK Date:	
Protect Period:	0						
Directions:	I-696 HWY TO 10 MILE RD EXIT TO JEFFERSON						

Features

Foundation:	Crawl						
Basement:	Unfinished						
Exterior Feat:	Fenced						
Exterior:	Brick			Construct Feat:			
Fireplc Fuel:				Fireplace Loc:	Living Room		
Interior Feat:	Cable Available						
Heating:	Gas, Forced Air			Cooling:	Central		
Wtr Htr Fuel:	Gas						
Water Source:	Municipal Water			Sewer:			
% Wooded:		% Tillable:		% Tiled:		Soil Type:	

Room Information

Room	Level	Dimensions	Room	Level	Dimensions
Bathroom	Entry		Bedroom	Entry	12 x 10
Bedroom	Entry	12 x 12	Breezeway		
Kitchen	Entry	16 x 9	Laundry	Entry	10 x 8
Living Room	Entry	20 x 13	Master Bedroom	Upper	19 x 13

Legal/Tax/Financial

Property ID:	1423360001	Oth/Sp Asmnt:		Tax Winter:	$47	Tax Summer:	$2,448
Ownership:	Private Owned, Short Sale - No			Terms Offered:	Cash, Conv, FHA, VA		
Legal Desc:	EAGLE POINTE ON THE LAKE SUBDIVISION LOT 158 LIBER 3, PAGE 37						
Subdivision:	Eagle Pointe On The Lake						

Agent/Office Information

Sub Agency:	Yes	Buyer Agency:	Yes	Trans Coordinate:	Yes	Access:	Appointment / LockBox
Sub Ag Comp:	4%	Buy Ag Comp:	3%	Trans Crd Comp:	3%		
Agent:	363821	LINDA KINT				Agent Ph:	(586) 337-2600
Office:	336321	RALPH ROBERTS REALTY LLC				Office Ph:	(586) 751-0000

Remarks

Pub Rmks: Location, location. Bungalow Style Home located close to I-696/I-94. Carpeted upper 3rd bedroom with plenty of room and storage space. Huge 2 car detached garage. Breezeway from garage to side door entry of home is a nice feature as well. This property is built on a crawl space. 3-d roof. Nice large privacy fenced in backyard. New kitchen, dishwasher, microwave, hot water heater. Floors refinished, freshly painted. Gorgeous bath.

REALTOR® Remarks: Call Showingtime for all showings #800-746-9464. New Paint, Refinishing of the Hardwood Floors on Entry Level and Carpeting the upstairs, New Kitchen, Lanscaping updated.

Data not guaranteed. Verify independently. All warranties, express or implied, disclaimed.
Copyright © Realcomp II Ltd. All rights reserved.

Figure 7-1: An MLS listing contains a lot of useful information.

Image courtesy of Realcomp II Ltd.

Nothing on the MLS is the gospel truth. Sellers and real estate agents alike often estimate room sizes or make mistakes when entering details. Approach all prospects with a discerning eye.

Weeding out potential time wasters

Just as an MLS listing contains words and phrases that highlight potential buying opportunities, listings commonly contain details that function as red flags, such as the following:

- **Inordinately high list price:** If the price is way out of line with prices of comparable properties in the same area, the seller may be delusional. Sellers who are emotionally attached to their homes can be difficult in negotiations. Keep an eye on the property to see whether the price drops.
- **Super cheap:** Either something is terribly wrong with the property or somebody made a typo. (However, don't assume that the price is too good to be true. Check it out for yourself.)
- **Flowery description of the property:** Under the Property Description or Remarks section of the MLS, watch out for phrases like "nicest home in the neighborhood" or "a real show stopper." When you're flipping a house to make some quick cash, the nicest, highest-priced house on the block isn't the best investment.
- **Neighborhood that's outside your farm area:** Don't be tempted by properties outside your farm area — the neighborhood you decided to focus on. These properties may look like great deals at first glance, but if the property is on the wrong side of the tracks, it may not be such a great deal in that area. Stick with the market you know best — your farm area.

Scanning the classifieds for key words

Local newspapers (and the websites of local newspapers), along with online classified services such as Craigslist, typically carry classified advertisements of homes for sale. When scanning these ads, look for words or phrases that clue you in to the fact that the property is a *dontwanner*, as in "The owner don't want 'er." As a flipper, you want the houses that current homeowners don't want because the homeowner is more motivated to sell and is likely to offer you a better deal. Phrases like "needs work," "must sell, owner relocating," and "fixer-upper" are like billboards broadcasting that the owners want to get out, move on, and cut their losses. These billboards are telling you to "Look at this house!" (See the section "Mining Special Markets for Dontwanners" later in this chapter for details on finding dontwanners.)

Beware of the following subliminal messages that warn you of potential trouble ahead:

- **Glitzy $100 ads:** The more money the seller invests in advertising, the less likely the person is to negotiate price. Give more consideration to the tiny $10 ads.
- **Words indicating a reluctance to negotiate:** If the ad includes the word "Firm" the owner has probably set a steep asking price and is unwilling to haggle. Don't waste your time with an owner who thinks his bungalow is worth a million bucks.
- **Ads that promise "cash back at closing":** Translated into plain English, this phrase means "con artist at work." The property owner or the front man is using the house as a pawn in a scam. Don't be the sucker who gets hooked into an illegal transaction. Don't even call. (See Chapter 1 for information about additional real estate scams.)

Poring over real estate magazines

Walk into just about any grocery store, restaurant, or gas station, and you see a rack of homes-for-sale magazines. Grab an armful of these publications and head to your local café to peruse the offerings. Most magazines organize the homes by area — such as north, south, east, and west — and may contain listings for well-known areas, such as homes around a local lake or reservoir.

TIP

Although homes-for-sale magazines may point you in the direction of a hidden gem, listings are often two to three weeks old — after all, printing and distributing the magazine takes time. Other real estate investors very likely have picked over the properties already. These ads, however, can help you locate a quality real estate agent, check out the asking prices for comparable properties in your target area, and acquire tips on how to make a property more marketable.

Scoping Out FSBOs: For-Sale-By-Owner Properties

Drive through any neighborhood, and you're likely to see some crummy-looking signs that say "For Sale" or "For Sale By Owner." No self-respecting real estate agent would ever think of planting one of these signs on a client's lawn, but for aspiring real estate flippers, these signs are like flashing Vegas neon. People who sell their own homes are often highly motivated and willing to deal with a serious buyer.

People commonly try to sell their own homes for one of three reasons:

- To save the sales commission they would have to pay a real estate agent
- To get rid of a house when they don't really know or care about its value

- To sell the house for a price that's so far above a realistic market value that no agent in her right mind would consider listing it

If you like the property, pull over and jot down the number or grab your cellphone and start dialing. If you're not comfortable approaching the property owner yourself, call your agent. The only wrong way to approach a FSBO (often pronounced "fizz-boh") that catches your eye is not to approach it at all.

WARNING! Avoid overpriced properties. If you run into a seller who's convinced that his run-of-the-mill shack is the neighborhood Taj Mahal, don't waste your time trying to convince him it's not. Just keep an eye on the property and approach the owner after the home has been on the market for a long time. The longer it lingers on the market, the more desperate the seller is to sell.

TIP For Sale By Owner (`www.forsalebyowner.com`) is a commercial website where property owners can list their properties without going through a real estate agent. If you're interested in FSBOs, check this site and similar websites.

Mining Special Markets for Dontwanners

As a house flipper, you're essentially a house recycler — you convert trash into cash. By trash, I mean properties that nobody wants — properties I call *dontwanners*. Real estate investors can score big profits on dontwanners by investing the time and effort into transforming them into *dowanners* — homes that prospective buyers find appealing.

Every neighborhood has its share of these trash-into-cash opportunities — "Your trash is my cash" — but finding them can be a bit challenging, especially if you don't know where to hunt for these hidden treasures. Here I show you how to spot the dontwanners in your neighborhood.

Cruising the neighborhood for dontwanners

Drive, walk, or bicycle around your neighborhood in a search for dontwanners. Some of the best properties may not even be for sale, so look for the following signs and symptoms:

- Overstuffed mailbox
- Porch littered with newspapers
- Overgrown lawn
- House looks vacant inside
- Cheap "For Sale" or "For Sale By Owner" sign

TIP

If you spot a dontwanner, try to contact the owners to see whether they want to sell the house. If someone's living in the house, knock on the front door and spark up a conversation. If the house is vacant, ask the neighbors if they know who owns it.

One good way to approach a prospective seller is to say: "Do you know anybody in the subdivision who's considering selling? I have a family member who's looking to buy a home."

Tapping into special markets

Some of the best opportunities don't show up in the MLS listings or even in the classifieds. You need to scope them out yourself by researching and networking in special markets, including the following:

- **Foreclosures:** Easy credit and an unpredictable job market have led many homeowners to assume more debt than they can handle. If the homeowner misses one or more mortgage payments, the bank or other lending institution that holds the mortgage typically begins the process of *foreclosing* — taking possession of the property. You can purchase properties at various stages in the foreclosure process: pre-foreclosure (from the homeowners), foreclosure (at auction), or post-foreclosure (from the bank that foreclosed on the property or at an auction). See Chapter 12 for details.
- **Bankruptcies:** Homeowners who file for bankruptcy rarely get to keep their house, and even if they do, they may not want it. As an investor, you may have the opportunity to purchase the property at any stage in the bankruptcy process: prior to the bankruptcy filing (directly from the homeowners), filing (directly from the homeowners, but creditors must approve the sale), liquidation (with approval of the trustee and creditors), and post liquidation (from one of the creditors).
- **Probate properties:** When someone who owns some stuff dies, the stuff often goes into *probate,* where the courts decide what happens to it. Because a house divided cannot stand, probate often results in the process of selling a house to turn it into liquid assets (cash), which the courts can more easily use to pay off outstanding debts, taxes, and administration fees. The court divides any remaining crumbs among the unsecured creditors, funeral expenses, and credit-card debt. Anyone with a claim has the chance to pick up a few leftover scraps.
- **Divorce:** When couples divorce, they often sell the property and split the proceeds, or one of them gets the house and doesn't want it or can't afford it. You may be able to purchase a property for well below the market price either pre-divorce, during divorce proceedings, or after the divorce.

TIP

Sometimes members of divorcing couples try so hard to hurt their partners that they hurt themselves. For example, if a spouse gets to live in the house but must split the proceeds with the ex when she sells the home, and if she really doesn't need the money, she may sell for significantly less than market value so the ex gets less money.

- **Government-owned properties:** Various government agencies at the federal, state, and county levels frequently acquire properties they must dispose of. For example, the departments of Housing and Urban Development (HUD) and Veterans Affairs (VA) obtain houses when borrowers fail to make their mortgage payments. In addition, states and counties often seize homes for the nonpayment of property taxes. If you know where to look, you can find government-owned properties at bargain-basement prices.

Bad news is good news

Bad news for homeowners is often good news for real estate investors. I'm not making light of this or trying to encourage future flippers to become cold-hearted opportunists, but this is a fact of life. And as long as you treat the distressed homeowners with respect and try to help them get what they need out of the deal, you can often become a part of the solution to their problems rather than the bane of their existence. Bad news includes the five D's of below-market prices:

- **Death:** When a homeowner dies, the homeowner's significant other often must sell the home, because he or she can't afford it or has no desire to maintain it alone. If the deceased homeowner was the sole owner of the property, another family member may need to dispose of the property, or the property ends up in probate and must be sold to distribute the proceeds to the beneficiaries named in the will.
- **Divorce:** Divorce strikes a serious blow to a couple's or a family's income. With a divorce, someone usually "gets the house," but that person usually ends up selling it in a hurry, usually for less than it's worth, because he or she can't afford to keep it. Often, a divorce leads to foreclosure.

  If you have a lead on a divorce, you can go to the county where the divorce was filed and look up the settlement to see how much each party was entitled to. You can use this information to make deals on both sides. Knowledge is key — the more knowledge you have, the more likely you are to turn a profit for yourself.
- **Debt:** Some homeowners simply take on too much debt. They buy a house they really can't afford or get buried in credit-card debt and face the terrible choice of having to declare bankruptcy or sell their belongings, including their home, to pay off the debt.
- **Drunkenness:** Although social drinkers can usually hold down a job and earn sufficient income to make their mortgage payments, those who drink to excess often lose sight of what's important and may be unable or unwilling to work a full-time job.
- **Drug abuse:** As with drunkenness, drug abuse often leads to foreclosure.

See Chapter 8 for more information about foreclosure properties and Chapter 9 for details about finding properties in the other special markets: bankruptcy, probate, divorce, and government-owned properties.

Job loss is another calamity that commonly results in the loss of a home. If one or more breadwinners are fired, laid off, or scheduled for fewer hours, the loss or reduction in income may undermine their ability to make monthly mortgage payments.

Chapter 8

Closing In on Foreclosure Properties

In This Chapter

- Understanding the overall foreclosure process
- Brushing up on local foreclosure regulations
- Picking the most desirable point of entry in the foreclosure process
- Walking through the steps of buying a foreclosure property
- Raising your profile to get more leads

Foreclosure is an unfortunate necessity that often wipes out any equity built up in the home, injures the homeowner's credit rating, and forces the homeowner and perhaps an entire family out of their home. The upside, if there is an upside, is that foreclosure provides an opportunity for the lender to recover the unpaid debt (or at least a portion of it), for homeowners to relieve themselves of their financial burdens and perhaps salvage some of the equity in their homes, and for you to purchase properties below market value.

As a real estate investor, you should know the basics of the foreclosure process so you can survive a foreclosure, if it ever happens to you, and profit from flipping foreclosure properties, if you choose to explore this area. And why should you explore it? Because foreclosures can be some of the best real estate deals in town.

This chapter introduces you to the foreclosure process, outlines the local rules you need to understand, and leads you step by step through the course of locating and purchasing foreclosure properties.

TIP: When dealing in foreclosure properties, you may or may not purchase the property through a real estate agent, depending on the point in the foreclosure process at which you decide to make your offer. You may purchase the property directly from the homeowners, at an auction, or from a bank. However, an agent who knows the foreclosure process in your area can be a valuable mentor and even present you with opportunities for purchasing pre-foreclosure properties.

Getting Up to Speed on the Foreclosure Process

A common misconception of foreclosure is that after the homeowner misses a payment or two, the bank immediately takes possession of the home and then turns around and auctions it off at a foreclosure sale. Actually, the process is more drawn out than that, typically falling in line with the following scenario:

1. Homeowner stops making mortgage payments.
2. After about 15 to 30 days, bank sends a gentle reminder.
3. Homeowner still doesn't make payments.
4. Bank continues to send notices.
5. Homeowner still isn't making payments.
6. Bank turns the matter over to its collectors, who continue to harass the homeowner with letters and phone calls.
7. After about three missed monthly payments, the bank gets pretty steamed and sends an official notice, typically written and signed by an attorney, warning that foreclosure proceedings are about to commence.
8. Homeowner doesn't reply or presents a solution that the bank deems unsatisfactory.
9. Bank posts a foreclosure notice in the local newspaper.
10. Property goes on the auction block for sale to the highest bidder.
11. Highest bidder pays for property and becomes official owner, or the bank buys the property and transfers it to its REO (Real Estate Owned) department, which prepares it for sale.
12. In some states, the high bidder immediately takes possession of the property. Other states have a *redemption period,* during which the homeowner can buy back the property by paying the full amount of the sheriff's deed price, which can be significantly less than the original loan amount. This period can last up to a year.
13. Previous owner moves out or is evicted.

Lenders generally don't like to foreclose on properties. They prefer that homeowners pay their bills. At any point before the foreclosure sale, the lender may, if the homeowner cooperates, set up an alternative payment plan commonly called a *loan modification.* With a loan modification, the lender may extend the term, lower the interest rate, forgive any payment penalties, and possibly even reduce the principal balance in order to reduce the monthly payments.

If you or a loved one is ever facing a foreclosure, contact the lender immediately to explore your options. Seek help sooner rather than later. Shame, anger, and denial may discourage you from seeking assistance, but the longer you wait, the fewer your options. As with any relationship, communication is key. Educate yourself and communicate with your lender. Check out *Foreclosure Self-Defense For Dummies,* by Ralph R. Roberts, Lois Maljak, and Paul Dorah, with Joe Kraynak (Wiley), and *Loan Modification For Dummies,* by Ralph R. Roberts, Lois Maljak, and Joe Kraynak (Wiley), for additional guidance.

Brushing Up on Local Rules and Regulations

Although the foreclosure process is similar in all states, laws and other details vary, as I explain in the following sections. Before you join in the game, know the rules and find out where to go for additional information and assistance. You can gather most of the information you need by visiting your county's Register of Deeds office or by talking to a real estate agent or other professional who's familiar with the foreclosure process in your area.

Don't rely on information from foreclosure gurus who appear on late-night TV infomercials for insight. They make buying and flipping foreclosure properties seem easy so they can sell their books and CDs. If it were as easy as they lead you to believe, everyone would be doing it. You can profit from foreclosures, but you have to invest some time in learning the ropes and establishing the right connections, as I recommend throughout this chapter.

Procedural stuff

Because the foreclosure process varies from state to state and from one locale to another, I can't describe the foreclosure process for your jurisdiction, but I can tell you what you need to find out:

- **Where to find foreclosure notices.** Foreclosure notices are often posted on properties or printed in a local newspaper or in a county's legal newspaper. You may also be able to register with your county's Register of Deeds to get on its mailing list.

  You may be able to find county-specific foreclosure information, including foreclosure notices, online. Search the web for "sheriff sale" followed by the name of your county and state. If the information you need isn't online, your search is likely to lead you to contact information for someone who can supply the information.

In states that require or offer judicial foreclosure as an option, all judicial foreclosures go through the courts, so you can search the court dockets for pre-foreclosure notices. (*Judicial foreclosure*, allowed in all states, requires that foreclosures go through the courts. With a *non-judicial foreclosure*, allowed only in certain states, the lender advertises and sells the property at a public auction without the courts being involved.)

- **The number of times a foreclosure notice is published before the property actually goes up for sale.** This number differs from state to state; Michigan, for example, follows a five-week process in which the foreclosure notice must be posted at least four times in a qualified legal publication.
- **Where, when, and by whom the foreclosure sales (auctions) are held.** Foreclosure sales are always held at the courthouse, by either the local sheriff or someone the sheriff hires. Get the location of the courthouse and the dates and times of foreclosure sales.
- **Terms of sale at the foreclosure sale, such as acceptable forms of payment and the amount of time you have to come up with the money.** For example, you may be required to pay for any property you win at auction immediately after the auction.
- **Whether the state has a mandatory redemption period, and if it does, how long it is.** A redemption period (the amount of time the current homeowners have to buy back the property) can be as long as 365 days.
- **How *liens* (claims against property as security for repayment) are handled.** Senior liens wipe out junior liens. For example, a house may have three liens — the mortgage (the senior lien or first position), a home equity line of credit (the first junior lien), and another junior lien from a contractor. After the foreclosure and redemption period, the two junior liens are wiped out. (The holders of the junior liens have a right to redeem the senior lien to protect themselves, so that their liens aren't wiped out by the foreclosure. Redeeming the senior lien consists of buying out the senior lienholder.)
- **How evictions are handled and how long they typically take.** Evictions may take 30 days or more. Offering homeowners cash for keys (a financial incentive for moving out) often expedites the process.

WARNING!

Be very careful not to bid on a junior lien. Sometimes, a junior lienholder can foreclose on a property before the senior lienholder forecloses. A foreclosure ad announces the foreclosure (looking no different than a foreclosure notice for a senior lien), and you can bid on the junior lien just as if it were a senior lien. If your bid wins, you end up the loser in many cases, because when the senior lienholder forecloses on the property, your junior lien is wiped out, and you end up with a worthless piece of paper. I've seen unwary investors lose more than $100,000 buying a junior lien. Sure, you have the right to redeem the senior lien, but that option is often cost prohibitive.

Different types of foreclosures

The foreclosure process varies depending on whether your state performs judicial or nonjudicial foreclosures:

- **Judicial foreclosure:** This type of foreclosure passes through the justice system — the state or district court. The bank or lender files a claim to recover the unpaid balance of the loan from the borrower. The courts decide the case, and, as you may guess, typically take a long time to resolve the issue — usually four to six months, but sometimes up to a year.
- **Nonjudicial foreclosure:** In so-called *deed of trust* states, a third-party trustee (typically a bank or trust company) holds the first lien position on the mortgage until the loan is paid in full. If the borrower defaults on the loan, the lender works through the trustee to foreclose on the property, and the entire process is typically wrapped up in the course of two to four months.

Taxes

Before purchasing a foreclosure property, you should also be aware of any taxes that the property owner owes and how those taxes are paid. Note the following:

- Property taxes follow the property. If you purchase a property on which taxes are owed, you owe them.
- Federal income taxes may be wiped off the records by the foreclosure. Attorneys for the lenders put the Internal Revenue Service on notice that the property is going through foreclosure. The IRS has a certain number of days to respond and has the right to pay off the senior lien, but it rarely does. In most cases, the IRS releases its lien.
- State tax liens pretty much follow suit with the IRS. Attorneys notify the state, and the foreclosure wipes any taxes owed off the books.

Picking Your Point of Entry into the Foreclosure Process

Foreclosures are drawn-out ordeals that typically span a period of several months to more than a year. As an investor, you're free to choose your point of entry. You can deal with homeowners directly before the foreclosure proceedings begin, wait around for the foreclosure auction to place your bid, or acquire the property from the bank's REO department or from the new owner after the messiness of the foreclosure has passed. The following sections explore the pros and cons of the available entry points.

Understand all phases of the foreclosure process before trying to carve out your niche. Flexibility and creativity are often key ingredients in working out a deal that's beneficial for all parties involved, and until you understand all phases, you can't put together an effective strategy.

Pre-foreclosure

Inserting yourself early in the foreclosure process, before it begins in earnest, is the most effective way to eliminate your competition and acquire the property for a decent price. After the foreclosure notice is posted, the competition begins to swarm, and other investors attempt to strike a deal with the homeowners, which can drive up the price. Of course, you have to be able to approach homeowners tactfully and be prepared to deal with heated emotions and plenty of complications. It's not for everyone.

In the following sections, I show you how to search for pre-foreclosure properties and work with homeowners tactfully.

Flipping with integrity

If you're an honest, hardworking individual, you can make a good living by flipping foreclosure properties and doing it with integrity. You may not turn every prospect into a transaction, but the more people you help, the more leads you receive. In many cases, the best solution for homeowners who are facing foreclosure is to sell their homes to an investor like you, but present the facts accurately and let the homeowners decide what's best for them. Your reputation depends on it.

Unfortunately, some investors who deal in foreclosure properties are nothing more than con artists, misrepresenting the facts to pounce on naïve and gullible homeowners. I know of one fellow in the Detroit area who shows up at houses in pre-foreclosure, befriends the homeowners, buys them *groceries*, prays with them, and then preys on them. He may find a house worth $125,000 that has a debt of $9,000 and offer a payoff of $22,000, convincing the distressed, unsophisticated homeowner that she has the right to live in the house forever. After he gets the deed signed over to him, he turns around and sells the house to another investor for a huge profit, never disclosing the fact that he has a "tenant" living in the property.

In this particular example, the homeowner could have sold the property and walked away with about $100,000 or even refinanced to cover the bills and retain ownership of the property. However, the con artist swooped in, scammed the homeowner out of more than $100,000, left the owner without a place to live, and passed the headache along to the unsuspecting investor. Don't con people out of their homes to make a quick buck. You can make a fair profit and still retain your integrity.

Finding pre-foreclosure properties

When a lender initiates the foreclosure process, the foreclosure goes public. To get a jump on the competition, try these heads-up strategies:

- **Interact with friends and neighbors.** You often obtain your best leads by talking with friends, neighbors, fellow church members, and others. Let them know that you buy homes. Let everybody know who you are and what you do, and let them come to you. (See "Advertising to Generate More Leads," later in this chapter, for more advice on networking your way to leads.)
- **Talk with lawyers.** The first person a homeowner contacts when the foreclosure process begins is often a lawyer. The lawyer may recommend that her client sell the property and can refer the client to you.
- **Talk with real estate professionals.** Real estate agents and other real estate professionals often know about foreclosures before they're made public.
- **Contact condo or homeowner associations.** Condo and homeowner associations frequently hear about a homeowner's financial woes long before the news becomes a matter of public record.
- **Advertise in the paper and online.** A small ad in a newspaper or online classified service such as Craigslist with your phone number and a statement such as "I pay cash for homes" or "We buy ugly homes" can lead distressed homeowners to you.

Approaching the homeowners gingerly

Attaining success at the pre-foreclosure stage hinges on your ability to establish trust with the homeowner. If you swoop down like a ravenous vulture, the homeowner is likely to hang up, slam the door in your face, and fling a few choice words in your direction. You have to build credibility. Ninety percent of the people who go into foreclosure lose less and benefit most by selling the house. It's the best option they have. Let them know this fact and help them decide whether their situation falls into that 90 percent category.

Stepping in at the pre-foreclosure stage isn't for everyone. The homeowners are often embarrassed, bitter, and reluctant to trust anyone . . . especially someone offering to help by buying their house out from under them. Approach gently and follow these guidelines:

- **Be honest.** If the homeowner has gobs of equity built up in the home and can refinance his way out of the problem, say so. You may not get this property, but you make a friend who can recommend you to others. Steering distressed homeowners into making a decision that's in your best interest and not in their best interest is wrong. The deal is good only if it's good for both of you.

- **Add a personal touch.** If you have the person's address, pay him a visit or hand-deliver a letter introducing yourself and explaining how you can help.
- **Take notes and pictures.** Getting past the front door to inspect the property is perhaps the biggest challenge you face. If the homeowner invites you in, ask to look at the property. Take notes and photographs, unless you get the feeling that it would upset the homeowner too much. In that case, take good mental notes. You need all the information you can get to determine the right price to offer.
- **Verify the facts.** What the homeowners tell you isn't necessarily true. Inspect the property as closely as possible, determine its true market value, and research the title closely, as you would before purchasing any property. (See Chapter 10 for more about researching distressed properties.)
- **Make a decision.** The longer you waffle, the more time another investor has to make her move. Decide quickly whether you want the property, and if you want it, make your offer . . . after checking the title and inspecting the property, of course.

Pitching your offer for a pre-foreclosure property is very similar to making an offer on any home that's on the market. If the homeowner listed the property for sale, your agent should present your offer in the form of a written purchase agreement to the listing agent. If the property is not yet listed, have your agent present the purchase agreement to the homeowner for consideration.

The more you assist homeowners through a difficult situation, the better your chance of acquiring the property and establishing yourself as an investor with integrity. When people hear that you helped so-and-so out of a tough jam, they're more likely to seek your assistance when they run into similar problems.

TIP

To keep yourself honest, take off your investor shoes and put yourself in the homeowner's shoes. Ask yourself whether what you say, suggest, and propose is in the homeowner's best interest. If it's not, don't do the deal.

Negotiating a short sale

A *short sale* occurs when a lender agrees to allow the homeowner to sell the home for less than the balance due on the loan and accepts the proceeds as full payment. For example, suppose a homeowner owes $175,000 to a bank and can no longer afford the payments on that loan. The homeowner wants to "get out from under the home" — sell it, pay off the mortgage balance, and move to more-affordable accommodations. Unfortunately, the best offer the homeowner gets on the home is $135,000. With a short sale, the mortgage lender allows the homeowner to sell the property for $135,000 and fork over that money to the lender as payment in full; the lender forgives the other $40,000 due on the loan.

That's the simple version of a short sale. More complicated versions arise when multiple lenders have claims against the property (liens on the property). For example, a homeowner may owe back taxes on the property and have a first mortgage with one lender, a home equity loan from another lender, and financing from one or more contractors for new windows, new carpeting, and a host of other goodies. When several parties have liens against a property, they must get in line to collect their money. In the event of a foreclosure, certain lienholders are paid before others: Property taxes are paid first, followed by the first-mortgage holder, followed by the second-mortgage holder, followed by any contractors. If no money is left after paying the first lienholder, the junior lienholders are likely to receive nothing. (Because of changes in how these situations are resolved, the second lienholder may receive some portion of the proceeds of the short sale.)

To further complicate matters, junior lienholders who stand to lose everything they're owed in the event of foreclosure have the opportunity to buy out the senior lienholder through redemption — paying that lienholder the total owed to the lienholder or by negotiating a payout of a lesser amount.

You can profit from short sales in various ways. For example, suppose three lienholders have a claim against a property, with A being the senior lienholder, B being the second-position junior lienholder, and C being in the third position. Depending on how much equity is built up in the property, the following scenarios are possible:

- You buy A's position (either at auction or directly from A) and wait for the redemption period to expire. B and C take no action, if you're very lucky, and their positions are wiped out.

  REMEMBER: When you're first getting started, I strongly recommend that you buy only A's so you own the controlling position. You're much less likely to lose your investment if you own A's. You can still profit by purchasing junior lienholder positions, but you usually buy out a junior lienholder only for the right to buy out the senior lienholder.

- You buy A's position. B buys you out to protect its position and waits for the redemption period to expire to wipe out C's position. You have to sell, but you don't have to discount, so you should at least get your money back. You get more money if you bought A's position for less than A's claim against the property; for example, if A holds a mortgage of $125,000, which you're able to get for $100,000, then B must pay you $125,000 to buy you out, and you earn a tidy $25,000.
- You buy A's position. C buys out both you and B to protect its position. Again, you have to sell, but C must pay you the balance on the loan you have claim to.
- Another investor buys A's position. You buy B's position, giving you the right to buy A's position from the other investor, which you do, forcing C to either buy you out or lose out entirely.

- You buy A's position and then buy B's and C's positions (typically by paying them less than the total of what they're owed via a short-sale agreement). Why buy out B and C? If the property has a lot of equity in it, buying out B and C prevents them from buying your position and prevents other investors from buying B's or C's position and then attempting to buy you out.
- You buy A's position, and then, during the redemption period, the homeowner redeems the property (buys you out). Again, assuming you paid less for A's position than the balance owed that position, you stand to receive the difference. For example, if A has a lien on the property for $125,000, and you bought A's position for $100,000, then the homeowner has to pay you $125,000 to redeem the property, and you earn $25,000.

Success in short sales requires a lot of wheeling and dealing and jockeying for position. Start by contacting all parties that have liens against the property to find out the payoff amount for each loan. After you know the position of each lienholder, the total payoff amount of all loans, and the maximum amount you're willing to pay for the property (see Chapter 12), you can begin to negotiate with the lienholders. For example, suppose the payoff amounts look like this:

Lienholder	***Payoff amount***
City Mortgage (first mortgage)	$84,349.42
Capital Source (second mortgage)	$39,208.16
Jackson Heating and Cooling	$10,680.00
Internal Revenue Service	$16,803.43
Total	**$151,041.01**

You decide the maximum amount you can pay for the property is $111,600. Now you're ready to plan your strategy for wheeling and dealing with the lienholders:

- The balance on the first mortgage from City Mortgage is $84,349.42. Because the estimated property value is $144,000, City Mortgage is highly unlikely to agree to a short sale. It would be better off owning the property. You're going to have to pay the full $84,349.42. That leaves you about $27,251 for paying off the other lienholders without exceeding your top offer of $111,600.
- Capital Source holds the second mortgage of $39,208.16. This is a perfect opportunity for a short sale. Capital Source stands to lose the entire amount if the foreclosure proceeds to conclusion and the homeowners fail to redeem the property. They may be willing to accept $24,000 to assign the lien to you, in which case the homeowners owe you the $39,208.16. This places you in a prime position to buy the first mortgage at auction. See the following section for details.

- Jackson Heating and Cooling holds a construction lien of $10,680. It's in a very weak position and is unlikely to buy the first mortgage of $84,349.42 to protect its position. It would be very likely to sell you its position for $2,000–$3,000.

WARNING!

- The IRS is also unlikely to invest $84,349.42 to protect its $16,803.43 position. However, if the IRS has a lien on the property, make sure the law firm handling the foreclosure gives the IRS 30 days' notice prior to the sale. Assuming notice was given, after the redemption period, this lien is dropped. If you don't check this, you could end up with a property with the IRS lien still attached.

Assuming your negotiations unfold according to plan, you pay City Mortgage $84,349.42, Capital Source $24,000, and Jackson Heating and Cooling a cool $3,000 (at the most), for a grand total of $111,349.42, slightly below your target of $111,600.

A variation on this scenario arises if you short the first mortgage — that is, pay the bank less than the principal remaining on the first mortgage. As of the writing of this book, if the first mortgage is shorted, the second lienholder is entitled to 6 percent or $6,000, whichever is less. For example, suppose you're buying a property that you can sell for $175,000 after fixing it up. The current value of the property is $125,000, and the owners owe $150,000 on the first mortgage and $50,000 on the second mortgage. You short the first mortgage for $125,000, and the bank holding the first mortgage pays all commissions, closing costs, and $6,000 to the second lienholder.

WARNING!

Don't start negotiating short sales until you've done your research on the property, as discussed in Chapter 12. Carefully research the title so you know all parties that have a lien on the property. For more about short sales, check out *Foreclosure Investing For Dummies*, by Ralph R. Roberts and Joe Kraynak (Wiley).

Foreclosure

The foreclosure process begins with the posting of the Notice of Default (NOD) in the county's legal newspaper, proceeds through the sale (typically at auction), and ends with the transfer of property from the previous owner to the new owner. At any step along this journey, you have the opportunity to acquire the property. The following sections show you how to acquire properties after the NOD is posted or at a foreclosure sale.

Perusing foreclosure notices

When a lender initiates foreclosure proceedings, the lender posts a foreclosure notice in the county's legal newspaper. (See Chapter 10 for more on foreclosure notices.) Contact your county's Register of Deeds office and ask where it posts foreclosure notices. You may be able to subscribe to the paper or register to receive the postings via e-mail.

The posting of the foreclosure notice provides you with another entry point into the process. With the foreclosure notice in hand, you now have more information at your fingertips, including the following useful tidbits:

- **Mortgagors' names (who owes the money):** This bit of information can help you track down the property owners and perhaps approach them before the property ends up on the auction block.
- **Lender's name (bank or mortgage company):** You may not need this information right away, but it could come in handy in the future if the lender ends up with the property after the auction and needs to sell it.
- **The amount that remains to be paid on the loan:** By knowing the amount remaining to be paid on the loan, you have a clear idea of what may be considered a reasonable opening bid.
- **The interest rate:** If the interest rate on the first mortgage is high, and you buy the first mortgage, you stand to gain a decent return on your investment even if someone redeems the property after the sale because whoever redeems the property must pay you back the amount of money you paid for the first mortgage plus interest. If the interest rate is 8 percent, that's higher than most banks pay.
- **Legal description of the property:** The notice doesn't provide you with a mailing address, but through the Register of Deeds office or your agent, you can figure out the mailing address from the legal description. After you know where the property is located, you can drive by or possibly even get inside to inspect it.
- **Length of the redemption period, if any:** This tells you how long the current owners have to buy back the house after the sale . . . and how long you'll probably have to wait before you can place the house back on the market.

TIP

If you live in a county that sees a fair share of foreclosures, the foreclosure listings may seem overwhelming at first. The trick to making the listings less cumbersome is to know what you're looking for and then weed out any listings that raise red flags. For example, if you find a property on Main Street with a mortgage of $200,000, and you know of no property on Main Street that you'd pay more than $150,000 for, you know that property isn't for you. If the same property is listed for $75,000, it may be worth investigating.

WARNING!

After you find a property that interests you, double-check to make sure that it's going to be sold. Sometimes, the foreclosure notice is posted, and then the homeowner files for bankruptcy or takes some other action to cancel or postpone the sale. Call the attorney listed in the foreclosure notice before you waste a lot of time researching the property (see Chapter 10 for more about conducting research). You may be able to obtain additional information from the attorney, such as the exact price, but don't count on it — the attorney is acting as a debt collector on behalf of the lender.

WARNING!

Hurry. The clock's ticking. You have about 30 to 90 days from the time the foreclosure notice appears in the paper before the property goes on the auction block. You also have more competition now that the foreclosure is public knowledge.

Taking part in the foreclosure sale

TIP

Many real estate investors choose to wait until the foreclosure sale to make their move, trusting that they can successfully outbid the competition. Before you choose to make your entrance at the foreclosure sale, sit in on a few auctions to get a feel for how they work. Talk to one or two veterans who actually purchase properties at auctions, and place your bid only after taking the following precautions:

- Research the title thoroughly to check for any liens on the property. (See Chapter 10 to find out how to research the title.)
- Make sure that you're bidding on a first mortgage or senior lien, not a second mortgage or junior lien. (This information is also on the title.)
- Accurately estimate the value of the property by researching recent sales of comparable properties.
- Inspect the property as thoroughly as possible with your own two eyes (as I explain in Chapter 10).
- Settle on the maximum amount to bid and don't exceed this amount no matter how keyed up you get over the property. (I show you how to rein in your impulses in the section "Settling on a maximum bid.")

I give you the nitty-gritty on placing bids at an auction in the section "Step 4: Bid on a property," later in this chapter.

WARNING!

Don't assume you're getting a good deal just because you're acquiring the property at an auction. Research a property and its title thoroughly before placing a bid. You can really get burned by not doing your homework.

Post-foreclosure

You may think that your chance of purchasing a property ends when the auctioneer hollers "Sold!" but the property can still change hands. Jumping in this late in the process may mean that you have to pay more for the property than you could have gotten it for by acting more aggressively early on, but after the property is sold or passed back to the lender, you can deal directly with the new owner . . . without a lot of emotional baggage. In the following sections, I show you how to contact the new owner: the lender or the investor who purchased the property.

Buying an REO property

In most cases, the lender buys back the property and, after the redemption period, transfers the property to its REO (Real Estate Owned) department, which prepares the property for resale. The lender may be willing to sell you the property before or after transferring it to its REO department. From the foreclosure notice (discussed earlier in this chapter), you can obtain the lender's name and the amount owed on the mortgage.

When you're ready to make an offer, have your agent draw up a purchase agreement to submit to the lender. Many times, the lender stipulates that you must add some standard addendums to the purchase agreement, such as a statement that you agree to purchase the property as is, subject to inspections. Your agent can help you determine which addendums to add.

You may have better luck purchasing a property from the REO department at the end of a month or quarter. In an attempt to make its numbers for a particular month or quarter, the REO department may be under pressure to clear bad loans off its books. It may accept an offer on June 25 that it rejected on June 3.

Contacting another investor

If another real estate investor won the bid, she may be willing to sell the property after she takes possession of it or even during the redemption period. If you purchase the property before the redemption period expires, keep in mind that the property owner can buy back the home at any time during the redemption period by paying the loan balance and any accrued interest.

In all real estate transactions, presenting an offer in writing (as a purchase agreement) is best. Sometimes an investor has a property already tied up with the seller through a purchase agreement, but the investor doesn't have the funds to close and wants to pass it off to another investor. This is called a *pass through transaction,* typically accompanied by a *bird dog fee* (a finder's fee), which can range from $5,000 to $10,000.

Paying a bird dog fee isn't something I recommend. You're better off putting that $5,000 to $10,000 to work on another property that you can buy directly from a homeowner or at auction.

Purchasing Foreclosure Properties Step by Step

Profiting from foreclosures isn't the slam-dunk proposition that many perceive it to be. For every story of someone buying a property and selling it at a 500 percent profit, I can tell three stories of rank beginners who lost their shirts making ill-informed decisions. The truth is that investing in foreclosure properties is risky.

Although you can't eliminate the risk, you can whittle it down to the point at which success becomes more probable than failure. The following sections present a step-by-step process of finding, researching, and purchasing foreclosure properties that reduces the risk.

Step 1: Find a property

The method for finding foreclosure properties depends on where in the foreclosure process you decide to look (I cover these stages in more detail earlier in this chapter):

- **Pre-foreclosure:** A homeowner may contact you directly, knowing that you're an investor who buys houses, or you may obtain leads from lawyers, real estate agents, friends, or acquaintances.
- **Foreclosure:** Search through the foreclosure notices in your county's legal newspaper or register to get on the mailing list.
- **Post-foreclosure:** Contact the lender's REO department or the investor who purchased the property at the foreclosure sale.

Step 2: Follow the paper trail

After you locate a property that looks promising, it's time to do your homework. Begin by researching the title to make sure that it doesn't contain any hidden surprises, and then dig a little deeper, especially if you're purchasing the property in a pre-foreclosure deal, to uncover additional details that can help you during negotiations. See Chapter 10 for details.

Step 3: Inspect the property

The first rule in flipping houses is to never buy a property without looking at it first, but that can be a bit tricky. In a foreclosure situation, the property owner may be less than enthusiastic about showing his home to someone who's ultimately going to take possession of it and evict him.

TIP

The least you should do is drive past the property, get a look at it from all sides, and snap some photos. The care and handling of the house's exterior and landscaping are often pretty good indications of how well the owner cared for the inside of the house. A house with a perfectly manicured lawn, trimmed hedges, and freshly painted garage reflects a pride of ownership that generally permeates the house.

If you can establish a good rapport with the homeowners, they may invite you in to look around, especially if you need to meet with them to go over some paperwork or explain their options to them. Do what you can to get inside the house, short of breaking in or appearing too pushy. After you're inside, follow the guidelines for inspecting a property, as I suggest in Chapter 11, to whatever degree possible.

REMEMBER

Stamp the following rule on your forehead: *Your eyes or no buys.* Never buy a property that you haven't visited and inspected yourself. If you decide to have someone else inspect the property, don't blame them if they miss something.

Step 4: Bid on a property (when buying at an auction)

You performed your due diligence. The price is right, the house looks great, and the title is clear. You're one bid away from financial freedom. Now it's time to place that winning bid, right? Not so fast. Assuming that you're entering the process at the foreclosure stage, read through the following sections to prepare for auction day.

Settling on a maximum bid

The single most important step in bidding on foreclosure properties is to establish your maximum bid — an amount you're not to exceed no matter what happens.

REMEMBER

To determine your maximum bid, use the same system I present in Chapter 12 to ensure that you stand to earn at least 20 percent.

If you're unable to get inside the house to inspect it, estimating the costs of repairs and renovations can be tricky. Use the following techniques to come up with some rough estimates:

- Assume the house needs painting inside and out and new carpet from wall to wall.
- Estimate high for older homes because they generally have more costly surprises, such as substandard plumbing and electrical systems.
- Remain cautious of brand-new homes that may not be finished on the inside.
- When in doubt, overestimate expenses.

REMEMBER

Always commit to a maximum bid before the auction begins. Otherwise, you may get caught up in a bidding war, win the bid, and lose your shirt. I take an assistant with me to keep me from bidding away my future profit.

Testing the waters

Sit in on a few auctions before placing your first bid. Observe other bidders to size up your future competition and discover their techniques and strategies. Bring your list of properties along with your maximum high bids and compare your bids with the winning bids. If your bids are way out of line, you may want to tweak the process you use to arrive at your estimates before you do any serious bidding. Don't talk yourself into raising the price you think you can sell the property for in an attempt to justify bidding higher than your maximum bid.

Surveying bidding strategies

TIP

Foreclosure auctions are like poker tournaments. Every bidder has a unique strategy and various techniques for psyching out the competition. Here are some common strategies you may want to look out for and try yourself:

- **Bore 'em into submission:** Keep outbidding the highest bidder by the minimum bid. If the minimum increment is $100, whenever someone makes a bid, bid $100 more. Just don't exceed your maximum.
- **Speak softly and carry a big wad of cash:** Quiet bidding often conveys confidence and can undercut the high-energy, emotional tone of the auction. It forces other bidders to ask, "What did he bid?" which can be a little unsettling and give you the edge you need.
- **Crank the volume:** Bark your bids as if you're a mad dog in control of the room. If you've ever had your parents yell at you, you know the effect this technique can have. It can rattle your opponent just enough to make him back off or make him think that you've lost your mind. Either way, you're in control.
- **Mix it up:** Go erratic, random. Don't follow a pattern. As long as your bids make sense to you without exceeding your cap, experiment and see what works best.

TIP

I was recently at a sheriff's sale and someone bid a dollar, I bid $500, then he bid $1,000, then I went to $1,500. He went to $2,000. My maximum bid was four grand. I jumped my bid to $4,000 instead of going to $2,500. He just shook his head and said, "No more." You can scare people off with this tactic.

Performing post-auction chores

Assuming you submitted the winning bid, you have to take several steps to pay for the property and protect your interest in it. Proceed through the following checklist to make sure that you've attended to all the details:

- **Follow through on the conditions of the sale.** Ask the Register of Deeds or whoever is holding the auction to supply you with a list of conditions to finalize the sale, and then attend to those conditions.
- **Pay any remaining balance due.** You must pay the entire balance right then and there.
- **Record the deed.** Upon payment, you receive the deed to the property. As soon as possible, take the deed to the county clerk's office or Register of Deeds and have it recorded to protect your legal claim to the property. In some counties the sheriff may record the deed, but make sure it gets done quickly.

  TIP: Ask the Register of Deeds or your real estate attorney to explain the recording requirements in your area.
- **Obtain title insurance.** Visit your title company and obtain title insurance for the property.
- **Obtain property insurance.** If any major damage occurs to the property during the redemption period, you want to have an insurance policy to pay for it. Contact your insurance agent as soon as possible to obtain a policy for the home.
- **Notify any taxing authorities who have liens on the property.** If the IRS or the state has an income-tax lien on the property, the foreclosing attorney usually notifies the IRS prior to the sale. Make sure the IRS notice accompanies the bidding paperwork. If the foreclosing attorney did not notify a taxing authority who has a lien on the property, consult the foreclosing attorney and your own attorney, if necessary.
- **Return any overbid money to the homeowners.** An *overbid* situation occurs if you bid more than is required to cover any liens on the property. When a buyer submits an overbid, the homeowners have the right to claim the overbid amount. All they have to do is go down to the courthouse, file a claim for the money, and it's theirs.

TIP: If someone outbids you at the auction, if your area has a redemption period, and if you're still interested in buying the property, consider writing a letter to the homeowners informing them of their redemption rights. You may be able to help the homeowners redeem the property, and then you can buy the property from them. Or, better yet, knock on their door, make sure you know what you're talking about, and try to swing a deal.

Step 5: Survive the redemption period

If you win the bid in some states, you pay off the mortgage and any taxes due on the property and immediately take possession of the property. In other states, you have to sit on the property until the redemption period passes, which can last up to 365 days.

The Rivercrest fire: Why you buy insurance

An investor I know bought a house for $80,000 that was worth $350,000. The owner was still in the house and in a 12-month redemption period. She had canceled her homeowner's insurance. One day, her children and her neighbor's children were playing with sparklers in the garage, without adult supervision. You can probably guess the rest. A fire started in the garage.

Fortunately, the fire department saved the house. The investor later found out that the owner had canceled her insurance, which would have covered her for the contents of the home, but as a result of her cancelation, she wasn't covered. The investor had the house insured, however, so the damage to the property was covered. I strongly recommend that all investors get insurance — it's important because incidents such as this aren't uncommon.

While you're waiting, you may be tempted to start working on the house. Don't. You may invest $10,000 in renovations only to have the property owner decide to redeem the property just before you wrap up the project.

During the redemption period, the deed holder (homeowner) still has control of the real estate. You can, however, gain a sense of security by offering the seller cash for keys and having them execute a *non-redemption certificate*. A non-redemption certificate is an agreement by the homeowner to not redeem the property.

WARNING!

Be very cautious when working with homeowners. You don't want to be accused later of taking advantage of homeowners while they were under duress.

REMEMBER

Never spend money on a house you don't own or that doesn't have a clear title. You can pay taxes and insurance and file an affidavit to add that amount to the balance required to redeem the property, but don't spend money on renovations until you take possession.

Advertising to Generate More Leads

At this point, you likely have more opportunities to explore than you have time to research, but after you have a solid support team in place, you may find that your flip-able property pool becomes overfished. To continue expanding your real estate investment business, you can either widen your net by reaching out to other neighborhoods (see Chapter 6 for details) or fish a little deeper by advertising for leads.

Unless you're afflicted with a bad case of tunnel vision, you've probably noticed ads, signs tacked to telephone poles, and billboards advertising in big bold letters **We Buy Homes**. Well-established real estate investors often post these ads to draw sellers to them instead of having to search for properties on their own. You can follow their lead by doing a little of your own guerilla marketing:

- Tack up flyers at local stores, but don't post them on telephone poles, vacant buildings, or lawns, because it's against city ordinances.
- Print and distribute business cards to people you meet in the area.
- Network with others by telling *everyone* what you're doing and by asking lots of questions.
- Visit neighborhood churches; they often know people in the neighborhood who need to dispose of property.
- Post an ad in the neighborhood newspaper or on Craigslist or other online venues — Private Lender Looking for Properties.
- Post your own billboard ad after you become well established.

Advertise only after you become well established and are comfortable flipping multiple properties at once. Otherwise, you may be overwhelmed with calls that you're unable to follow up on. This inability to get back with potential leads can quickly damage your reputation as someone who can help distressed homeowners get out from under a house.

Chapter 9

Scoping Out Properties in Special Markets

In This Chapter

- Finding and buying probate properties
- Digging up leads on properties in bankruptcy
- Buying properties from various government entities
- Remembering to do your homework

Bargain hunters often discover great deals in retail stores, but they know that some of the best deals are available outside of the normal channels — on eBay, at flea markets and garage sales, in thrift stores such as Goodwill, and simply by networking with friends and family members to get second-hand goods they're no longer using.

The same is true when you're hunting for bargains in the housing market. Sure, you can find bargains in the Multiple Listing Service (MLS) or by cruising the neighborhood for For Sale By Owner signs, but some of the best deals aren't listed. You can find these unlisted properties in special markets. The biggest special market is the foreclosure market, which I cover in Chapter 8. In this chapter, I introduce you to other special markets, including probate, bankruptcy, and government-owned properties.

Acquiring Properties in Probate

When someone who owns some stuff dies, the stuff often goes into *probate,* where the courts decide what happens to it. Because a house divided cannot stand, probate often results in selling a house to turn it into liquid assets (cash), which the court can more readily use to pay off outstanding debts, taxes, and administration fees. The court divides any remaining crumbs among the beneficiaries of the estate.

In the following sections, I step you through the process of finding and buying properties in probate.

Finding probate properties

The first step in acquiring probate properties is finding properties in probate. Tap the following sources for leads:

- **Probate attorneys:** The best way to discover properties in probate is to contact probate attorneys. They handle estates, and they want to get paid, so they need the services of real estate investors like you to help them liquidate properties. Be sure to ask for references and check those references to find reputable attorneys.
- **Classifieds:** Check the classifieds in your local newspaper for announcements of probate sales.
- **County clerk's office:** Your county clerk's office should have information about probate hearings and estate sales. See if you can get on a mailing list to receive this information via e-mail.
- **Obituaries:** To get a jump on other investors, check the obituaries to find out about recently deceased residents in your area, and then skip to the next section to begin your research.
- **Auctioneers:** Check the auctions category in the phone book for auctioneers who specialize in estate sales. (You can usually get a property for a lower price by purchasing it before it ends up on the auction block, where bidders can drive up the price.)

TIP: Add the names and contact information of helpful probate attorneys and others to your contacts list and keep in touch with them so that when good deals cross their desks, you're the first person they call.

Digging up the death certificate for more info

However you happen to hear about the passing of a resident in your area, the first order of business is to get hold of a copy of the death certificate, which may provide additional useful information.

Death certificates are a great resource for information on the owner. A death certificate includes information about a person's background, family, age, and more. Laws vary by state; in Michigan, anyone can obtain a death certificate from the clerk of the county in which the person died. Visit the county clerk's office or visit its webpage to find information regarding who can obtain a death certificate, and the process and cost involved. You may be able to download a request form online, complete the form, and send it to the county clerk's office with payment.

If you can't track down the death certificate, try performing an Internet search for the person's name followed by "obituary" and search the obituary sections of local newspaper websites for the person's name. (Often, newspaper obituaries are not indexed by Internet search engines, so you have to perform your search on the newspaper's website.) That may lead you to the funeral home, where you can find out which county issued the death certificate. You can then head down to the Register of Deeds office for that county to obtain additional information regarding ownership of the property.

Finding out who can sell the property

After you find a probate property, you need to figure out who's authorized to sell the property. Head down to the Register of Deeds in the county in which the property is located and look up the deed for the property, as I explain in Chapter 8. The deed should indicate who's authorized to sell the property or at least provide you with a lead on how to find that individual. What you do next depends on what you find out from the deed:

- If the only person who owns interest in the property is deceased, then only that person's estate can sell the property. If the estate is open, search the probate court's records to find out who's managing the estate (or the name of that person's attorney). The estate will be on record at the county probate court, usually in the county where the individual lived. Go online and find the probate court's website. The court may have an online search tool you can use to look up the case to get contact information; otherwise just call the court and ask. Don't be afraid to call any attorney who's involved; the attorney is usually willing to discuss the matter and can give important details on what's required to purchase the property, the condition of the property, title issues, and the names of the various parties involved.
- If the deed shows that the property is owned by a trust, only the trustee of that trust can sell the property. Locating this individual (usually a child of the deceased) may be quite a challenge. Again, the attorney involved is a great resource. Often, the deed transferring the interest to the trust contains contact information for the estate-planning

attorney who drafted the trust. Call the attorney for information on who the trustee is and say that you'd like to make an offer on the property. Be sure to ask questions regarding who has the authority to sell, whether the person is interested in selling, and what obligations are owed on the property.

TIP

If you can't track down the person authorized to sell the property, check the death certificate; it may contain the name of the *informant* (usually a close relative) who provided information about the deceased person to the funeral home so the death certificate could be completed. If that doesn't get you anywhere, visit `zabasearch.com` or `ancestry.com` and use the site's search tools to locate and obtain contact information for the next of kin.

Contacting next of kin

Don't feel uncomfortable contacting the relatives of a deceased individual regarding their real estate. In most cases, these relatives will welcome your interest, and there's nothing wrong with asking. Find out who's in charge of selling the property and what the various people who have a stake in the property want out of the sale. By engaging in conversation, you can usually obtain a sense of how eager everyone is to sell.

TIP

The more heirs to the estate there are, the better for you, because each heir needs to give up less for you to get a bargain on the property. For example, if you want to buy a $150,000 property for $100,000 and you're dealing with only one heir, that heir has to give up $50,000 in agreeing to the deal. However, if five heirs are involved, each stands to receive $20,000 and has to give up only $10,000. Negotiating a discount from multiple people is easier than doing so with a couple, such as a husband and wife.

Keeping tabs on overbids

WARNING!

Probate sales can be a little tricky, especially in states that allow *overbids.* An overbid occurs when the property sells to the highest bidder at an auction and then another investor bids higher than the winning bid. The overbid typically must exceed the winning bid by 5 percent or more, so someone can't just bid an extra dollar and get the property. Still, if you're bidding on a probate property, overbids are a concern. If you're in a state that allows overbids (ask a probate attorney), don't assume the sale is final just because you were the high bidder at the auction. Keep tabs on the property until the sale is final.

REMEMBER

Probate overbids differ from foreclosure overbids. In foreclosure, an overbid is an amount paid for a property over and above what's required to pay off any liens on that property. In probate, an overbid is a bid in excess of the original winning bid by the required amount.

Scooping Up Bargains in Bankruptcy

Dealing in bankruptcies can be extremely complicated — even more so than trying to acquire a foreclosure property. In most cases, you can't simply deal with the homeowner or bid at an auction. You have to work with the homeowners' attorney or the court-appointed trustee, who's committed to selling the property for fair market value or at least a fairly decent price. Even if you obtain the attorney's or trustee's approval, creditors may oppose the sale of the property in court.

In the following sections, I reveal tips and tricks to improve your odds of success in finding and buying bankruptcy properties.

WARNING!

Acquiring bankruptcy properties can be a royal pain, which is exactly why most real estate investors avoid them like the plague. If you're a novice investor, I suggest you do the same. However, because so many investors steer clear of properties in bankruptcy, the opportunities are more plentiful for anyone who can learn the ropes. Just make sure you have an attorney who specializes in bankruptcy in your corner.

Brushing up on bankruptcy laws

Filing for bankruptcy stops everything . . . or in legal parlance, it *stays* everything. It stops foreclosure (only temporarily). It freezes the bill collectors in their tracks. It transforms the bankruptcy filer's loose collection of assets into an estate, from which nothing can move until the bankruptcy courts and trustee can resolve disputes.

In the following sections, I explain the differences among the main types of bankruptcy you're likely to encounter. Consult an attorney who specializes in bankruptcy for specific rules that apply to bankruptcies in your area. Pay close attention to any rules governing what you can and cannot do as an investor.

Selling assets through Chapter 7 bankruptcy

Homeowners filing for Chapter 7 bankruptcy hand over control of all of their assets to a court-appointed trustee. The court empowers the trustee to liquidate the assets in order to pay any claims against the estate, including back taxes, unpaid mortgages, and credit-card debt.

When you're negotiating for the purchase of a home that's part of a Chapter 7 bankruptcy, you deal with a court-appointed trustee. You may present your offer to the homeowners, but that offer must state that it's subject to the trustee's approval.

Restructuring debt through Chapter 13 bankruptcy

In Chapter 13 bankruptcy, people seek to *restructure* their debt — that's a fancy way of saying that they work out some sort of deal with the people to whom they owe money (the *creditors*). Restructuring may include selling some assets, including the bankruptcy filer's home, assuming they own a home.

When you're negotiating for the purchase of a home that's part of a Chapter 13 bankruptcy, you deal with the homeowner's attorney and must present your offer to the attorney.

Cramming down debt in a Chapter 11 bankruptcy

Chapter 11 is more of a business bankruptcy. Unlike Chapter 7 bankruptcy, which requires a business to cease its operations, under Chapter 11, the court allows the debtor to continue doing business as *debtor in possession* subject to court oversight and jurisdiction.

High-net-worth and high-income companies use Chapter 11 to restructure their debt and come up with a plan to pay their creditors. If a plan can be brokered, the company gets a fresh start and is allowed to pay its outstanding debts in monthly installments. The court may also allow the debtor to *cram down the debt*; if the debtor owes more on an asset than it's currently worth, the court may reduce the outstanding balance to the amount the asset is worth. Cram downs help reduce the total debt owed.

Knowing when to purchase

Knowing when to purchase a property is often the key to acquiring it. Following are the various stages in the bankruptcy process, along with some tips on how to more effectively position yourself at each stage:

- **Debtor in possession stage:** Upon filing for bankruptcy, the homeowners remain in possession of the property and can accept offers and negotiate the sale. The bankruptcy attorney or court-appointed trustee, however, is legally obligated to notify the creditors, and they must approve the sale. At this stage, you're unlikely to obtain the property for a price significantly below market value.
- **Liquidation stage:** At the liquidation stage, control of the property is transferred to the trustee. Unless the judge objects, the trustee is in control of the property and chooses the most attractive offer. This is usually the best time to make your move. Although a creditor can object at this point, the trustee has the power to overrule the objection. Of course, the trustee also has the power to reject your offer and hand the property over to one of the creditors. Dealing with the creditors is often your key to acquiring the property at this stage.
- **Post liquidation:** If one of the creditors buys or is given the property during the liquidation stage, you may be able to purchase the property from the creditor. This is another excellent opportunity to purchase the property, especially if you've established a solid relationship with the creditor.

WARNING!

Never contact the homeowners before consulting an attorney who's well-versed in bankruptcy law in your area. In some cases, you may be able to work out a deal that's acceptable to both the homeowners and their creditors, but this is like tip-toeing through a minefield. If the homeowners perceive you as working on behalf of the lenders to circumvent their bankruptcy protection, they can have you hauled into court, and you're likely to find yourself paying a hefty penalty.

Tracking down houses in bankruptcy

Bankruptcy is hush hush, because attorney-client privilege prohibits attorneys from sharing a client's information with anyone, let alone publishing client information. In addition, free sites don't publish personal bankruptcies except in certain cases when the bankruptcy is linked to a probate case. In other words, you're unlikely to find out about a bankruptcy unless it's linked to a celebrity or other high-profile person. Your best chances of discovering houses in bankruptcy come from the following three sources:

- `Pacer.gov`, a subscription service that provides *public access to court electronic records* (PACER)
- Court-appointed bankruptcy trustees
- Personal bankruptcy attorneys

Digging up additional info

`Pacer.gov` is also a great service for digging up valuable information about a property in bankruptcy, including the following golden nuggets:

- Names of the people filing for bankruptcy
- Whether the husband and wife filed jointly
- Whether bankruptcy was filed under Chapter 7 or Chapter 13
- The name of the trustee, if a trustee was appointed
- Whether the house is included in the bankruptcy
- The home's stated value, if included in the filing
- How much of the equity can be protected
- The names of any creditors who've been contacted and whether any of the creditors filed an objection at the confirmation hearing
- The acting attorney's name and contact information
- The schedule for proceedings
- If the bankruptcy hasn't been confirmed, when the property will be placed back on the foreclosure docket
- Whether the lender has moved to lift the stay

Dealing with the gatekeepers

To acquire a property that ends up in bankruptcy court, you have to serve at least two masters — the bankruptcy attorney or trustee and the homeowners. You may also need to deal effectively with any creditors who have a stake in the sale of the property. In bankruptcy, the legal people are your main contacts, but if you were working with the homeowners prior to the date on which they filed for bankruptcy, you can leverage your relationship with them to influence the decisions. Following are suggestions on how to team up effectively with court-appointed trustees, personal-bankruptcy attorneys, homeowners, and creditors:

- **Bankruptcy trustees:** In deed of trust states, the court appoints a trustee to settle the estate. Realize that this person has a court mandate to sell the property for as much money as possible in a relatively short period of time. As an investor, the best approach is to present a fair offer that gives you a sufficient profit and doesn't turn the trustee against you. If your offer is laughable, you not only risk losing this property, but you also jeopardize any future relationship with the trustee.

- **Bankruptcy attorneys:** How to negotiate effectively with a bankruptcy attorney depends on the attorney and the situation. If the attorney is pressuring the homeowners to sell quickly and put the bankruptcy behind them, all you may need to do is pitch your offer and hand over the cash. On the other hand, if the attorney knows how to play the legal system and is dedicated to serving the clients' needs, and the client wants to stay in the home as long as possible, you'd better play nice with the attorney. A good bankruptcy attorney can keep her clients in the house for months or years, while you're footing the bill.
- **Homeowners:** After the homeowners file for bankruptcy, you may not be able to deal with them directly. If you're allowed to contact the homeowners, do so respectfully and keep their needs in mind. Always keep their attorney or the bankruptcy trustee in the loop. And never talk to the homeowners directly without your own attorney's consent.
- **Creditors:** Creditors often stand to lose the most from bankruptcy, so they may be willing to team up with you to help you get the property while they recoup a portion of a bad loan. Find out what they're looking for and seek ways to meet their needs while earning a decent profit for yourself.

The key to working with a trustee is to get the name of the attorney the trustee is working with and reach out to the attorney. The attorney helps the trustee make quick decisions. Even though the trustee wants to take your deal, he has to get it approved by the bankruptcy court. Approval is subject to higher and better offers. In Chapter 7, the trustee attorney loves for potential buyers to come forward because his compensation is tied to the amount of money he gets for his clients — the unsecured creditors. It's a win-win because the trustee attorney has nothing to lose but a lot to gain by working with you.

In Chapter 11 bankruptcy, you deal with a debtor in possession. This person has an obligation to run the business in a manner that benefits the creditors and the business. If the debtor-in-possession's plan isn't confirmed, everything is subject to the court's approval. If the plan is confirmed, then the debtor in possession can make the decisions.

In Chapter 13 bankruptcy, the homeowners/debtors decide what to do with an asset subject to court approval. You negotiate with the homeowners and their attorney, but the deal is subject to court approval. For example, if the homeowners receive $20,000 from the sale of the home, they can use that money to restructure their debt, prepay the debt they owe, or combine the two strategies. What they choose to do, however, must be consistent with the court-approved plan for paying off the debt.

Planning for delays

You may inadvertently encounter properties in bankruptcy, especially if you're investing in foreclosures. If you buy a foreclosure property at auction, the homeowners file for bankruptcy, and the court grants a stay, you may be stuck holding a house and paying the bills while the homeowners remain in possession well past the expiration of the redemption period.

In the worst-case scenario, your profit is limited to the interest you charge the homeowners on the purchase price you paid. If the homeowners manage to redeem the property, they must pay you the purchase price plus interest and reimburse you for any property taxes and homeowner's insurance you paid out of pocket.

To sweeten the deal and increase your profit on the property, often the best approach is to pitch a deal to the homeowners' attorney or the bankruptcy trustee. Following are a couple of suggestions on deals that the homeowners and the court may find appealing:

- **Offer to lease the property to the homeowners.** The homeowners and the courts typically want to avoid a situation in which the homeowners are evicted and have no place to live. By offering to lease the property to the homeowners for a fixed period of time, you demonstrate your sensitivity to their needs and give them extra time to find new living arrangements.
- **Structure a buy-back deal.** To avoid a long bankruptcy delay, consider selling the property back to the homeowners at a profit that's perhaps less than what you had hoped for. Why would the homeowners be willing to buy back the house? Because challenging the sale can be costly both in time and money. If the attorney involved can see the benefit of a sure deal that will cost less in the long run, she may be willing to accept it, particularly if accepting the offer ensures she'll get paid. A sure deal looks pretty good next to the alternative — a lengthy and expensive courtroom battle.

REMEMBER

If you do decide to work in the bankruptcy arena, develop a strong knowledge of how bankruptcy works in your area and don't go it alone — hire an experienced bankruptcy attorney to guide you and prevent you from making costly mistakes. To find the best bankruptcy attorney, go to a trustee firm. Meet with whoever assists the trustee and helps with the firm's real estate ventures. All law firms across the country are looking for more business, so you should have no trouble finding a qualified bankruptcy attorney who's willing to work for you.

Finding Government-Owned Properties

The government often plays a supporting role in the real estate business. It insures or secures loans, and when homeowners default on those loans, the government has to step in, foreclose on the property, and then sell it to recover some or all of its loss. When citizens fail to pay their taxes, the government may seize the homeowner's real estate to cover the bill. Law-enforcement agencies often get in the act by seizing homes of convicted drug dealers and other criminals.

Nobody likes to think of the government kicking people out of their homes, but that's a tragic reality that some homeowners face when they experience a significant financial setback, commit a serious crime, or make poor financial decisions.

Anyone with enough money or financing can purchase these homes, either through designated real estate agents or by bidding on the properties at auction. To begin your hunt for government-owned properties, check out the following leads:

- **HUD homes:** First-time buyers often finance their homes through the federal government, primarily by way of loans insured by the Federal Housing Administration (FHA). When the property owner fails to make mortgage payments, the FHA initiates a foreclosure, which commonly results in the agency taking possession of the house and reselling it through a real estate agent registered with the Department of Housing and Urban Development (HUD). The only catch, and it's a biggie, is that HUD sells homes "owner-occupied," meaning you have to commit to living in the home for at least 12 months before selling it. (After the 12 months, you can sell to anyone you choose, including someone who doesn't plan on living in the home.) Investors who say they'll live in these homes but then don't are committing fraud and can end up behind bars. To find HUD homes, contact a local HUD-approved real estate agent or visit `www.hudhomestore.com` to search for and bid on properties.
- **VA repos:** When a homeowner defaults on a Department of Veterans Affairs (VA) loan, the VA repossesses the property and places it back on the market. To find VA repos, contact a VA-registered real estate agent in your area or visit `HomeSales.gov`.
- **Freddie Mac homes:** Freddie Mac, the nickname of the Federal Home Loan Mortgage Corporation (FHLMC), is a government-sponsored organization that promotes homeownership by making mortgage loans

affordable, especially to first-time homeowners. You can search for Freddie Mac homes at HomeSteps (www.homesteps.com) or by contacting a local real estate agent who lists Freddie Mac homes.

- **Fannie Mae homes:** Fannie Mae, the Federal National Mortgage Association (FNMA), is Freddie Mac's older sister, and it does pretty much the same thing as Freddie Mac — it promotes homeownership by making affordable mortgage loans available. To search Fannie Mae's listing of real estate owned (REO or bank-owned) properties, visit HomePath.com, where you can also bid on properties.
- **FDIC properties:** The Federal Deposit Insurance Corporation (FDIC) is a government agency that insures savings deposits at member banks. When a bank fails, the FDIC acquires any properties the bank owns and puts those properties up for sale. It's sort of like foreclosing on the bank. You can check out what the FDIC has to offer by visiting www.fdic.gov/buying/owned, but don't expect to find a huge selection.
- **IRS seizures:** When a home goes into foreclosure, the IRS usually releases any lien it has on the property. Occasionally, however, the IRS redeems the property to sell it and recover lost tax revenue. To find out about properties that the IRS has for sale and obtain information about upcoming auctions, visit www.treasury.gov/auctions/irs, scroll down the page, and click Real Estate. Just don't expect to find much real estate for sale.
- **DOT properties:** The Department of Transportation (DOT) commonly purchases real estate when building or widening roads or making other improvements to the infrastructure. If the property is not destroyed during the construction project, DOT puts it up for sale. Contact your state's DOT for leads on properties it may currently have for sale. It may list the property with a particular broker, post notices in specific legal publications, or offer them for sale online.
- **Treasury auctions:** The U.S. Department of the Treasury conducts about 300 auctions each year to sell property it seizes as a result of violations of federal laws it enforces or for the nonpayment of federal taxes. Visit www.treasury.gov and search for "property for sale" to find a link to the Treasury Auctions page.
- **USDA real estate for sale:** The U.S. Department of Agriculture lists properties it has for sale at www.resales.usda.gov. This site displays links to single-family and multi-family properties along with any farms or ranches the USDA has in inventory. Simply click the link and follow the trail of maps to your state and county to find out whether any USDA properties are for sale in your neighborhood.
- **U.S. GSA property disposals:** The U.S. General Services Administration often lists government-owned properties that you can't find anywhere else. Visit propertydisposal.gsa.gov and use the Property Search

tool near the bottom of the home page to look for available properties. This site provides access to information about properties owned and for sale by the federal government, such as land and buildings made available by military base closings or U.S. Marshals Service property seizures.

If you stumble upon what looks like a great deal, make an offer subject to a satisfactory home inspection. Delaying your offer until you can have the home inspected opens the possibility that another buyer will swoop in and buy the property. By making your offer subject to a satisfactory home inspection, you can get your offer in and then back out if the property needs a lot of work. Present your offer, but make sure it has a good contingency clause you can use for an emergency exit.

Buying Properties at Tax Sales

Taxing authorities don't mess around when citizens don't pay their taxes. They simply send a few notices, and if the homeowners don't come up with the cash or work out a payment plan, the taxing authority seizes the property, puts it up for auction, and attempts to collect the taxes from the sale proceeds. Taxing authorities show little leniency, and the homeowners rarely dodge the bullet by claiming bankruptcy.

Your county treasurer's office or property-tax division is the best place to start your search for information about tax sales, particularly property-tax sales. Visit the treasurer's office or whichever county office handles the tax sales and try to obtain the following information:

- **Bidder's packet:** Many counties put together a bidder's packet with general information for investors. For a small fee, you can obtain most of the basic information you need about tax sales in your county.
- **Property list:** As the date nears for the property-tax sale, the county treasurer may offer a list of all the properties to be auctioned. The problem with such a list is that it's generally in progress up until the date of the sale.
- **Regulations:** If your bidder's packet doesn't contain information about how redemptions are handled for property-tax sales, ask. (See Chapter 8 for more about redemption — the right a homeowner has to buy back the property after the sale.) Different states and counties may handle this differently. For example, in some states homeowners who lose their property in a tax sale have no redemption rights. Find out the rules that govern tax sales in your area. Tax-sale rules are defined by the state and are administered by the county.

The rules and regulations regarding tax sales are very complex and vary from state to state. The entire delinquent tax foreclosure process can take anywhere from three to seven years from the time a homeowner stops paying taxes until the time the government takes possession of the property and puts it up for sale. In that time, the taxing authority attempts to contact the homeowners and anyone else who has a lien on the property, giving them the opportunity to pay the back taxes. In most cases, someone who has an interest in the property ponies up the money and takes controlling interest in the property. Contact your real estate attorney to find out more about how tax sales are handled in your area.

Regardless of which special market you choose to tap for properties, perform your due diligence in researching the property and its paper trail. You need to inspect the property with your own eyes and visit your county's Register of Deeds to dig up information about the title and other details. See Chapter 10 for additional guidance on researching properties.

Part III

Evaluating Properties and Crunching Numbers

Home Inspection Checklist

Property Address: ______________________________

Area	**Comments**	**Estimated Costs**	**Estimated Time**
EXTERIOR			
Roof			
☐ Shingles & Underlayment			
☐ Underlayment			
Gutters & Siding			
☐ Missing or Damaged Gutters			
☐ Aluminum Siding			
☐ Vinyl Siding			
☐ Brick			
☐ Other			
Windows			
☐ Glass			
☐ Screens			
☐ Frames & Sills			
Driveway			
☐ Trip Hazards			
☐ Gravel			
☐ Asphalt			
☐ Concrete			
Landscaping			
☐ Backyard			
☐ Front & Side Yards			
Doors			
☐ Screens			
☐ Storms			
☐ Entry Doors & Frames			
Porch			
☐ Front Porch & Stairs			
☐ Back Porch & Stairs			
Garage			
☐ Roof, Siding, & Gutters			
☐ Doors & Windows			
☐ Foundation & Floor			
☐ Electric			

web extras

Buying a property at the right price is key to earning a decent profit from it. Visit `www.dummies.com/extras/flippinghouses` for a more detailed Property Analysis Worksheet that can help you calculate your maximum purchase price.

In this part...

- Gather all the information you need to know about a property in order to make a well-informed purchase decision.
- Inspect properties with your own eyes so you know the property exists and have a general idea of what condition it's in.
- Dig up vital information about distressed properties at your county's Register of Deeds and assessor's offices.
- Find out how to come up with a ballpark figure for the cost of repairs and renovations.
- Calculate the most you can pay for a property in order to earn at least a 20 percent profit after you fix it up and sell it.
- Get tips on pitching offers and counteroffers to get the price and terms you want.
- Avoid the common mistake of haggling your way out of what would have been a great deal.
- Discover how to use weasel clauses that enable you to back out of a deal if you discover unsettling issues.

Chapter 10

Researching Distressed Properties

In This Chapter

- Investigating a property's vital statistics
- Gathering legal documents at the Register of Deeds office
- Inspecting the property from the street
- Checking your list to ensure you have everything you need

A large part of real estate *investing* consists of *investigating* — knowing what you're about to buy before you lay your cash on the line. You need to know how much the property is worth, how much is owed on it, whether it has any additional liens or encumbrances on it, whether the property is in violation of any building codes or has any environmental hazards, and whether the person selling the house is the legal owner.

TIP

For each property you consider buying, create a separate folder with a photo of the property, its address, and all publicly accessible information available for that property. This chapter shows you the type of information you need and provides instructions on how to dig it up and gather it into a file to create a *property dossier* (pronounced daw-see-ay) — a collection of photos, documents, and other information regarding the property.

In addition to assisting you in determining whether the property is worth your time pursuing, this information becomes critical if you need to assist homeowners in pre-foreclosure, negotiate with homeowners and lenders, or bid on a property at auction.

REMEMBER

This chapter focuses on researching distressed properties — properties in foreclosure, probate, bankruptcy, and so on. If you're buying through the normal channels — through an agent who's listed the home in the MLS — certain protections are in place, so extensive research isn't required. The sellers are legally required to disclose any defects in the property, you can arrange for the home to be professionally inspected, and, as long as you purchase title insurance, the title company performs its due diligence in confirming the seller is the legal owner of the property and identifying any creditors who have liens against the property.

Creating a Property Dossier

For every property I investigate, I create a dossier. I use different-colored folders to keep data for my top prospects separate:

- Green: Sheriff sale
- Red: Chapter 13 bankruptcy
- Yellow: Chapter 7 bankruptcy
- Blue: Bankruptcy carve-outs, where the secured lender carves out money to give to the bankruptcy trustee who has control of the asset, so the trustee will transfer his interest to the investor/buyer
- Orange: Short sale

I recommend a similar strategy, but feel free to be creative — just make sure your system keeps all the data on each house separate and easily accessible. If you prefer to go paperless, you can even store the information in separate folders on your computer.

However you choose to organize your property information, make sure each folder contains the following items:

- An 8-by-10-inch photograph of the property taped to the front of the folder for quick reference
- A map showing the location of the property (search MapQuest or Google Maps)
- An exterior inspection form (see "Checking Out the Property" for a blank form)
- An interior inspection form, if you're able to get inside the house (see Chapter 11 for a blank form)
- The foreclosure notice or notice of default (NOD) if the property is in foreclosure (see "Picking details off of a foreclosure notice" later in this chapter)
- A foreclosure information sheet containing key details from the foreclosure notice
- The title commitment and 24-month history in the chain of title or the minimum last two recorded documents
- The last recorded first mortgage, so you know how much the homeowners currently owe on the property
- Records of other liens on the property, such as second mortgages, construction liens, and tax liens (property tax liens are especially important, because if you buy the property, you're responsible for paying any back property taxes)

- A copy of the deed with the current homeowners' names, which should match the names on the title (if the names don't match, find out why)
- The city worksheet on the property showing the history of the property
- The property's state equalized value (SEV) — the value of the property on which its property taxes are based
- MLS listings of at least three comparable properties that have recently sold or are currently for sale, so you have a general idea of how much a buyer is likely to pay for this property
- A legal pad to keep names, phone numbers, e-mail addresses, notes, and a log of all correspondence, whether mail, e-mail, or fax, complete with dates and times

If you're not sure where to get all of this stuff, keep reading. The rest of this chapter explains how to gather the documents you need to build a property dossier.

TIP

If you're bidding on one or more properties at auction, bring all of your property dossiers to the auction. You may have researched 20 properties and narrowed down your prospects to the top three, but take all 20 folders with you, because you never know what will happen come auction day. You may have ruled out a $250,000 house that had a $260,000 mortgage on it, but then, when the auction rolls around, it may open with a bid for $170,000. By quickly referencing your property dossier and doing some basic math, you realize that you can pick up $80,000 in equity. Because you've done your homework and you have your dossier with you, you may be the only one in the room who knows what that house is worth. When that happens, you're like a fox in the henhouse.

This strategy works for us every single week. We get a house because we already have a file on it. Prospective buyers who haven't done their homework have only one hour to research the property. By doing our research in advance, we simply have to review the file and get the check to buy the property.

Checking Out the Property

An investment property may seem like a steal on paper when it's actually a gutted shell of a home in the center of the low-rent district. Until you see the property for yourself, you have no idea what it is, what kind of homes surround it, or what condition the home is in.

REMEMBER

Before you plop down your money or borrowed money on a property, always inspect it as closely as possible with your own two eyes, carefully record your observations, and add the details you gather to your growing property dossier.

In the following sections, I provide an exterior home inspection form to complete, and I lead you through the process of performing your due diligence in the field.

Note: If you're researching a foreclosure property, you may need to do a little detective work to find out where the property is located. The foreclosure notice may provide only a legal description of the property, which doesn't include a street address. See "Finding the property," later in this chapter, for details.

Doing a drive-by, walk-around inspection

The least you should do (and the most you can do in some situations) to inspect a property is to drive over and walk around the property . . . at a safe distance, of course — I'm not suggesting that you trespass. Even if you can't get inside to take a closer peek, the drive-by, walk-around inspection provides you with enough preliminary information to develop a ballpark estimate of the property's value and rule out any really bad properties.

Whenever you visit a property in person, you're at some risk. The homeowners, and sometimes their dog, may not appreciate uninvited visitors, especially if you trespass. Keep your distance. Knocking on the front door is usually okay, but if the homeowners ask you to leave, respect their wishes. If you want to work with the homeowners in pre-foreclosure, you can send a letter introducing yourself and explaining how you may be able to help them.

As you perform your drive-by, walk-around inspection, complete the exterior inspection form provided in Figure 10-1. (I don't write very neatly, so I take along a digital recorder, record my observations, and then burn the audio clip to a CD to add to my file. You may want to type notes on a laptop or other portable electronic device.) You may be unable to collect all of the information requested on the form, but collect as much information as possible without becoming too pushy if the homeowners confront you.

If the home is currently listed for sale, call the agent and take a tour of the inside of the house. In Chapter 11, I provide an inspection form for the interior of the property — take the form with you and fill it out.

Exterior Property Evaluation

Owner: ____________________

Home Phone: __________ Work Phone: __________ Pager/Mobile: __________

Address: ____________________

Distinguishing Feature of Property: ____________________

Property is: ❑ Vacant ❑ Owner Occupied ❑ Tenant Occupied

Tenant Info: How Long at Home? ______ Monthly Rent: __________

Neighborhood Details: ❑ Brick ❑ Frame ❑ Mix

Block Club? ❑ Yes ❑ No

# of burn-outs: ___ #of board-ups: ____ #of vacant lots: ____ %ownership: ________

Neighborhood Rating: ❑ Poor ❑ Fair ❑ Good ❑ Excellent

Neighborhood Listings:

Address: ______________ Phone: ________ Asking Price: __________

Address: ______________ Phone: ________ Asking Price: __________

Address: ______________ Phone: ________ Asking Price: __________

House Details:

Garage: ❑ Yes ❑ No # of Cars: ____ Condition: ❑ Poor ❑ Fair ❑ Good

Driveway: ❑ None ❑ Solid ❑ Ribbon ❑ Asphalt ❑ Alley

Condition: ❑ Poor ❑ Fair ❑ Good

Roof Type: ______ Age: ______ Condition: ❑ Poor ❑ Fair ❑ Good

Type of Construction: ❑ Brick ❑ Frame ❑ Aluminum ❑ Block

❑ Asbestos ❑ Vinyl ❑ Brickote ❑ Stucco

Condition: ❑ Poor ❑ Fair ❑ Good

Year Built: ______ Square Footage: __________ Number of Bedrooms: ___

House Style: ❑ Tudor ❑ Bungalow ❑ Ranch ❑ Split-Level

❑ Colonial ❑ Cape Cod ❑ Multi-Family: __________

Foundation: ❑ Basement ❑ Slab ❑ Crawl ❑ Piers

Storm Doors/Storm Windows/Screens Condition: ❑ Poor ❑ Fair ❑ Good

Window Condition: ❑ Poor ❑ Fair ❑ Good Lot Size: ________

Fence: ❑ Chain ❑ Wood ❑ Wire Landscape: ❑ Poor ❑ Fair ❑ Good

Porch: ❑ Cement ❑ Wood ❑ Brick Condition: ❑ Poor ❑ Fair ❑ Good

Steps: ❑ Cement ❑ Wood ❑ Brick Condition: ❑ Poor ❑ Fair ❑ Good

Door: ❑ Wood ❑ Steel Condition: ❑ Poor ❑ Fair ❑ Good

Recommendation: ❑ Cash Buy ❑ Re-Fi ❑ Listing ❑ Short Sale ❑ Pass

❑ Other: ____________________

Reasoning/Notes: ____________________

____

____

Figure 10-1: Personally inspect the neighborhood and the exterior of the property and record your observations.

Figure by Wiley Composition Graphics

Never pass up the opportunity to talk to a neighbor. If a neighbor wanders out to ask what you're doing, strike up a conversation and try to find out more about the homeowners and the condition of the property. No nosy neighbors? Then consider becoming a little nosy yourself and knocking on doors. A neighbor may have recently been inside the house. If you can't get in to inspect the property, a second-hand report from a neighbor is the next best thing. In some cases, you may even stumble across a neighbor whom the homeowner has anointed to be caretaker; if he or she has keys and is willing to show you around, you've struck gold!

Snapping photos

Every real estate investor should own a high-quality digital camera with a 3x or better zoom lens to take snapshots of prospective investment properties. As you walk around the property, take a couple of photos of each side of the house, the landscape, and surrounding houses. The photo documentary you create is priceless. If you inspect dozens of properties, you're not likely to remember a specific house. A few photos can bring you right back to the day when you first inspected the property.

If possible, take your photos in the late morning or early afternoon, when the homeowners are more likely to be at work and the kids in school. You may avoid a confrontation with the homeowners and keep the kids from asking their parents embarrassing questions, like "Why is that lady taking pictures of our house?"

If your camera has a time-stamp feature that places the date and time on every photo, turn on the time stamp so you can coordinate your photos with your property data sheets, which I explain later in this chapter. As soon as possible after snapping the photos, print them or take them to your local photo shop to have them processed. Stick the photos in your property dossier for later reference.

Following the Paper Trail

Every property has records on file that indicate the location of the property, who owns it, any liens against the property, its assessed value, taxes paid and due on the property, and so on. If the property is in foreclosure, additional information may be available on the foreclosure notice. Before you even think about purchasing a distressed property, you need to dig up this essential information so you know exactly what you're getting . . . and getting yourself into. When researching a property's records, here are some of the most important facts you need to find out:

- Which lenders hold the first and second mortgages and any junior liens, such as a construction lien or a lien for homeowners association fees.
- Whether the property has any property-tax liens. Property taxes follow the land, so if you buy the property, you owe the taxes. Search the county records for any taxes due on the property.
- Whether any outstanding water or sewer bill is attached to the property. Water and sewer bills may follow the property, too.
- Whether the property has any federal or state income-tax liens against it. If it does, closing the deal may be impossible, because dealing with the IRS and state almost always leads to a dead end.
- Whether any of the owners has filed for bankruptcy, in which case you need to work through the bankruptcy trustee.
- If the owners are divorced, you need to check the court records to see what the property settlement was. If you're dealing with the ex-husband but the divorce decree says that the ex-wife gets the house, you're dealing with the wrong party.

In the following sections, I point you to the sources of key information and provide a couple of forms to complete to record the essential data in a format you can quickly reference later. But first, I want you to get some experience by digging up information on your own home.

Honing your title acquisition and reading skills

To hone your skills at gathering data related to distressed properties, consider practicing on your own home first. Of course, unless you're currently in foreclosure, you won't have access to a foreclosure notice (lucky you), but you can practice researching your title, mortgage, and other documentation relating to your property. You may have several of the documents you need to practice on in the closing packet you received when you purchased your home, but don't cheat by referring to those documents. If you still live with family members, then research your parents' home; it'll still make sense and you'll understand things more quickly. Go out in the field and see what sorts of publicly accessible data you can gather on your own:

1. **Head down to your local title company.** You can find a list of title companies in your phone book.
2. **Meet with one of the representatives and explain that you're reading this book called *Flipping Houses For Dummies*, and you want to know everything they can teach you about titles.**

   See "Researching the property's title," later in this chapter, for additional details.
3. **Request a title commitment on your own property.** A *title commitment* is a promise by the company to provide title insurance after conducting a title search, assuming that the search doesn't dig up any problems with the title. The title commitment may take a couple of days to prepare. Most title companies can e-mail the title commitment or policy to you.
4. **Visit your county courthouse and track down the Register of Deeds or County Recorder's office.**
5. **Ask nicely to see everything recorded against your house since the time the title shows you took ownership of it.** You should be able to obtain the last two recorded documents — perhaps the deed and the mortgage showing when you purchased the property.
6. **Now, compare the title commitment you received from the title company with the documents you picked up with your own detective work.**

You should notice a big difference in the documents. The title commitment won't include all the information from the documents you picked up at the county courthouse. Instead, it extracts the essential details and presents them in a more easily accessible format, showing:

- Homeowner's names
- First mortgage
- Any second mortgage or other liens against the property
- Property taxes paid or due
- Delinquent sewer or water bills or other services supplied by the municipality

Picking details off of a foreclosure notice

When a foreclosure notice or notice of default (NOD) is published, like the one shown in Figure 10-2, you have a wealth of information at your fingertips.

ROBERTS & KRAYNAK, P.C.
Attorneys and Counselors
1313 Mockingbird Ln., Ste. 200
Dellingham Farms, MI 48025

THIS FIRM IS A DEBT COLLECTOR ATTEMPTING TO COLLECT A DEBT. ANY INFORMATION WE OBTAIN WILL BE USED FOR THAT PURPOSE. PLEASE CONTACT OUR OFFICE AT THE NUMBER BELOW IF YOU ARE IN ACTIVE MILITARY DUTY.

ATTN PURCHASERS: This sale may be rescinded by the foreclosing mortgagee. In that event, your damages, if any, shall be limited solely to the return of the bid amount tendered at sale, plus interest.

MORTGAGE SALE - Default has been made in the conditions of a mortgage made by JOHN Q PUBLIC and JANE Q PUBLIC[5], husband and wife, original mortgagor(s), to Federal City Mortgage Co D/B/A Commonwealth United Mortgage Company[6], Mortgagee, dated March 4, 2008, and recorded on April 10, 2008 in Liber 55555 on Page 617[12], in Oakland county[3] records, Michigan, on which mortgage there is claimed to be due at the date hereof the sum of Four Hundred Seventy-Two Thousand Seven Hundred Fifty-Eight And 23/100 Dollars ($472,758.23)[7], including interest at 5.625% per annum[8].

Under the power of sale contained in said mortgage and the statute in such case made and provided, notice is hereby given that said mortgage will be foreclosed by a sale of the mortgaged premises, or some part of them, at public venue, at the Main entrance to the Court House in Pontiac at 10:00 AM, on **JANUARY 31, 2016**[10].

Said premises are situated in Charter Township of West Bloomfield, Oakland County, Michigan, and are described as:

Homesite No. 55, Amberleigh Condominium, according to the Master Deed recorded in Liber 55555, Pages 665 through 730, Oakland County Records, as amended, and designated as Oakland County Subdivision Plan No. 1555[4] together with rights in the general common elements and the limited common elements as shown on the Master Deed and as described in Act 59 of the Public Acts of 1978, as amended

The redemption period shall be 6 months from the date of such sale[11], unless determined abandoned in accordance with MCLA 600.3241a, in which case the redemption period shall be 30 days from the date of such sale.

Dated: December 30, 2015[2]
For more information, please call:
FC F 555.555.5555
Roberts & Kraynak, P.C.[9]
Attorneys For Servicer
1313 Mockingbird Ln., Ste. 200
Dellingham Farms, MI 48025
File #055000F05[1]

Figure 10-2: Collect important details about the foreclosure property from the notice of default (NOD).

Figure by Wiley Composition Graphics

Burned by hidden details

Recently, an investor, Uncle Ray, purchased a condo lien at a sheriff sale. A *condo lien* enables the condo association to foreclose on a property for unpaid association fees, just as a bank can foreclose on the condo if the owner doesn't make the mortgage payments. Uncle Ray did his homework; he researched the title, which showed a condo lien against the property that the condo association was about to foreclose on. Unfortunately, the records didn't show that the property also had a mortgage lien. In other words, the bank held the first mortgage, and the condo lien was in the second position.

Uncle Ray bought the condo lien and waited for the redemption period to expire. When it did, he thought he owned the property free and clear. That's when Uncle Ray discovered the mortgage and realized that he had thrown his money away.

Uncle Ray couldn't have known. I researched the file carefully. The way the information was indexed and recorded made it impossible to spot that mortgage.

The moral of this story is that with big risks come big rewards, but big risks often lead to big disappointments, too. Your goal should be to minimize the risks and the disappointments.

The foreclosure notice presents you with the following details (the numbers in superscript in Figure 10-2 correspond to the superscripted numbers next to the items in the following list):

- **Case or reference number[1]:** Some attorneys include a case or reference number in the foreclosure notice to simplify the process of searching for information in their database.
- **Insertion date[2]:** The date may appear in the notice itself, but if it doesn't, use the date of the publication in which the notice is posted. In the legal news, the advertisements are listed under subtitles to indicate the order of the posting — first, second, third, and so on.
- **County[3]:** The county in which the property is located is your key to unlocking other details about the property. Using this bit of information, you know which county's Register of Deeds office to visit to research the title and mortgage and find the property's address. (Start off working in the county where you live.)
- **Legal lot, subdivision, and city[4]:** The legal description of the property doesn't provide the property's mailing address, but from the legal description, you can find the mailing address. See the next section, "Finding the property," for details.
- **Name of the mortgagor[5]:** The mortgagor is the borrowers, typically the homeowners, but if someone else borrowed the money to pay for the home, the mortgagor may be a different person.

- **Name of the mortgagee[6]:** The mortgagee is the lender who is foreclosing on the property.
- **Amount owed on the mortgage[7]:** The NOD or foreclosure notice always states the exact amount the homeowners currently owe on the first mortgage. They may owe additional sums on other loans, such as a second mortgage or home-equity line of credit.
- **Interest rate of loan[8]:** The longer the amount owed on the mortgage remains unpaid, the more the amount increases by the specified interest rate. The interest rate can help you calculate the amount owed as it increases over time.
- **The mortgage company's attorney[9]:** The mortgage company attorney's name and contact information is useful in enabling you to double check the sale date and the opening bid and contact the mortgage company to work out a deal.
- **Mortgage sale date[10]:** This is the date on which the attorney for the lender expects the mortgage to be auctioned. This date can change, but jot it down so you can keep track of it.
- **Length of the property's redemption period, if applicable[11]:** If your area has a mandatory redemption period, it should appear in the foreclosure notice. Using the date of sale and redemption period, you can determine the last day the homeowners can redeem the property.
- **Liber and page number of the recorded mortgage that is in foreclosure[12]:** This tells you where to find the mortgage document. (*Liber* means book.)

Pick the details off the foreclosure notice and transfer them to the relevant blanks on the Foreclosure Information Sheet shown in Figure 10-3. (Later, in this chapter, in the section "Researching the property's title," you add details to complete this sheet.)

If you're buying properties directly from homeowners who contact you prior to the beginning of foreclosure proceedings, you can gather most of the information you need to complete the foreclosure information sheet from the homeowners. Just be sure to verify the information by inspecting the title and other records, as I explain in the following sections.

WARNING!

Multiple names on a foreclosure notice doesn't mean they're all owners. Sometimes certain people have to sign for specific rights, such as dour or courtesy rights. (*Dour rights* refer to what a wife of the owner gets if her name's not on the title. *Courtesy rights* are essentially dour rights for men. In Michigan, women can buy real property without their husbands, so Michigan essentially has no courtesy rights.) You have to look at the last deed on record, as I explain next, to find out who owns the property. Nothing is more frustrating than taking time with someone who doesn't actually own the property.

Foreclosure Information Sheet

Date: ___________

Foreclosure Notice

Case or Reference Number: ___________

Insertion Date: ___________ Thru:

County: ___________

Legal Lot: ___________

Subdivision: ___________

City: ___________

Mortgagor (Homeowners): ___________

Mortgagee (Lender): ___________

Mortgage Amount: ___________

Interest Rate: ___________

Mortgage Company's Attorney: ___________

Mortgage Company's Attorney Phone Number: ___________

Mortgage Sale Date: ___________

Redemption Period: ___________

Last Day to Redeem: ___________

Register of Deeds (Title)

Property Address (Ask Clerk): ___________

Mortgagor Names: ___________

Price Paid for Property: ___________

Deed Warranty Names: ___________

Previous Mortgagor (Previous Title): ___________

Price Paid for Property (Previous Title): ___________

Current 1st Mortgage Mortgagee (Lender): ___________

Original Mortgagee (Lender): ___________

Register of Deeds (1st Mortgage and Note)

1st Mortgage Loan Amount: ___________

Interest Rate: ___________

Date Recorded: ___________ Liber: ___________ Page: ___________

Mortgagee (Lender): ___________

Address: ___________

(continued)

Mortgage Assumable? ☐Yes ☐No

Register of Deeds (Second Mortgage and Note)

2nd Mortgage Loan Amount: ______________________________

Interest Rate: ______________________________

Date Recorded: ____________ Liber: ______ Page: ______________________________

Mortgagee (Lender): ______________________________

Address: ______________________________

Mortgage Assumable? ☐Yes ☐No

Register of Deeds (Additional Mortgages or Liens)

Junior Lien Holder 1: ______________________________

Address: ______________________________

Junior Lien Holder 2: ______________________________

Address: ______________________________

Tax Lien: ______________________________

Address: ______________________________

County Tax Assessor

Sidwell (Tax ID #): ______________________________

Taxable Value (SEV): ______________________________

Property Tax Formula: ______________________________

Unpaid Property Taxes: ______________________________

Property Tax Lien? ☐Yes, Amount: ________________ ☐No

State, County, City or Town Property Worksheet

Building Permits: ______________________________

Code Violations: ______________________________

Other: ______________________________

Other Information

Opening Bid: ______________________________

Homeowner's Phone: ______________________________

Estimated Property Value: ______________________________

Total Owed on Property: ______________________________

Estimated Equity in Property: ______________________________

Figure 10-3: Record information from the foreclosure notice and public records on the foreclosure information sheet.

Figure by Wiley Composition Graphics

Digging up details at the Register of Deeds office

Whether you're planning to bid on a property at auction or purchase the property directly from homeowners, a trip to your county's Register of Deeds office is a necessity. The Register of Deeds or County Recorder records most of the legal paperwork for a property, including the title work, deed, and mortgage. In the following sections, I point out the essential information you need to scrounge up from this most important source.

The records you need to research can be recorded on any of several types of media. You may be pulling out folders, flipping through pages in a book, or looking for records on microfilm or a computer screen.

TIP

Many counties have websites where you can access a great deal of information about properties, including the owner names, parcel ID number, property address, taxable value, and so on. Some sites even include aerial photographs of the property that outline the lots on which properties are built.

Finding the property

The foreclosure notice describes the location of the property through a legal description rather than simply providing a mailing address. Isn't that just like lawyers? Fortunately, you can use the property description to track down the mailing address by employing one of the following strategies:

- Ask the clerk at your county's Register of Deeds office.
- Ask your real estate agent or attorney.
- Contact your title company. If you have a good relationship with the company, the staff may be willing to look up the address for you.
- Use a land-data software program to search a database of property information. Land-data software programs are available in some areas and on the web.

Sometimes the person who owns the property isn't living there. In that case, look up the property-tax records to find the owner (the person paying the property taxes) and the owner's address.

TIP

Some companies, such as HomeInfoMax (`www.homeinfomax.com`), provide online search tools that can assist you in finding a property's address based on its legal description. However, most online tools don't cover all counties and typically charge per search. You can get the information for free by doing a little legwork or dialing the phone. When you have the address, plug it into the online mapping program you use and print a map of the property's location.

Obtaining the property's title and other key documents

When most homeowners buy a property, they agree to buy the property from the seller before any mention of the title. Prior to closing on the transaction, they hire a title company that inspects and insures the title to protect the buyer from any messy legal battles over who owns the property.

When buying foreclosure properties, however, inspect the title before you decide to pursue a property. If anything about the title smells fishy, you may want to do a little extra research or simply cross the property off your list.

You can do your preliminary title research yourself by heading down to your county's Register of Deeds office and asking the clerk to provide you with the information recorded on the title for a particular property. At the bare minimum, obtain a copy of the deed and any other recorded documents for the current and previous owners. If possible, obtain copies of all documents recorded back to when the current owner came into ownership. Look for anything opened from that day, such as a loan taken out on the property.

WARNING!

Although you can do this research yourself, and you really should do it yourself to get the hang of title research, I recommend that when you're first starting out, you consult a title company for a second opinion and order a title commitment. When you feel comfortable doing your own research, you can take on more of the burden.

Researching the property's title

Inspect the title work and deed for the following critical pieces of data and record them in the corresponding spaces on the foreclosure information sheet (see Figure 10-3):

- **Mortgagors' (homeowners') names:** Note whether the mortgagors' names match the names actually listed as the property's title holders. Differing names raise a red flag — make a note of it.
- **Price paid for the property:** Depending on how long ago the current homeowners purchased the property, this can provide some indication of the property's current value.
- **Deed warranty names:** The names on the deed should match the homeowners' names on the title. If they don't match, the difference raises a red flag — make a note of it.
- **Previous mortgagor:** Check the previous title and jot down the names on the title. Note any chinks in the chain of ownership. If the title work shows that Johnson sold the property to Davis and then Howard sold it to Pinkerton, who did Davis sell the house to? This gap indicates a problem in the chain of ownership. Consult with your title company whenever you notice any irregularities in the chain of title.

- **Current first-mortgage mortgagee (lender):** The first-mortgage mortgagee is the bank or other lending institution that holds the first (senior) lien on the property. By obtaining the lender's name from the title, you can begin the process of tracking down the lender.
- **Original first-mortgage mortgagee (lender):** In many cases, a lending institution loans the homeowners money to buy the property and then sells the mortgage almost immediately to another lending institution. The title typically includes the name of the original lender. When you start making calls, having this information at your fingertips helps convince the person you contact that you know what you're talking about.

If the property has a second mortgage on it, record the same information for the second mortgage. In a foreclosure situation, you may be able to work with the second mortgage lender to shore up your position. See Chapter 8 for additional details on collaborating with lenders.

Gathering information from the mortgage and note

The mortgage and note are recorded along with the title when someone purchases a property. These documents include important details about the senior lien, so be sure to record these details on your foreclosure information sheet:

- **First mortgage loan amount:** How much did the homeowners borrow to finance the purchase of the property?
- **Interest rate:** Knowing the interest rate on the first mortgage can assist you in calculating the homeowners' current monthly payments and providing them with refinance options.
- **Date recorded, liber, and page number:** With the date recorded, liber, and page number, you can access the information much more quickly.
- **Mortgagee (lender):** You may have already obtained the mortgagee's name from the title, but check the mortgage for any discrepancies. Also jot down the mortgagee's address for future reference.
- **Mortgage assumable:** The mortgage note contains language indicating whether someone other than the borrower can assume the mortgage. You may have to read the note very closely and perhaps even consult your attorney for guidance on how to make this determination.

Uncovering facts about additional lender liens

Although the first (senior) lien is the most important, the property may have other liens from second or third mortgages or construction liens that you should know about. Unless the homeowners very recently took out another loan using the property as collateral or the Register of Deeds is way behind in recording documents, records of these liens should be accessible.

Protecting yourself against mortgage fraud

By carefully researching the properties that interest you, particularly the legal documents associated with them, you protect yourself not only from inadvertent errors but also from con artists who may try to fleece you. Con artists often manipulate the legal documents and file false documents as part of their scams. Sometimes, they can even sell a house they don't own or sell a house several times to different buyers. To protect yourself from falling victim to a real estate scam, take the following precautions:

- Check the records to see if the mortgage on the property was recently paid off. Sellers rarely pay off mortgages right before they sell, so any document that shows the mortgage as having been recently paid off is likely to be a phony document.
- Be wary of an investor who's pitching you a great deal on a property. Con artists often target novice investors in double-sales scams.
- Analyze the title commitment for suspicious transactions.
- Ask your title company for a 24-month property history, including mortgages.
- Purchase title insurance as soon as possible and pay for it up front. Sometimes this is your only protection.

On your foreclosure information sheet, record the names and addresses of any additional lien holders. The date on which a lien was recorded should alert you to the fact that a particular lien is a junior lien. The liber and page number on which the junior lien was recorded should also be higher than that of the senior lien because the junior lien was recorded later.

Uncovering unpaid property taxes and other tax liens

When homeowners get behind on their taxes, government agencies at the federal, state, and county level can place additional liens on the property. While researching the title, inspect it for any of the following additional liens:

- Federal (IRS) income-tax liens
- State income-tax liens
- Property-tax liens
- Any other liens

TIP

Additional liens, most importantly liens for overdue property taxes and federal taxes, are a good sign that the homeowners will be unable to redeem the property. They're probably too deeply in debt to catch up on their payments.

Gathering tax information at the assessor's office

In addition to checking the title for any property-tax liens, head down to the county treasurer's or assessor's office and ask for the following:

- The property's tax ID number (sometimes called a *sidwell number*).
- The taxable value of the property — you may have to visit the county assessor's office for this tidbit. The taxable value of a property is referred to as the state equalized value (SEV). The assessor uses this number to calculate property taxes.
- The property tax formula. Currently in Michigan a house is generally worth 2 to 2.5 times the SEV, so a house with an SEV of $200,000 is usually worth $400,000 to $500,000. Ask the assessor what formula he or she uses. This can often provide you with a rough estimate of the property's market value.
- Whether property taxes are currently paid up and whether the assessor's office has a property-tax lien on the property.

Getting your hands on the property worksheet

Every town, city, or county in the United States keeps a worksheet on every property showing when it was built, any building permits issued on the property, code violations, inspection reports, and so on. Find out who keeps the property worksheets and obtain a copy of the worksheet for any home you're considering buying. On your foreclosure information sheet, record the following data from the property worksheet:

- **Building permits:** Building permits provide a record of all approved property improvements. If you inspect the property later and discover an improvement that was performed without a permit, this may be a warning that the improvement doesn't conform to building codes.
- **Code violations:** If the property has any code violations recorded against it that have not been resolved, you want to know about it so you don't unknowingly take possession of a property that you're responsible for bringing up to code later.
- **Other interesting tidbits:** The property worksheet may include additional information about health-code violations that warn you to inspect the property more closely before purchasing it.

Chapter 11

Inspecting the Property and Estimating Rehab Costs

In This Chapter

- Packing important tools for your inspection trip
- Identifying perfect quick-flip opportunities
- Distinguishing a cash cow from a money pit
- Ball-parking the cost of renovating the property

Before you even consider making an offer on a property, examine the property inside and out to evaluate its potential and then draw up a preliminary list of improvements that would make the property marketable at an attractive yet profitable price. You can inspect the property during an open house or showing or during a private visit with your agent, who can assist you in determining which renovations could add the most value to the home and help you decide whether the property is a good investment.

In this chapter, I take you through a preliminary inspection and point out the features of the landscape and house that should draw your focus. I highlight the types of defects you should avoid at all costs, areas of a home that are often packed with potential, and the types of renovations that really boost a property's resale value. By the end of this chapter, you should be able to walk through a house in 15 to 30 minutes, give it the thumbs up or thumbs down, and walk away with a list of repairs and renovations and an estimate of their costs.

No problem is a real deal breaker if you know about it. You can calculate the cost of fixing a problem into your offer so you're not losing any money and have a good chance of earning a decent profit. The situation you want to avoid is buying a house when you don't know about an issue. A thorough inspection of the premises and estimates for repairs and renovations is critical in determining how much to offer for a house.

Packing for Your Inspection Mission

REMEMBER

A house inspection isn't just a pleasure trip. You're on an information-gathering mission to find the property with the most potential and estimate the cost of making the property marketable and maximizing your profit. To complete your mission successfully, plan ahead and pack the following essential tools:

- Pen or pencil
- Clipboard
- Camera, preferably digital with extra batteries
- Flashlight, with extra batteries, for checking dark nooks and crannies (test it beforehand to make sure that it works)
- Circuit tester to check the outlets (a circuit tester has a three-pronged plug on one end and indicator lights on the other end that show whether the outlet works and is wired properly)
- Step ladder
- One copy of the home inspection checklist in Figure 11-1 for each house you plan to visit (you may want to create your own checklist with more space for comments)
- Screwdrivers (Philips and flathead)
- Tape measure for measuring rooms, doorways, ceilings, and so on (a laser distance measurer is a good investment)

TIP

If you don't like the idea of writing everything down, consider carrying a small digital recorder (or a smartphone that can record audio) in your pocket or purse so you can record comments during your walk-through. A house-inspection trip typically brings you in contact with at least three or four properties, and when you're done looking, you're too exhausted and overwhelmed to remember important details. Don't rely on your memory alone. Consider walking through the house once to get a general idea of what needs to be done and then a second time recording your observations for future reference.

Home Inspection Checklist

Property Address: ____________________

Area	**Comments**	**Estimated Costs**	**Estimated Time**
EXTERIOR			
Roof			
☐ Shingles & Underlayment			
☐ Underlayment			
Gutters & Siding			
☐ Missing or Damaged Gutters			
☐ Aluminum Siding			
☐ Vinyl Siding			
☐ Brick			
☐ Other			
Windows			
☐ Glass			
☐ Screens			
☐ Frames & Sills			
Driveway			
☐ Trip Hazards			
☐ Gravel			
☐ Asphalt			
☐ Concrete			
Landscaping			
☐ Backyard			
☐ Front & Side Yards			
Doors			
☐ Screens			
☐ Storms			
☐ Entry Doors & Frames			
Porch			
☐ Front Porch & Stairs			
☐ Back Porch & Stairs			
Garage			
☐ Roof, Siding, & Gutters			
☐ Doors & Windows			
☐ Foundation & Floor			
☐ Electric			
INTERIOR			
Electrical			
☐ Fuses/Circuit Breakers			
☐ Wiring			
☐ Switches			
☐ Junction Box Covers			
☐ Faceplate Covers			
Plumbing			
☐ Water Pipes			
☐ Wastewater Pipes			
☐ Hot Water Heater			
☐ Floor Drains/Sump Pump (Basement)			

(continued)

Heating & Cooling			
☐ Furnace/Radiators/Boilers			
☐ Duct Work & Vents			
☐ Filters			
☐ Air Conditioning			
☐ Humidifier/Dehumidifier			
Living Room/Family Room			
☐ Floor/Carpet			
☐ Walls			
☐ Ceiling			
Laundry Room			
☐ Floor/Carpet			
☐ Walls			
☐ Ceiling			
☐ Washing Machine Connect			
☐ Laundry Tub			
Kitchen			
☐ Floor			
☐ Walls			
☐ Ceiling			
☐ Light Fixtures			
☐ Cabinets/Countertops			
☐ Sink			
☐ Stove			
☐ Refrigerator			
☐ Dishwasher			
Bedrooms			
☐ Floor/Carpet			
☐ Walls			
☐ Ceiling			
Bathrooms			
☐ Floor			
☐ Ceiling			
☐ Walls			
☐ Tile			
☐ Cabinets			
☐ Countertop			
☐ Lights			
☐ Tub/Shower/Enclosure			
☐ Toilet			
☐ Sink & Vanity			
☐ GFIs (Ground Fault Interrupters)			
Basement			
☐ Stairs & Handrail			
☐ Watertight Foundation			
☐ Windows & Lighting			
☐ Finished			
Attic			
☐ Insulation			
☐ Vents			
Other			
Total Estimated Costs			
Total Estimated Time			

Additional Comments

Figure 11-1: A home inspection checklist is an essential inspection tool.

Figure by Wiley Composition Graphics

Finding the Perfect Candidate for a Quick Makeover

When you're flipping your first or second property, look for the easy score — a property that looks a lot worse than it is. These houses are typically sold below market value because nobody wants them and the owners aren't motivated enough to do what's necessary to make somebody want to buy them. In short, look for a good, solid house that requires no major repairs and looks ugly. The following sections help you spot the signs of an ideal candidate. For full details on quick-flip renovations, head to Chapter 15.

TIP

My team does a lot of *white-boxing*. We buy houses that are cosmetically challenged but in pretty good shape and give them a quick makeover. We paint the walls white, install new light-switch and electrical-outlet covers, lay new carpeting, spruce up the landscaping, and so on to give the property a nice, clean, well-manicured look.

Poor but promising curb appeal

REMEMBER

If you go to look at a property and your first impulse is to drive past, that's a good sign that curb appeal is lacking. Either the house looks ugly from the street or you simply don't see it. The house has no pop. Assuming the shell of the house is sound — the roof, gutters, windows, and siding don't need to be replaced — you can often improve the curbside appeal with a few quick and affordable do-it-yourself improvements.

Figure 11-2 shows a potentially perfect candidate, although a closer inspection could prove otherwise. The house appears to be in good shape, but it doesn't really stand out from the street. However, some landscaping and light touches on the exterior can change all that!

Cosmetically challenged, inside and out

Often, homeowners' poor taste is enough to turn away prospective buyers. The owners paint their house with colors that should be illegal. They install carpeting that clashes and tile that can turn your stomach. They install a pink bathtub and paint the walls yellow.

Photo courtesy of Ralph Roberts Realty

Figure 11-2: This house is a potentially perfect candidate for a quick makeover.

TIP

Fortunately for you, cosmetically challenged houses are often a good buy, assuming they're in decent condition. Simply by decking out the house in a new, neutral color scheme, you can raise the resale price by thousands of dollars and attract a steady stream of house hunters who previously couldn't stomach looking at the property.

A second-rate showing

Homeowners often lack the energy, motivation, and expertise required to properly *stage* their home for a showing. Staging, as I discuss in Chapter 21, is the process of beautifying your home for prospective buyers. Think of it as primping yourself for a hot date. A properly staged home draws more interested buyers and commands a higher sales price, which is exactly what you *don't* want when you're bargain hunting.

TIP

When looking for a property to quickly flip for a profit, keep an eye out for poorly staged homes. The poor staging reduces your competition as a buyer, enables you to make a low-ball offer, and provides you with the opportunity to raise the resale price just by doing a little clean-up and redecorating.

Assessing Potential Curbside Appeal

Poor curbside appeal isn't necessarily a bad thing. It's often one of the main reasons you can purchase a property below market value. What you're looking for at this point is potential. When you pull up to the curb, don't scramble out of the car and sprint to the front door. Linger for a few moments, observe the outside of the house, and ask yourself the following:

- **Is the house visible from the street?** If it's visible, good. If you can do something relatively easy and inexpensive to increase its visibility, that's good, too. If the house is hopelessly hidden, that's bad.
- **Is the house on a busy thoroughfare?** If it is, that can be a good thing if the location provides convenient access to stores, schools, and work. It can also be a drawback because people may worry about the noise and traffic.
- **Is the house near a park, school, or golf course?** Each of these places can be a big draw.
- **Is the exterior of the house inviting?** Can you make it more inviting without spending too much money? A little landscaping, including trimming trees and shrubs, mowing, and edging, can do wonders and doesn't cost a lot of money.
- **Are the sidewalks and driveway structurally sound?** Sidewalks and driveways can be solid and still look awful. Pulling weeds, patching cracks, and resealing an asphalt drive are easy, inexpensive fixes. If you need to install a new concrete drive or sidewalks, that can get costly.
- **What's the garage look like?** If the house doesn't have a garage, you may be able to add one, depending on how much land you have to work with. If the garage looks worse than it is, some minor improvements can give it the pop it needs.
- **How does this house stack up to neighboring houses?** Can you make affordable adjustments to make it the prettiest peacock on the block?
- **Does the house look as though it requires a greater investment than you can afford, both in time and money?** Bottom line: If the house strikes you as a money pit, walk away. Don't play the hero and try to salvage a hopeless home.

TIP

Be sure to include the entryway in your curb-appeal assessment. A home's entryway is the bridge to an oasis. When a visitor passes through the front door, he should feel as though he's entering a new and better world. If the front porch is cluttered, the doors are ugly, and you enter feeling as though you're getting shoved into a closet, consider options for making the entryway more inviting.

TIP

And don't forget the backyard! Homeowners often treat the backyard like a pristine nature preserve. This undeveloped space often provides you with the pure potential you need to unleash your creativity, add living space, and significantly boost the property value. You may want to consider adding or improving a patio, deck, or attached garage.

Check out Chapter 16 for full details on perking up a house's curb appeal.

Taking a Big Whiff, Inside and Out

Nothing turns away a prospective buyer like a foul odor, so when you start looking at properties, get your sniffer up to snuff. Take a big whiff inside and out to check for any of these foul smells:

- Gas smells may indicate a leaking gas line. Contact the gas company to report a possible gas leak.
- Sewage odors outside may point to problems with a septic tank or nearby sewer line. Indoor sewer odors may indicate a plumbing problem.
- Doggy doo is a common fragrance in backyards populated with one or more dogs. A little scooping can fix this problem. In addition, watch out for indoor pet odors from cats, dogs, or other animals and for decaying flesh from dead animals somewhere in the house — perhaps in a crawlspace, in a duct, or between the exterior and interior walls.
- Cigarette smoke is a real turn-off for many buyers.
- Mold and mildew may be in damp areas in the house. (The notorious black mold isn't typically black, but usually you can smell it.)

None of these malodorous problems is a deal breaker, assuming you can locate the source of the smell and remove it without too much expense. Don't dismiss a bad smell, however, until you know what's causing it. If the seller is trying to mask bad smells by burning candles and incense or by using an assortment of air fresheners, try to smell past the cover-ups and pick up the scent in other rooms of the house.

TIP

When you run into a pet odor, replace the carpet, but before laying the new carpet, sand and stain the flooring below the carpet to kill the odor. If you lay new carpet over the odor, eventually that nice new carpet will pick up the odor.

Lots of companies specialize in treating odors; they are quick and inexpensive and do a very thorough job of eliminating offensive smells.

Inspecting the House for Big-Ticket Items

Almost every property that's flip-able can use a fresh coat of paint, new carpeting, and some tender loving care. You expect that, and you budget it into the cost of the property. Unexpected defects in big-ticket items, however, can quickly bust your budget and drastically cut into your potential profit. Many of these items are costly to repair or replace and, unfortunately, the repairs don't increase the value of the property.

Although you should have the property professionally inspected before you close on the deal (see Chapter 13 for details about professional inspections), you can often save yourself the time and money by catching any major problems on your first visit. The following sections point out the most common and expensive problem areas.

Focusing on the foundation

Every house rests on a foundation, typically a basement or concrete slab. Inspect the foundation, inside and out, for any of the following symptoms of a sick foundation:

- **Cracked foundation or walls:** Almost all foundations have cracks, but large cracks that run down the entire length of the basement wall or along the floor are symptoms of costly structural problems. Check inside the house for cracked walls that may also point to foundation problems.
- **Bowed walls:** Check basement walls for any signs of bowing, indicating that water and dirt are pushing in the foundation.
- **Warped floors:** Uneven floors may be a sign of underlying structural problems. If a floor is sinking, you may see the tops of the walls separating from the ceiling or cabinets pulling away from walls.
- **Spongy floors, particularly under wall-to-wall carpeting:** Be mindful while you walk to discover any spongy areas that may point to trouble. If the house has a basement or crawlspace, check the joists and the condition of the floor from the underbelly of the house.
- **Mold/mildew:** Mold and mildew on basement walls is often a sign of a leaky basement. The basement may appear to be dry now, but when the rain starts pouring down, you may have an indoor pool in your basement.
- **Recently installed paneling:** Recently installed paneling or drywall may indicate a foundation problem that the owner is trying to cover up.

TIP

Dampness in a basement isn't always a sign of a serious problem. Clogged gutters or downspouts that fail to direct the water away from the house are common causes of dampness too — problems that are much easier and cheaper to correct. Note the problem and be sure to mention it when you have the home inspected.

Checking out walls and floors

Walls and floors are particularly susceptible to water damage in bathrooms. To check for water damage in the floor, press your foot down near the base of the toilet or try rocking the toilet back and forth. The toilet moves if the sub-floor it's anchored to is rotting.

If the bathroom is tiled, press lightly on the tiles around the bathtub, shower, and sink. In homes with drywall, moisture often softens the drywall and causes it to crumble. Note any serious damage you find, but don't rule out the house just yet.

Examining the siding

Visually inspect the outside of the house and note the type of facing — brick, wood, vinyl, aluminum, or stucco. Compare it to the neighboring properties. Inspect the facing and note any damage or signs of aging:

- **Brick:** Worn or missing mortar
- **Vinyl:** Cracked, warped, or peeling siding
- **Aluminum:** Dented or peeling siding
- **Wood:** Rotted, cracked, or missing boards
- **Stucco:** Cracked, bowed, or peeling stucco

Chapter 16 has information on retooling a house's siding.

Giving the roof and gutters the once-over

As you inspect the home's facing, let your eyes wander up a little higher to check out the roof and gutters. Note any of the following potential problems:

- Bowed or damaged roof, indicating a problem with the underlying structure of the roof.
- Damaged or aging shingles. Shingles curling at the edges are often a sign that the house needs to be re-roofed.

- Obvious patches. An obvious patch or an area with shingles that don't match the color of surrounding shingles may indicate that the roof leaked in the past and may be damaged beneath the shingles.
- Two or more layers of shingles. You can usually lay one layer of shingles over another, but if the home needs a new roof and it already has two or more layers of shingles, the roofers will need to strip off the old layers first, which can nearly double the cost of roofing the house.
- Gutters pulling away from the house. You may be able to re-attach the gutters, unless the facing board they're anchored to is rotten.

TIP

Listen to your contractors. We recently did a house that needed a new roof, to the tune of $8,500. The contractor noted that only the front side of the roof needed to be replaced; the back had about ten years left of life. We spent $4,400 on the front roof and saved a bunch of money.

Head to Chapter 16 for additional details about new roofs and gutters.

Glancing at the windows, inside and out

Windows are not only a functional part of every house — letting in light while insulating the house and acting as a barrier against the natural elements — but they also play an aesthetic role — accenting both the interior and exterior. Inspect windows for both function and appearance, and note the following:

- Any broken panes
- Torn or missing screens
- Windows painted shut
- Rotted wood, especially window sills

Chapter 18 has information about updating windows.

Evaluating the plumbing

As you walk through a house, turn the faucets on and off, flush the toilets, and check for the following common plumbing problems:

- **Clogged drains.** Leave the faucets running for several seconds to see whether the water backs up.
- **Leaking drains or pipes.** Check under the cabinets for any signs of leaking drains or pipes. Water stains on the ceilings and walls are often a sign of leaking pipes.

- **Dripping faucets.** Drips are relatively easy and inexpensive to fix, but note them.
- **Leaking toilets.** Try rocking the toilet or press your foot down near its base to make sure that the floor isn't rotted.
- **Low water pressure.** Water should flow faster than a trickle, especially if the house has an upstairs bathroom.
- **Broken water heater.** Make sure that you're getting hot water and visually inspect the water heater for rust, leaks, and other signs of damage.

Exploring the electrical system

A home's electrical system delivers power to every light, appliance, and gadget in the house. Fortunately, most homes built in the last 30 years or so have reliable electrical systems built to code. If the outlets function, the lights don't flicker, and the home was built in the last 30 years, you can be fairly confident that the electrical system is acceptable. Even so, you should always check for the following:

- The condition of the electrical box. An old electrical box with fuses instead of breaker switches may need to be replaced.
- The type of wiring used. The best wiring is installed in conduit (metal tubes that completely insulate the wire). Many homes use flexible cables insulated in white plastic, which are also acceptable. Older knob-and-tube wiring strings the wires around porcelain knobs and usually doesn't meet modern building codes. Aluminum wire (silver rather than copper) may also be a problem in some areas.
- The use of lots of extension cords, indicating that the house has too few outlets or outlets that aren't working.
- The functionality of the outlets inside and out.
- The functionality of the lights. Turn on all the lights to make sure that they work.

Checking out the furnace and air conditioner

When examining a house for investment purposes, compare what the house has to what it needs to bring it up to neighborhood standards. If most homes in the area have forced-air heat and central air conditioning, and the house you're looking at has radiant heat with no ductwork, adding central air conditioning can be costly, but it can also add real value to the property.

Visually inspect the furnace and air-conditioning unit to determine their approximate age and any obvious damage. You may not be able to test the air conditioning if you're looking at a house in the winter, but you can check the furnace year-round by turning it on and cranking up the thermostat.

Check the seller's disclosure for the approximate age and condition of the furnace and air conditioning system. (Ten years is considered old, but I've seen furnaces last up to 30 years if they're good and well-maintained.) Also, turn on the furnace fan at the thermostat and check the vents around the house to make sure the furnace fan is working.

Adjusting your eyes to the lighting

Some houses feel more like caves than homes. Even on a bright, sunny day, little light penetrates, and the house has insufficient lighting to compensate. As your eyes adjust to the lighting in various houses, observe what well-lit houses have that ill-illuminated houses lack. Focus on the following items:

- **Windows:** Compare the number, size, and positions of the windows.
- **Window dressings:** Some drapes and blinds are more translucent than others. What style of window dressings are used in well-lit houses?
- **Colors:** Dark walls, trim, carpet, and furnishings absorb light, often making a house seem darker than it really is.
- **Floor plan:** A house that's chopped into tiny rooms often prevents outside light from penetrating into the inner recesses.
- **Landscaping:** Trees and shrubs can filter out just enough light while shading the house and improving privacy, or they can blanket the house in gloomy darkness.
- **Skylights:** Modern homes often incorporate skylights to draw daytime lighting into a room and make it appear more open. Skylights don't necessarily add value to a home; if you're inspecting a home that has skylights, look for signs of leaks around the skylights, such as a patched or discolored ceiling. Skylights may also be a source of heat loss in the winter.
- **Light fixtures:** Well-lit homes typically have plenty of overhead light fixtures, track lighting, or recessed lights. Poorly lit homes rely on lamps, which tend to cast shadows and consume living space.

Discovering Some Promising Features

Some houses are like army barracks. They're neat and clean and well suited for sheltering a family, but they're no work of art. A handful of homes are more inspired. They have a couple of features that take your breath away . . . in a good way — perhaps a lush garden in the backyard, a master bedroom with a fireplace and built-in entertainment system, or a huge kitchen that opens into a living and dining room area complete with a fireplace. Keep an eye out for the following special features:

- **Rooms with character and class:** Real estate agents often use the word "character" to mean "old," and they're typically justified in doing so. Older homes tend to have more character — interior walls of brick, tin ceilings, hardwood floors, sculpted plaster ceilings ten feet high, and so on. But some newer homes have their own classy features, as well, such as fine woodwork, an open-concept floor plan, or built-in shelves. Look for features that have marketing potential — that will draw prospective buyers to see the home.

  TIP

  Also note any rooms that fall short of the standard. These are the rooms that you can improve to make the house more attractive to potential buyers.

- **Hardwood floors:** Valuable hardwood floors are often concealed beneath wall-to-wall carpeting, especially in older homes. You may be able to peel up a corner of the carpet in a closet to see what's underneath without damaging the carpet. If you find a hardwood floor, you're in luck. Hardwood flooring costs two to three times as much as carpeting laid over plywood, so it's definitely a bonus in terms of the property's value.
- **Large, open kitchen:** A large, open kitchen is better than a cramped one. A large, open kitchen that opens to a living room and dining room is even better. Best, perhaps, is a large kitchen that's closed off from the rest of the house but has the potential of being opened up with the removal of one or two walls. If you can buy the house at a bargain price, removing those walls could significantly improve its marketability.
- **Large bathroom:** People don't generally hang out in the bathroom as much as they do in the kitchen, but they like to have at least one large bathroom to relax in. The minimum size for a bathroom is about 5 feet by 7 feet, and no matter how you arrange the toilet, shower, and sink, that feels a little cramped. An extra foot (5 x 8) significantly increases your choice of tub or shower. Any additional space makes the bathroom a more marketable feature.
- **Two or more bathrooms:** An extra bathroom or even a half bath is a big bonus, making the home more attractive to more people.
- **Room to add a bathroom:** If a home has only one bathroom, look for possible spaces you can convert into a bathroom or half bath — for example, one corner of the basement.

  TIP

  You can usually improve the marketability of a home by cleaning the bathrooms. A thorough cleaning, some fresh caulk, and a coat of paint may be enough to transform a vile health hazard into a sparkling, nearly new bathroom. With a little extra money, you can retile the floor and walls, resurface the tub, or install a new shower stall.

- **At least one large bedroom:** Consider a 10-x-10-foot bedroom the bare minimum. When you consider that a queen-sized bed hogs about 35 square feet of floor space and a small dresser consumes another 5 or 6 square feet, a 100-square-foot bedroom quickly fills up. Of course, the larger the better.

  A master suite, complete with a walk-in closet and an attached bathroom, is a big plus because it appeals to married couples who have or are planning to have children. In homes that don't include a master suite, consider ways of converting existing spaces into a master suite; for example, you may be able to combine two neighboring bedrooms and a bathroom. However, you need to weigh the tradeoffs of having more bedrooms versus more room in a master bedroom.

- **At least two bedrooms:** A two- or three-bedroom house is much more marketable than a one-bedroom house. Even if a prospective buyer doesn't need the second bedroom, most will appreciate having an extra room for a home office or study or for overnight guests.

- **Lots of closet space:** Although some people barely notice the closet space (or lack thereof) in a home until they move in, others quickly rule out homes that are lacking in closet space. Some buyers won't even consider a home that doesn't contain at least one walk-in closet. When checking out homes to buy, opt for homes with plenty of closet space.

  Hallway closets are also a big plus for storing linens, cleaning supplies, and other stuff. Again, the bigger, the better.

- **Laundry room:** A main-floor laundry room is a big plus. Most buyers don't want to have to run up and down the stairs to do their laundry. In some cases, converting an extra small room on the main floor into a laundry room is a smart move. The room should be large enough to hold a washer, a dryer, a shelf for storing clothes, and one or two people to fold the laundry.

  Step into the laundry room and perform the usual inspections of the ceiling, walls, and floor to look for any damage or water stains that could indicate plumbing problems. Make sure the water pipe connections for the washing machine are present and that the threads on the connectors aren't stripped. If the room has a laundry tub, note its condition and whether it needs to be replaced. Also note the size of the room.

- **Attic:** If the house has an accessible attic, climb up there and note whether it has a floor (yes or no), adequate insulation (which you may not see if the attic has a floor), and sufficient venting for the roof. Is the attic large enough to convert into another room? Also inspect the underside of the roof for any damage and note it on the roof section of your inspection sheet.

- **Basement:** Head to the cellar to inspect the stairway and handrail. Carefully check the outside walls for water or structural damage (walls bowed in or covered with mold or mildew). Is the basement finished or partially finished? Note the types of improvements you could make to the basement to enhance its appearance and functionality.

- **Bonus rooms:** Bonus rooms include family rooms and dens — any attractive, spacious, and comfortable area that's conducive for friends and family members to hang out and enjoy one another's company or some peace and quiet. A fireplace is a big bonus, as long as it's in working order. Be sure to have the chimney inspected and get an estimate of any required repairs before you close on the house.

A single overpowering feature can often sell a home, so as you tour homes, look for these hidden gems. When comparing houses, give more weight to a house with character than a house that's simply neat and tidy.

Some houses are begging for reconstruction. They're either too chopped up to allow smooth movement or they have too few rooms to make them marketable. Always look for houses with great floor plans so you don't have to invest in any major surgery, but if you can't find a house with a good floor plan, look for one that has a floor plan you can reconfigure affordably. If you're debating between two houses — one with three bedrooms and one with two bedrooms that you can convert into a three-bedroom house — all other things being equal, go with the three-bedroom house. See Chapter 19 for details on reconfiguring spaces and other structural renovations.

Arriving at a Ballpark Figure for Repair and Renovation Costs

As you inspect a property and figure out what needs to be done before placing it on the market, you need to come up with a ballpark figure for the costs of repairs and renovations. After you gain some experience, you'll know the approximate costs of most repairs and renovations. For example, I know that a 1,500-square-foot house costs about $1,500 to paint because where I flip houses in Michigan, painters charge about $1 per square foot. Some offer better deals. Kitchen rehabs cost between $5,000 and $10,000, furnaces/air conditioners cost about $1,000 to $5,000, and so on.

When you're starting out in the flipping biz, however, you may have no idea how much different repairs and renovations cost. Until you get up to speed, consider having a contractor walk through your properties and inspect them with you. If the contractor knows that you're interested in flipping properties and will hire her to perform the repairs and renovations, assuming you purchase the property, she may see her time as a small investment that will lead to a steady stream of work.

Chapter 12

Calculating Your Profit and Maximum Purchase Price

In This Chapter

- Making money no matter how the housing market performs
- Setting your sights on a target resale value
- Factoring the purchase price, holding costs, and other expenses into your profit estimate

Real estate investors follow the credo, "You make your profit when you buy; you realize it when you sell." In other words, if you purchase a property for a low enough price, you ensure yourself a profit at the time of purchase. Pay too much for a property, and you have a tough time turning a profit, if you ever do.

This chapter offers the guidance you need to answer the big question you face every time you're about to make an offer or bid on a property: What's the most I can pay for this property to earn a profit of at least 20 percent after all is said and done?

Doing the Math to Ensure a Profitable Flip

Although late-night TV real estate gurus dangle the promise of easy money in front of investor wannabes, a 50 percent profit from a flip is rare, although it does sometimes happen. Investors who consistently see 50 percent or higher profits are either very good or involved in some dishonest scheme.

A good rule of thumb is to shoot for a 20 percent profit over and above your total investment in the property. If, at the end of the project, you invested

$100,000 and sold the property for $120,000, you've done well. By total investment, I mean every penny you paid to purchase, repair, renovate, hold, and sell the property:

- Purchase price plus any closing costs or other fees you pay when you buy the property
- Holding costs from the time you buy the property until the time you sell it, including monthly interest payments on the loan plus property taxes, homeowner's insurance, and utilities
- Repair and renovation costs
- Real estate agent commissions you pay to market and sell the property
- Any costs or fees you pay at closing when you sell the property

Adjusting for market conditions

Shooting for a 20 percent profit in real estate is like trying to hit a moving target; housing values in your area may be going up, going down, or holding steady. To give yourself a better chance of hitting the 20 percent mark, adjust the percentage to your market conditions:

- 20 percent in a market where homes values are rising
- 25 percent in a market where home values are steady
- 30 percent or more in a market where home values are declining

This doesn't mean you're going to make 10 percent *more* in a declining market than in a rising market; it means that you set your goal 10 percent higher in a declining market so you can hit your target of making a 20 percent profit. In other words, you figure in more of a profit buffer when property values are falling.

WARNING!

Don't even think of buying into an area where the market is in a steep decline and shows no signs of recovering. Wait for the market to bottom out and exhibit signs of improvement before you dive in.

Crunching the numbers

When you have a pretty good idea of the cost of renovations, holding costs, real estate commissions, and other expenses (read the rest of this chapter for details), you're ready to calculate a maximum price to offer for the property:

1. **Start with the future sale price of the home after improvements.**

   Base your estimate on recent sale prices of comparable homes in the same area, as I explain in "Estimating a Realistic Resale Value," later in this chapter.

2. **For an estimated profit of at least 20 percent, divide the amount from step 1 by one of the following:**

   - 1.20 in a market where home values are rising (to shoot for a 20 percent return on your investment)
   - 1.25 in a market where home values are steady (to shoot for a 25 percent return and likely see a 20 percent profit)
   - 1.30 in a market where home values are declining (to shoot for a 30 percent return and likely see a 20 percent profit)

3. **Subtract any back property taxes you'll be responsible for paying when you purchase the property.**

4. **Multiply the estimated costs for repairs and renovations by 1.2 (to account for unforeseen expenses) and subtract that amount from the total determined in Step 3.**

5. **Subtract monthly holding costs for the expected duration of the project.**

   For example, if monthly holding costs are $3,000 and you expect to spend six months renovating and selling the property, $3,000 × 6 = $18,000.

6. **Subtract agent commissions and/or marketing and advertising costs for selling the property.**

7. **Subtract any closing costs you expect to pay when you sell the property.**

   The resulting amount is the maximum you can afford to pay for the property.

For example, to flip a house you expect to sell for $200,000 in a flat market, you may buy the house for $120,000, spend $20,000 fixing it up, and use $10,000 for other expenses (loan interest, insurance, utilities, selling costs, unexpected bills, and holding costs). Your total investment is $150,000, which is 75 percent of the estimated resale value. If you sell the house for $200,000, you earn a 25 percent profit, but if the market sours and you're able to sell the house for only $180,000, you earn a 20 percent profit.

In an increasing market, you can invest a maximum of $160,000 (80 percent of $200,000) in the property. In a decreasing market, you invest a maximum of only $140,000 (70 percent of $200,000) in the property. After you decide how much you can afford to invest overall, adjust the purchase price accordingly. Don't expect to make up the difference in your other expenses (including renovation and holding costs).

The maximum purchase price isn't necessarily the price you want to offer for the property. This is simply a fairly safe amount to offer to be relatively certain you'll earn a 20 percent return on your investment. Of course, the less you pay for a property, the better.

Estimating a Realistic Resale Value

You start house hunting by looking at neighborhoods and houses in your price range (see Part II for the scoop on house hunting). When you're guesstimating profits, though, you start your journey at the end by determining a realistic ballpark figure for the home's resale value after improvements. The key term here is *realistic.* Overestimating the resale value of the house can be as devastating as discovering termites in the floorboards; it can cause you to overpay for a house and almost guarantee low or no profit or even a loss.

To estimate a realistic resale value for a house, imagine the house all fixed up and then research the actual sale prices of comparable homes that have recently sold in the same neighborhood. Assuming that you're comparing apples to apples — this house to comparable homes in the same area with the same amenities — you should come away with an accurate estimate. What if the market takes a nose dive? By following the guidelines in the previous section, you're already taking into account potential market fluctuations.

Your goal as a house flipper is to purchase the worst house on the street for the lowest price possible and convert it into the best-looking house on the street at the highest price the market can bear. Anything you can do to add *wow* to the home, especially in terms of curbside appeal, can boost your bottom line. However, don't invest so much in renovations that you spend yourself out of a profit. Nobody's likely to pay $250,000 for a home in a neighborhood where the next best property sold for $200,000 regardless of what that $250,000 home has to offer.

Accounting for Expenses

The tough part of deciding how much to pay for a property is accounting for all the costs involved in buying, fixing up, holding, and selling the property. Many beginners don't account for all the costs and often overlook holding costs — loan payments, homeowner's insurance, utilities, property taxes, homeowner association fees, and so on — from when you take ownership of the property until you sell it.

The following sections serve as a checklist to make sure you account for all of the costs associated with buying, renovating, holding, and selling the property.

Unpaid property taxes and water bill

If you purchase a property at a tax sale or in foreclosure, you're responsible for paying any property taxes or water bills that are past due — an amount of money that may be significant. Prior to making an offer or bidding on a property, you should know of any past-due property taxes and other claims against the property, such as the water bill, that stay with the property even after foreclosure. For more about researching a property, see Chapter 10.

Closing costs

Unless you've negotiated with the seller to pay all or a portion of the closing costs, you're responsible for paying them. Your real estate agent, lending institution, or title company can provide a detailed estimate of closing costs, which, if you're taking out a typical loan to finance the purchase, typically include the following items:

- **Loan origination fee:** If you finance the purchase through a bank or other lending institution, it may charge a fee for establishing the loan. (See Chapter 5 for details about financing your purchase.)
- **Discount points:** Some lending institutions charge discount points — a percentage of the total amount borrowed — to provide you with a lower interest rate or wring another few hundred (or thousand) bucks out of you.

  Avoid loans with discount points. You usually have to hold a property for several years to justify the monthly savings, and when you're flipping houses, holding a property for several years isn't your goal.
- **Appraisal fee:** The lending institution charges you this fee to have an appraiser ensure that the property is worth at least the amount you're borrowing to purchase it. (See Chapter 13 for more about appraisals.)
- **Title insurance:** Even if you researched the title or hired a title company to do it for you (see Chapter 4), the bank may require you to pay for title insurance or a mortgage policy (sometimes called a mortgagee policy). If your lender doesn't require title insurance, buy a title insurance policy yourself; title insurance is essential for protecting your investment.
- **Insurance and taxes:** If you take out a loan that requires you to pay taxes and insurance out of an escrow account, you may need to pay a prorated share of insurance and taxes upfront.
- **Deed recording fee:** Whenever a property changes hands, the name on the deed changes and must be recorded. Yes, you're charged for this, too.
- **Credit report charge:** The lending institution does a financial background check on you called a *credit report* and then charges you for the privilege. (See Chapter 5 for details about credit reports.)
- **Closing fee:** The title company typically charges a closing fee.

Most closing costs originate with the bank or other lending institution. By financing the purchase through the seller or with money from private investors, partners, friends, or family members, you can trim closing costs considerably. See Chapter 5 for details on these options.

Cost of repairs and renovations

Eager house flippers often underestimate the cost of repairs and renovations. They're so enthusiastic about purchasing the house, selling it, and counting their money that they forget how much a carpenter or plumber charges per hour and the cost of materials at the local hardware store. Repairs and renovations are costly, and if you wait until you take possession of the house before obtaining estimates, you're already too late.

If you're still interested in a house after you take a quick tour of it, do a second, more thorough inspection of the premises to determine the repairs and renovations you want to make. (See Chapter 11 for details on the process of inspecting a potential flip.) List all the repairs and improvements needed to bring the property in line with your projected resale price (see "Estimating a Realistic Resale Value," earlier in this chapter). Estimate the cost of repairs by doing the following:

- Flag any repairs you can do yourself. These are zero-labor repairs, but you may need to visit your local hardware store to check out prices for materials.
- Ask a member of your team who has more experience with construction projects to walk through the house with you and offer estimates and advice. (See Chapter 4 for details on building your flipping team.) To prevent the negativity of naysayers from undermining your vision, keep in mind that you're taking the risk and making the final decisions.
- Call one or two local contractors to obtain ballpark estimates for any repairs or improvements you can't do yourself. You may be able to hire a general contractor to walk through the house with you and provide a professional opinion.

  If you can't look at the wiring in a house and come up with a pretty good guess at what it would cost to bring it up to code, you'd better consult somebody who can.
- Research estimated costs online. Contractors.com at `www.contractors.com` features a tool for estimating the costs of bathroom and kitchen renovations, room additions, decks, roofs, and other improvements. LetsRenovate.com at `www.letsrenovate.com` offers a toolbox packed with calculators for estimating the costs of repairs and renovations and the return you can expect on your investment.

Tally the estimated costs of repairs and renovations and multiply the total by 1.2 to add 20 percent for unexpected expenses.

You can trim the costs of repairs and renovations in several ways:

- Trade your services for free labor. Bartering (or trading services) may have tax consequences, so check with your accountant. Chapter 4 has info on finding an accountant to work with.
- Do some of the labor-intensive work yourself.
- Negotiate with the property owner to share the costs.

Chapter 14 has more details on planning and prioritizing your renovations, including tips on tagging do-it-yourself projects and knowing when to hire professionals for certain tasks.

Holding costs

As a homeowner, you're well aware of the monthly costs of owning a home, but when you first begin flipping properties, you tend to overlook the monthly expenses, such as your house payment, homeowner's insurance, and property taxes. Reality hits after you've owned the property for four or five months and begin running out of cash. By then, your 20/20 hindsight leads only to panic and despair.

To keep the property, you need money to pay the mortgage, property taxes, and insurance. And if you plan on using any power tools on the premises, you'd better pay your electric bill, too (in addition to other utilities).

If you're using the home you're flipping as your primary residence, you can safely skip this section. For you, holding costs are actually *living expenses* — the normal amounts you pay to have a roof over your head.

A great way to project holding costs is to assume, on average, an amount of $100 a day. This amount works for most houses and provides for any surprises along the way. If it takes you a total of six months to flip a property (including rehab and resale time), total holding costs break down as follows:

- $100 per day
- 6 months × 30 days per month = 180 days
- 180 days × $100 per day = $18,000 (in other words, $3,000 per month)

Of course, holding costs vary depending on several factors. To establish a more accurate estimate of your monthly holding costs, add your total estimated monthly bills for each of the following items:

- **Loan payments:** Mortgage payments and payments on any home-equity loans you use to finance renovations make up a significant chunk of your monthly holding costs.
- **Homeowner's insurance:** Ask your insurance agent for a quote and explain your plans, including whether you plan on living in the house, to properly insure the property. (A typical homeowner's policy allows for a home to be vacant only a certain number of days.)
- **Property taxes:** Set aside enough money per month to pay the property taxes when they're due. If you pay property taxes out of an escrow account, this amount may already be part of your mortgage payment.
- **Utilities:** Gas, electric, water, sewer, and trash bills are all part of your monthly holding costs. The seller should be able to provide averages for last year's bills, or you can contact the various utility companies to gather the information you need. (If nobody is living in the house, certain utility bills will be lower than normal.)
- **Neighborhood association fees (if applicable):** You may prepay these fees at closing and chalk them up as part of your closing fees, but if that's not the case, be sure to include them (if applicable) as part of your monthly fees.
- **Maintenance:** If you pay somebody for mowing the lawn, watching the house, and letting real estate agents inside to show the home, include this amount as part of your holding costs.

Err on the safe side. Budget sufficient funds to hold the house for three to six months beyond the date on which you expect to place the house back on the market. Few experiences are more demoralizing than renovating a house and then losing it in foreclosure because you underestimated your holding costs and can't make the monthly loan payments (or cash calls if you're working with hard money borrowed from a private investor).

Holding costs can be a great motivator for completing the project on schedule. The faster you flip, the less you pay in holding costs, and the sooner you can redeploy your funds on another venture.

Marketing and selling costs

When you place your rehabbed house back on the market, you incur additional expenses for marketing the house before you sell it and selling the house when you close the deal. These costs vary depending on whether you sell the home yourself or through a real estate agent:

- **Agent fees:** Attempting to sell your home without the help of a real estate agent can backfire, drastically restricting your number of potential buyers. Even if you choose not to use an agent, the agents hired by prospective buyers may not show your home unless they can get their 3 percent cut at the time of sale. Count on paying 3 percent to 7 percent of the sale price in agent fees. If you don't use an agent, add $250 to $1,000 for attorney fees.
- **Marketing fees:** If you choose to sell the home yourself, you can count on investing 1 percent to 2 percent of your list price in marketing fees. Whether you list your home in the classifieds or on a For Sale By Owner (FSBO) website, you pay for advertising. You also need a few bucks for a For Sale sign and for finger foods for your open house. (See Chapter 21 for more about marketing a property.)
- **Home warranty:** Supplying a warranty for the house can make it an attractive deal while protecting you against any lawsuits in the event that some undiscovered defect in the property rears its ugly head after the sale. If you decide to offer a warranty, budget enough to cover its cost. The cost of a typical home warranty ranges from $400 to well over $600 depending on the add-ons.
- **Closing fees:** A title company typically manages the closing and charges $300 or more for the service. Ask your title company for a more specific estimate.
- **Title insurance:** Insuring the title ensures that you're not liable for any hidden liens against the property. Title insurance can cost hundreds of dollars, so shop around for the best price and service.
- **Deed preparation:** The cost of preparing the deed usually goes to the seller and is typically about 50 bucks.
- **Transfer tax:** Your state, city, or town may levy a transfer tax on the exchange of property. The amount varies depending on your location, so consult your accountant.
- **Delinquent water or sewer bills:** At closing, you must pay any water or sewer bills that are in *arrears* (overdue or unpaid).
- **Other charges and fees.** You may be charged other fees depending on local requirements and on the closing company you're using. These fees may include a Title Insurance Enforcement Fund Fee (TIEFF) and a Closing Protection Letter (CPL) fee.

TIP

Don't list your house while you're rehabbing it, but feel free to talk to people during this time and pass out your business cards. If a buyer falls into your lap through your neighborhood contacts, contact a real estate agent or attorney to complete the transaction. Check out Chapter 22 for more details about negotiating the sale of your rehabbed house.

Income tax

The taxes you owe on the profit you make from flipping houses are ambiguous at best. Of course, you pay taxes only on the money that remains after expenses, but the percentage you owe on your profit varies depending on several factors:

- If you flip your primary residence in which you lived two of the past five years and you earn $250,000 or less ($500,000 or less for a couple), you walk away with your entire profit scot-free, at least according to the tax laws that were in effect when I was writing this book.
- Owning the investment property for at least one year and one day qualifies your profit as a *long-term capital gain,* taxable at a rate of 0 to 20 percent (plus a 3.8 percent Medicare surcharge if your ordinary income places you in one of the top two tax brackets). *Long-term* is longer than one year plus one day. *Capital gain* is whatever you make on the sale of an asset that has increased in value. (See Chapter 23 for details.)
- Owning the investment property for less than one year and one day qualifies your profit as a *short-term capital gain,* taxable at the same rate as the rest of your income from work-related activities (plus a 3.8 percent Medicare surcharge if your ordinary income places you in one of the top two tax brackets); the tax rate on your net profit could be as high as 43.4 percent.
- If flipping is your main line of business, the IRS considers you to be a dealer, so you can't treat your profits as long-term capital gains. The IRS treats your profits as income, subject to income tax and self-employment tax. You may find yourself paying 35 percent or more in taxes! This may be reason enough to keep your day job and flip houses in your spare time.
- If you lease the property, any income you receive from the rental, minus the cost of owning and maintaining the property, is considered ordinary income and is taxed at the same rate as your work-related income.

WARNING!

The tax figures provided here are accurate during the writing of this book, but tax rules can change at any time. Consult your accountant for accurate estimates on the amount of taxes you can expect to owe on your profits.

House flippers often boast about how much they make flipping properties, but the real measure of success is not your gross profit but your net profit — how much you get to keep *after taxes.* To determine your net profit, simply subtract your taxes from your gross profit. Chapter 23 discusses tax issues in greater depth and offers techniques for trimming your taxes to keep more of your earnings and boost your net profit.

Chapter 13

The Art of Haggling: Negotiating a Price and Terms

In This Chapter

- Laying the foundation for fruitful negotiation
- Brushing up on facts about the seller
- Preparing an attractive offer that doesn't sell you short
- Adding weasel clauses to your offer to protect your interests
- Using home inspection results to your advantage
- Tying up the loose ends and closing the deal

The housing market doesn't have a "no haggle" policy. You pay for a property whatever you can convince the owner to accept. You negotiate. You compromise. You make trade-offs. You haggle until all parties either agree on the terms of the deal or agree to disagree and part company.

Negotiating requires patience and persistence, excellent communication skills, and an ability to look beyond the sale price and grasp all the factors that affect the deal — including the closing costs, costs of necessary repairs, date of possession, which appliances stay with the house, and the seller's motivation for selling.

In this chapter, I show you how to prepare an initial offer that's reasonable enough to bring the seller to the bargaining table, yet low enough to give you some haggle room. I recommend adding conditional clauses to your offer to give yourself a safe exit if something goes wrong. And I reveal negotiating secrets that can add thousands of dollars to your bottom line and ensure your long-term success.

REMEMBER: A house is worth only what a buyer is willing to pay and a seller is willing to accept. Your success at negotiating hinges on your ability to accurately estimate what you can afford to pay and what the seller will accept. Check out the latest editions of *Negotiating For Dummies,* by Michael C. Donaldson (Wiley), and *Home Buying Kit For Dummies*, by Eric Tyson, MBA, and Ray Brown (Wiley), for even more info and guidance.

Planting the Seeds for Successful Negotiation

Negotiation begins long before you make an offer on the house. It begins when you choose a real estate agent to represent you.

When you choose an agent, make sure that the agent represents your interests; can keep the lid on sensitive information, such as how much you're really willing to pay for the property; and has a good poker face. An agent who represents both buyer and seller or one who tends to wag his tongue is a poor choice. See Chapter 4 for tips on selecting the best agent for your needs.

Strongly consider hiring a Realtor. Realtors are members of the National Association of Realtors (NAR) and are bound by its code of ethics not to disclose any confidential information they may have about their buyer, including how much he's willing to pay. Using a Realtor ensures that sensitive or confidential information remains confidential.

Negotiation continues when you start looking at and talking about a property. As you walk through a property to check it out, remain dispassionate. You may see a two-bedroom house with attic space that you can convert into a third bedroom for $5,000, adding $25,000 to the value of the house, but you don't have to yell "KA-CHING!" in front of the seller or his agent. Contain your glee until you get home.

You're better off letting the seller or seller's agent overhear a few mildly negative comments about the property, such as the following:

- It's a nice house, but the asking price is a little steep considering all the work it needs.
- The bathrooms need to be completely remodeled. That'll cost a few grand.
- The furnace looks old. It'll probably need to be replaced.
- It looks like the roof has two layers of shingles already. It'll have to be stripped first.

Don't trash-talk the house, because it may turn the owners against you. But making subtle comments about work that needs to be done can help prepare the seller for a lower offer. When you're looking at a house to flip, if you can't say something bad, don't say anything at all. And if you can't be chatty without disclosing sensitive information, zip your lips.

Digging Up Pertinent Information about the Seller

You researched the property thoroughly, but details about the property make up only about half the information you need before you present your offer. The second half consists of information about the sellers and the reason they're selling. Talk with your agent and do a little detective work to obtain answers to the following questions:

- **Why is the homeowner selling?** The answer to this question can help you determine how eager the homeowner is to sell the property (and how low you can go on your offer). Maybe the seller has just been laid off or needs to relocate to keep her job. Perhaps the seller's busybody mother-in-law just moved in down the block. Maybe something's going on in the neighborhood that will convince you not to buy the property. Finding out why the seller is selling can help you during negotiations, but don't count on getting a straight answer. You may be able to pick up clues in casual conversations with neighbors, the seller's agent, and even the sellers. Listen closely.
- **How soon does the homeowner need to move?** Did he already purchase another house? Has he scheduled a moving date? If he sells the house now, will he need additional time to find a new house or apartment? By knowing the current owner's situation, you may be able to present your offer in a way that goes beyond the seller's monetary needs, perhaps by highlighting the fact that you can move ahead immediately.
- **How much equity does the homeowner have in the property?** If the owner stands to cash out $70,000, she may be more willing to compromise on price if you can offer something in return, such as a quick, trouble-free closing. If, on the other hand, she has little or no equity in the house, she may be less willing to negotiate on the price. (Check out Chapter 5 for more information about equity.)
- **Did another buyer already bid on the property?** If so, how much did he bid? Why did the deal fall through? You can learn lessons from previous offers that can help you make your offer more attractive. For example, if the previous offer fell through because the buyer couldn't come up with the cash to close, you may be able to offer less with more earnest money to prove that you're serious and that you have the cash on hand to seal the deal.

- **If you're purchasing the property from a bank's REO department, do they have an addendum to the purchase agreement?** If so, obtain that addendum and review it in advance. The addendum can inform you of any special conditions that apply to the sale, such as types of financing permitted. (See Chapter 8 for more about buying an REO property.)

Don't expect your agent to supply you with information about previous offers on the property and details of why a particular offer fell through. Laws in most areas discourage disclosing sensitive information that may provide one party with an unfair advantage. Realtors are also required to follow a strict code of ethics that prevents them from disclosing sensitive information. It's a Realtor/client privilege. If you happen to strike up a conversation with the sellers or their agent, listen closely to what they say; they may let slip a valuable nugget of information.

You can find out a great deal about the seller's situation by looking around the house on your first walk-through. If the property seems a little run-down but the seller has two satellite dishes on the roof, a big flat-screen TV, and a boat in the backyard, he may value the latest toys and gadgets more than he values the house. To the seller, selling the house may be an opportunity for him to buy more stuff or pay off the stuff he already has.

Real estate revenge

Every once in a while you happen upon a deal that's just too good to be true. I was looking at houses to flip and, while touring one couple's home, I noticed that the closets had only women's clothes. This is always a good sign that the marriage is on the rocks or the couple is divorced.

I visited the courthouse and obtained a copy of the divorce decree. The entire process, including the time I spent driving to the courthouse and back, took me less than an hour. From the divorce decree, I discovered that the wife and children were allowed to live in the house until the youngest child turned 18. The wife was then required to sell the house and send the husband 50 percent of the proceeds. She was given the sole right to determine the price of the house. Well, the wife was getting remarried to a relatively wealthy man, and she didn't really care about the money. What she cared about was sticking it to her ex, so she was willing to sell the house for $20,000 less than it was worth!

Fortunately, I was in the right place at the right time and was able to cash in on the irrational vengeance of a messy divorce. The Freedom of Information Act entitles you to access to public records. (Check out `www.usdoj.gov` for more information.) You can view these documents and sometimes have them printed for a small cost. When you're looking for an edge at the negotiating table, leave no stone unturned. You may just stumble upon a minor detail that saves you a major amount of cash.

Making an Offer They Can Refuse (but Will Consider)

Preparing an offer (also known as a *purchase agreement*) on a property is like deciding how much to raise the bet in a hand of poker when you're holding a royal flush. Raise too much, and everyone folds. Raise too little, and someone may see your raise and end the betting long before you suck enough chips into the pot for a big payout. You want the betting to go on long enough so you can get more of what you want.

When preparing an offer, your goal isn't necessarily to have your first offer accepted. If it is, you may be paying more for the property than you should. Your goal is to offer just enough to persuade the homeowner to counter your offer and to show you're serious. In other words, you want to make an offer they *can* refuse but will consider and counter.

If a seller accepts your opening bid, it doesn't necessarily mean that your bid was too high. Don't get the heebie jeebies and start second guessing your decision. You did your homework, you made an offer on a property that you know you can profit from, and you got lucky. The homeowner accepted your bid. Now it's time to move forward. Delay can lead to downfall.

The following sections highlight the most important factors to consider in preparing your offer, including price, earnest money, conditional clauses, and other enticements. I also explain the best ways to pitch your offer and steer you clear of common negotiation pitfalls.

All offers and counteroffers must be in writing. With real estate transactions, the written word rules. Verbal agreements are worthless. The saying in the industry is "Buyers are liars, and sellers are worse." Get everything in writing. Your real estate agent can supply you with the form you need to officially present your offer.

Calculating a price

Before you make an offer on a property, you already know the maximum amount you can pay for it, based on how much you think you can sell it for; estimated costs for buying, renovating, holding, and selling the property; and your desired profit. (Chapter 12 shows you how to calculate your maximum purchase price.) But your maximum price isn't necessarily the price you want to offer. When settling on a price to offer, the following three strategies are most effective:

- **Leave a little haggle room.** Offer 3 percent to 5 percent below the price you're willing to pay to allow some room to negotiate. You don't want to offer a price so low that the owner dismisses the offer outright and refuses to sell — or, even worse, goes with another investor's offer — but you don't want to price yourself out of a profit. This strategy works well in most cases.
- **Make a firm offer.** Make your best offer, let the seller know that this is your best offer, and stick to it. I've seen firm buyers remain firm and have the seller reject the initial offer only to come back three weeks later, highly motivated to sell. If you can remain firm, this strategy may be the best for you. Some buyers stick to this strategy in every case. Others do it only when they know they can profit from the property even if their best offer is accepted and they're pretty sure that it's the best offer the buyer is likely to receive.
- **Make a low-ball offer.** A good time to make a low-ball offer is when you're already working on a project and don't really need another property. If you get the house for a steal, great. If you miss out, you really haven't lost anything.

TIP

Consider including a one-page letter that explains how you arrived at the price you're offering. For example, you may point out that comparable homes in better condition are selling for more, but that this house needs a new roof, which would cost about $8,000; a remodeled kitchen, which would run about $10,000; and new carpeting, which would cost about $3,000. You may actually be able to get the work done for a lot less by doing some of the labor yourself, but it's okay to quote what the seller would have to pay to have the work done professionally. Don't jack up your estimates — the seller may have estimates of her own, and you don't want to look like a swindler. Chances are you're telling the seller what she already knows. Your letter simply shows that you're no dummy — you've done your homework.

Proving you're earnest: Money talks

The old saying that "money talks" is especially relevant when you're pitching an offer on a house. Every offer should include earnest money that demonstrates how serious you are about purchasing the property. A $5,000 earnest money deposit speaks louder than a $500 deposit.

I can't offer you any hard and fast rules on what to offer in the way of earnest money. That depends on several factors, including how much cash you have on hand, how badly you want the property, and how much you're offering as a purchase price. In general, earnest money in the range of $1,000 to $5,000 is sufficient. The more you put down upfront, the stronger your position at the bargaining table.

As long as you deposit the earnest money with the title company (see Chapter 4 for more about title companies) or another reputable and insured real estate professional, your deposit is safe. In most cases, the seller's broker holds the earnest money. With REO sales (see Chapter 8), the bank may require that the listing broker or title company holds the deposit. Either way, the money is safe unless you default on the purchase agreement. When the deal closes, the money is credited back to you. If the deal doesn't close, you get the money back, assuming, of course, you lived up to your end of the bargain — you were diligent in seeking financing, you showed up for the scheduled closing, and you had a good reason to back out of the deal.

Another way to show that you're serious about the deal is to provide proof of your financing along with your offer. Proof of financing may consist of a preapproval letter from your lender. If you're offering cash and have a good chunk of it sitting in a bank account, you may include a copy of your bank statement with your account numbers blacked out. A signed and notarized statement from a private lender can also function as proof of financing. Head to Chapter 5 for details on securing financing for a flip.

Dangling additional enticements

Although the purchase price is the high-profile part of any offer, a real estate transaction isn't always all about money. Sellers have other needs. They may need some extra time to move, a new place to move to, some ready cash, or maybe even a good used car to get to work. By knowing the seller's needs and her motivation for selling (see "Digging Up Pertinent Information about the Seller," earlier in this chapter, for details), you can often sweeten the pot by addressing her most pressing needs. Check out the following sections for tips on providing additional enticements to the seller.

Helping the seller move on

Instead of approaching a negotiation as a contest, consider it a collaboration between you and the seller with the goal of meeting everyone's needs. You need to acquire a property at a price below market value. Find out what the seller needs most:

- If the seller needs more time to move, consider giving him 30 days of free rent and then start charging him if he stays any longer. Taking a loss of a few hundred dollars to gain thousands later is often a wise choice. In the meantime, you can start lining up your contractors and planning renovations (see Chapter 14 to get started).
- Help the seller find a new place to live if she doesn't know where to go. As you become more involved in real estate, you establish connections with other owners and landlords and can often refer sellers to other people who can assist them.

- Refer the sellers to a probate attorney if they need legal assistance.
- Advance the sellers some money so they can secure alternative housing, or assist them with getting a Section 8 voucher if they qualify for subsidized housing. (You can find out more about public housing vouchers and track down your local public housing agency through the Department of Housing and Urban Development (HUD) at `www.hud.gov`.)
- Call around to car dealers if the sellers need affordable transportation.

If the seller isn't ready to sell right away, don't get pushy. You may lose the house for good. Consider purchasing the property on contract (granting you the option to purchase the property at a later time), as I explain in Chapter 3. That takes the heat off the seller and provides you with a future project.

Do whatever you can — if it's aboveboard and reasonable — to help the sellers get on with their lives, but don't cross the line. Helping distressed sellers get on with their lives versus plying them with favors so you can steal their property may seem like a fine line, but it's a line between right and wrong, between legal and illegal.

Laying down cash

In real estate, cash is king. Think of it like a deck of playing cards. Cash is king. Fifty percent down is a queen. Thirty percent down is a jack. Twenty percent down is a ten. Ten percent down is a nine. Five percent down is an eight. And zero percent down is a joker. To have the winning offer, you want to lay down a king.

Offers with large down payments in cash always have an edge over other offers because they have less risk of falling through at the last minute because of the buyer's failure to obtain loan approval.

You may be wondering — if cash is king, what's an ace? Con artists consider an ace to be an offer of cash back at closing, but that's actually the joker, and if you get caught, that joker can lead to jail time. Working out a deal in which the seller agrees to sell you the property for more than it's worth so you can get a big fat loan and split the proceeds with the seller is a form of fraud.

Convincing the seller to sweeten the deal

When you're offering less than market value for a house, asking the seller to throw in the stove and refrigerator sounds a little pushy. But sometimes the purchase price is all the seller sees. He's so focused on getting that purchase price a little higher that he really doesn't care about those expensive appliances.

Before you present your offer, you may not be entirely sure about how stuck the seller is to the sticker price. So, when you present your offer, consider asking the seller for additional items. If he won't budge on the price, he may be willing to negotiate on these other items, which can boost your bottom line. Here are some ideas on what you can ask for:

- **Seller to pay for all or some of the repairs.** If the home is in need of some costly repairs, ask the seller to pay for all or a portion of the repairs. Whatever you save in repairs decreases your total investment in the property and increases your bottom line.
- **Seller to leave all appliances.** If the appliances are relatively new and in good condition, ask the seller to include the appliances. A refrigerator, stove, microwave, and washer and dryer can represent thousands of dollars. Whether you're planning to rent or sell the house, saving money on buying the appliances later can be a big plus.
- **Seller to pay a portion of closing costs.** The seller can legally pay up to 6 percent of closing costs. Although that may not represent a huge chunk of change, it can help you recoup a little if you have to give in on the purchase price.
- **Seller to waive reimbursement of tax proration.** In some states, the seller pays property taxes in advance. When you buy the property, you normally pay back to the seller any taxes he paid for months that you will own the house. Because the seller already parted with this money, he often doesn't see it as a loss if you ask him to waive the reimbursement. This waiver can save you thousands of dollars, depending on the time of year and the tax amount on the property. In other states, homeowners pay taxes in arrears — the homeowner pays last year's taxes this year. In these states, the seller typically gives money to the buyer at closing to cover taxes for any months the seller lived in the house.

To the seller, everything that affects the bottom line — the amount of cash she walks away with at closing — becomes her main focus. Asking the seller to leave appliances and waive the reimbursement of tax proration is often less of an issue for the seller than asking for a significantly lower sale price. These items are often open for negotiation.

You can often distract the seller by asking for something you know the seller won't negotiate. Suppose the seller has a boat stored in the garage. He loves this boat, and you know that he probably doesn't want to sell it. List it on the purchase agreement. When the seller sees it, he says, "No way is he getting my boat!" You agree to take the boat off the purchase agreement, and the seller okays the deal, giving you what you really wanted in the first place.

Protecting your posterior with weasel clauses

Weasel clauses (more officially known as *conditional clauses*) are legal phrases in the purchase offer that enable you to weasel out of the offer if something goes wrong. Although they're designed to help buyers back out of a deal when they can't get their financing approved or in the event that the home inspection uncovers a serious problem with the property, they're often used as escape clauses when a prospective buyer gets cold feet or finds a better deal. Make sure that your offer contains the following weasel clauses:

- **Financing must be approved.** If you're taking out a loan to pay for the property, make the purchase conditional upon your financing being approved. Buying property you can't pay for is a sure way to end up in foreclosure. If you have cash on hand to pay for the property, don't worry about this clause. (See Chapter 5 for more about financing.)
- **Sale is subject to closing on another property.** If you're counting on the proceeds from the sale of another property to finance the purchase of this property, stipulate that your offer is conditional upon the closing of the transaction on the other property. If you add this condition, include a copy of the offer you have on the other property so the seller knows you have an offer pending on that other property.
- **Property must pass inspection.** To ensure that you don't get stuck with a termite-infested house or a house that has foundation problems, make your offer conditional upon the home passing inspection. Not only does this clause provide a safety net, but it also buys you time to obtain estimates on repairs and renovations. See "Inspecting the house from the ground up," later in this chapter, for more about inspections.
- **Property must have a clear title.** A clear title ensures that the property has no liens against it and that the person selling the property actually owns it. Never submit an offer without this condition. (Chapter 4 has the scoop on hiring a title company to do a title search for you.)
- **Property must appraise at the sale price or higher.** To ensure that the property is worth what you're offering, make your offer conditional upon the appraisal. See "Ordering an appraisal," later in this chapter, for details on the appraisal process. (This shouldn't be an issue, because if you've done your homework you should know that the property is worth more than what you're paying for it.)

- **Buyer's attorney must approve contract.** A clause that gives your attorney ten business days to inspect and approve the contract provides you with additional time to seek a qualified second opinion. (See Chapter 4 for details on finding an attorney.)

Note: When I represent the seller, I hate these clauses. I try to get rid of these to help protect my seller's transactions. When I represent buyers, I use them.

Conditional clauses may protect you, but too many of them can sink the deal. Many purchase agreements have built-in conditional clauses required by local governing agencies or associations. Familiarize yourself with the purchase agreement used in your area so you're not adding redundant clauses that raise red flags. Your agent can provide you with a copy of the purchase agreement used in your area.

Pitching your offer

When you're ready to make an offer on a property, work closely with your agent to put the offer in writing and then submit the offer through your agent. Pitching your offer through an agent provides you with several advantages, including the following:

- The agent can act as the bad guy, presenting a low-ball offer without making the homeowner despise you personally.
- You lessen the risk of communicating sensitive information, verbally or through your body language.
- You have more time to react. When a seller voices an objection or presents a counteroffer, the agent acts as a buffer and gives you time to compose yourself and come up with a rational response.
- A skilled agent can often present your offer more effectively than you can. Agents are in sales.
- Your agent can provide you with a second, expert opinion.
- You can focus on the offer while your agent attends to the minor details of making sure that everything is properly recorded.

Representing yourself during negotiations is like playing Texas Hold'em with your cards facing out to the seller. A savvy seller can gather a lot of information about you by what you say and how you act that can cost you thousands of dollars. Hire a real estate agent who's an experienced and gifted negotiator and make yourself readily available to your agent during the negotiation process. Your agent may have a limited amount of time to present your counteroffer, and the more responsive you are, the more serious you appear to the seller.

Handling counteroffers

When the owner proposes a counteroffer, you have two more pieces of valuable information. You now know:

- That the owner probably hasn't received a much better offer
- More about what the homeowner wants, as described in the counteroffer

A counteroffer typically specifies the amount of time you have to respond. This amount of time can range from several hours to several days, but it's usually a day or two. If the counteroffer is reasonable and contains the price and terms you need to successfully flip the property, accepting it outright is always an option. Don't get greedy. If the numbers and terms don't meet your requirements for turning a profit (as discussed in Chapter 12), consider countering the counteroffer. You and the seller aren't limited by a set number of counteroffers, so you can go back and forth until you reach an agreement.

Use the guidelines I give earlier in the chapter for presenting your initial offer to structure your counteroffers, and keep your eye on the bottom line. If the seller doesn't budge on the price, counter with an offer that requests additional items — appliances, repair costs, closing costs, and so on. Look at the whole picture and make sure that after all is said and done, you can pay for the house, flip it, and still walk away with a profit of 20 percent or better.

Don't make a counteroffer without considering the potential consequences. A counteroffer makes the purchase agreement a non-binding contract. The seller is no longer bound by the agreement to sell you the property. The agreement only becomes binding when the seller accepts it. Your last counteroffer could cost you the deal.

Having another prospective property lined up can also help you during the negotiation. Tell your agent that if you can't come to terms on this property by a certain deadline, you want to look into making an offer on a second property. This tactic applies some gentle pressure on the seller. You make your offer, but you also let the seller know that you can take it away at any time.

Ducking common negotiating pitfalls

Some people are terrible negotiators. They're too open. They get rattled by uncertainty and silence. They overreact. They get emotionally involved. They convey a sense of eagerness and enthusiasm that prevents them from thinking straight. And then they make critical errors. Following is a list of common negotiating pitfalls that you should avoid:

- **Overbidding:** Don't present everything you have to offer on your opening bid. If the seller says "No," you have nothing more to offer. However, some investors do well by presenting their best offer upfront and then sticking with it. If you're going to make your best offer upfront, make sure you're the type who can stick.
- **Excessively underbidding:** A low-ball offer is one thing, but make sure that your pitch doesn't end up in the dirt. It can turn the seller against you, make any competitive offers look that much better, and, if you do it often enough, make your agent wonder whether it's in her best interest to work with you.
- **Bidding against yourself:** Don't submit another, higher offer until the seller responds to your initial offer. Some buyers get the jitters when they don't hear back immediately from the seller, and they submit a higher offer. When you do this, you're bidding against yourself and often pay more for the property than you have to.
- **Making a take-it-or-leave-it offer:** An ultimatum is counterproductive in negotiations. You want to open the lines of communication, not shut them down.
- **Talking too much:** You have two ears and one mouth, so listen twice as much as you talk. Ask questions, but don't offer information about why you're buying the property or what you intend to do with it. If you can't restrain yourself, you're better off saying nothing — just smile and talk about the weather. If you're just making chit-chat, never talk about sex, religion, politics, or schools.
- **Responding to an unofficial counteroffer:** To be official, a counteroffer must be recorded on the purchase agreement, and the seller must initial any changes. If the seller or seller's agent comes back with a note or phone call saying he'll consider the offer "if . . . ," make him put it in writing.

REMEMBER

Keep a copy of all offers and counteroffers. If the seller rejects your offer, keep a copy of that, too. Write "Rejected" across it and file it with any other information you have on the house. If a seller comes back later claiming that you agreed to purchase the property, you want to have proof that you didn't.

Tending to the Details: Inspections, Appraisals, and Walk-Throughs

Just because the seller accepted your offer doesn't mean that you have a done deal. Now's the time to test those conditional clauses I tell you about earlier in this chapter. You need to schedule a home inspection, have the property appraised, and do one final walk-through before closing, as I discuss in the following sections.

Inspecting the house from the ground up

Immediately after the seller accepts your offer, schedule a home inspection. (Chapter 4 explains how to find and select a home inspector.) The inspection ensures that the house doesn't have any hidden surprises, such as foundation problems, a faulty electrical system, or substandard plumbing. In the following sections, I explain different areas of concern to examine and show you how to put the inspection results to good use.

Although some experts recommend staying out of the inspector's way during the inspection and waiting for the written report, I strongly recommend that you schedule the inspection for a time when you can be present, preferably during daylight hours, so you have a clear view of the external features of the house. You should be there to hear specifically what the inspector has to say during the inspection. Take notes or carry a recorder for later reference, and pack a digital camera so you can take a picture of any defects the inspector points out and reference them later.

Examining areas of concern

If the inspector raises any doubts about a big-ticket item, such as the condition of the roof or furnace, or if she recommends additional tests or inspections, schedule follow-up inspections. For example, if the furnace is old, call in a heating and air-conditioning contractor to inspect it more thoroughly. (Chapter 4 has information on finding contractors.) The cost of repairs to any of these items varies depending on the nature of the problem and material and labor costs in your area. Areas of concern often include the following:

- **Foundation:** The entire house rests on the foundation. If it shows signs of water damage or serious settling, have it professionally inspected. Fixing the problem may be a simple matter of repairing the gutters to direct more water away from the foundation (inexpensive), or it may involve jacking up the house and pouring a new foundation (extremely expensive).
- **Electrical system:** If the home inspector points out any concerns about the electrical system, have a licensed electrician inspect it. An electrician can tell you whether the system is up to code and, if it's not, provide an estimate on the cost to bring it up to code.
- **Plumbing and septic:** A home inspector typically checks the plumbing to ensure that the water pressure is sufficient, nothing is leaking, and drains are freely flowing. If the plumbing appears to be substandard, have a licensed plumber inspect it. If the septic system is more than ten years old, have that inspected, as well.
- **Aging big-ticket items, including furnace, air conditioning, and roof:** If something is old but working, don't assume it's okay. Have a licensed

contractor check it out. Even if a furnace is heating the house, it may be leaking carbon monoxide or have other problems that the inspector doesn't notice.

- **Attic and insulation:** Make sure that the inspector checks the attic. Does it have sufficient insulation? Does the insulation contain asbestos? Does the underside of the roof show any signs of damage or leaking?
- **Grading:** Does the ground slope down away from the house as it should? Poor grading can funnel water right into the home's foundation and is costly to fix.
- **Lead-based paint:** In some homes built before 1978 and many homes built before 1960, lead-based paint may be present. You can pick up a test kit at your local hardware store to test for lead. In some cases, correcting this problem can be cost-prohibitive — because you must disclose the presence of lead-based paint on your seller's disclosure, it can drive a lot of potential buyers away.
- **Asbestos:** Commonly used to insulate furnaces and water pipes, asbestos is a health hazard that's costly to deal with. If it turns up in a home inspection, obtain a couple of estimates on having it removed and then calculate that into your rehab costs.
- **Radon:** Radon is a cancer-causing gas that can be a problem in some areas of the country; it often requires that the foundation be sealed and vented or even completely replaced, which can cost thousands of dollars. Your local environmental protection agency can tell you whether radon is a problem in your area.
- **Toxic mold:** If the home shows any signs of moisture damage or mold stains, have it tested for toxic mold and determine the cost of eliminating the mold and its cause. The presence of toxic mold (often called *black mold,* even though it's not always black) is enough to kill a deal — fixing the problem can cost as much as the purchase price of the house. If you suspect mold to be a problem, call a certified mold remediation specialist for additional testing and any necessary treatment.
- **Lead pipes or lead in water:** Some homes built before 1940 have lead pipes or copper pipes joined with lead solder. If lead is a concern, call your local water company to have the water tested. The cheap fix is to install a water filter for the drinking water. More-expensive fixes call for replacing the pipes or installing a whole-house water filtration system.

REMEMBER

The home inspector is sort of like your family doctor. She can give you a quick examination to tell whether you're generally healthy or not, but if you have any specific complaints that she's uncertain about, she refers you to a specialist. The home inspector can tell whether everything is functional, but if you or the inspector has a specific concern, consult a specialist.

TIP

If you're buying a property that the seller winterized, the gas, water, and electricity may be shut off, preventing an inspector from doing a thorough job. In this case, request that all utilities be turned on for the inspection.

Moving forward with the inspection results

You can use the home inspection results to your advantage in the following ways:

- If the home inspection turns up serious, expensive problems that the seller refuses to fix, you can back out of the deal.
- If the home inspection identifies required repairs, you can lower your offer to accommodate the cost of those repairs both in terms of time and money or demand that the seller pay for those repairs.
- You can ignore the little stuff and further endear yourself to the seller by avoiding the urge to nitpick.

WARNING!

If the inspection uncovers some issues that tempt you to submit a new counteroffer, realize that a counteroffer essentially places the property back on the market. I've seen many investors lose out on a good deal by being too picky.

Ordering an appraisal

If you're borrowing money from a bank or other lending institution, you don't have to worry about ordering an appraisal. The lender does it for you and adds the cost to the closing costs. Actually, the lender does the appraisal not to protect you but to protect the lender's investment. Even so, you should request a copy of the appraisal. The appraisal can either confirm or refute your belief that you're not overpaying for the property. Submit your request in writing; normally, the form you need is in the package you receive at closing.

When you're purchasing the property with your own cash or with money from a private lender, consider ordering an appraisal to ensure that the property is worth what you think it's worth (an *as-is appraisal*) or what it will be worth after repairs and renovations (an *as-repaired appraisal*). In most cases, your agent's advice is sufficient, assuming he has a thorough knowledge of the market, but if you have any doubts, a professional appraisal can put them to rest. I give you tips on finding an appraiser in Chapter 4.

If the appraisal shows that the house is worth way more than you offered, pop the cork on that bottle of champagne and start celebrating. If the appraisal comes back showing that you offered too much for the house, you then have several options:

- Buy the property anyway. An appraisal is an opinion, so don't ignore it entirely, but take into account that the appraisal could be 5 percent to 10 percent lower or higher than a buyer is likely to pay.
- Assuming you made your offer conditional on the property appraising for a certain amount of money, and assuming the property appraises for less than that, back away from your original offer and submit a new, lower offer. (This action places the property back on the market, so it's a little risky — you could lose out on the deal.)
- Ask the seller to throw in an added enticement to get you to go through with the offer.

Taking one final walk-through

The day before closing, walk through the house one last time to make sure that it's in the same condition or better than when you placed your offer. Until you close on the deal, the seller owns the house, and anything that happens to it is his responsibility. If the hot-water tank bursts the day before closing, you're entitled to a new hot-water tank at the seller's expense. If the wind picks up and the roof blows off, that's on the seller's tab.

TIP

Pack your digital camera and a notepad and document anything that looks out of the ordinary — any new problems that arose after the inspection.

Crossing Your Eyes and Dotting Your T's: Closing the Deal

When you attend a closing, the title company's closing agent hands out a bunch of forms and contracts and tells you to read everything, make sure that you understand it, and sign and initial the documents as directed. Except for a handful of control freaks, nobody reads through all those forms, but you really should. People can hide all sorts of zingers in a legally binding contract.

TIP

To be safe, you or your attorney should read, understand, and agree to everything stated on a document before you sign it. To keep closings from taking much more than an hour, I recommend that you ask the title company for the closing packet in advance and read everything or have your attorney or your agent look at the paperwork before the scheduled time. (You may have only 24 hours before closing to review the paperwork.) Write up a list of questions along with any errors you find and have them addressed before closing. If you wait until closing, some serious delays are likely to occur.

Don't sign anything unless you have read it and understand it! Pay close attention to the following items:

- **Your name:** Make sure that the documents include your legal name and not your nickname.
- **Your Social Security number:** These documents are official records and are likely to show up on your credit report, so make sure that your Social Security number is correct.
- **Information on the 1003:** If you're taking out a loan to purchase the property, you receive a 1003 (commonly referred to as a ten-oh-three) at closing. This is your loan application, and it includes your name, Social Security number, annual salary, and other details about your finances. The loan officer presents this information to the mortgage company. Giving false information is mortgage fraud, so make sure that all the information is correct before you sign the form. You can't leave this one up to your attorney to verify; read it yourself and correct any errors before you sign.
- **Mortgage and interest rate:** If you're taking out a loan to purchase the property, make sure that the mortgage amount and interest rate recorded on the form is the same as what the lender or loan officer quoted you. Have any necessary corrections made *before* you sign the form.

WARNING!

If you're a flipper and you're taking out a loan, make sure that it has no early-payment or prepayment penalty. Nothing is more shocking than reselling the house and finding out at the closing that the $200,000 loan you took out to purchase the house has an extra $6,000 added to it as a 3 percent penalty for paying off the loan in fewer than three years. Double-check for any prepayment penalties before closing.

Part IV

Fixing Up Your Fixer-Upper

Renovation Planner

Project	Start Date	Completion Date	Materials Cost	Labor Cost	Total Cost

Total Materials Costs		$_________
Total Labor Costs	+	$_________
Total Materials and Labor Costs		$_________
20 Percent for Sales Tax and Unexpected Costs	x	1.2
Grand Total		$_________

When renovating a property, it's easy to get carried away and blow your entire profit on upgrades. Visit `www.dummies.com/extras/flippinghouses` for a true story of an investor who spent nearly his entire profit by over-renovating.

In this part...

- Plan and budget for repairs and renovations at least as carefully as you plan a two-week vacation.
- Choose renovations that are likely to give you the most bang for your buck.
- Find out how to *whitebox* a property — perform essential repairs and make the home look new and smell fresh.
- Make a great first impression by significantly improving a home's curb appeal.
- Update and upgrade kitchens and bathrooms, the two rooms that sell houses.
- Boost a property into a higher price bracket with moderate to major renovations, and know when not to.

Chapter 14

Prioritizing and Planning Your Renovations

In This Chapter

- Looking for local trends in home renovations
- Ranking the importance of your renovations
- Assigning renovation duties
- Drawing up a tentative budget
- Scheduling renovations and keeping them on track

Prioritizing and planning renovations is like planning for a vacation. You have a limited amount of time to complete the trip, a list of activities you want to accomplish during that time, and a certain amount of money set aside to pay for it. With a vacation, you need to schedule flights and car rentals well in advance, plot your journey from point A to point B, and pack sufficient clothing, necessities, and accessories for a comfortable journey. Repairing and renovating a property requires the same foresight and attention to detail. You need to prioritize your list of projects, order materials well in advance, schedule the work, hire workers, and make sure that everything gets done on time and on budget.

In this chapter, I steer you toward valuable resources that can help you train your tastes and choose the renovations that are most appealing to the majority of house hunters in your area. Then, I lead you through the process of prioritizing and planning your renovations to complete your projects in a reasonable amount of time without spending too much money.

REMEMBER

Before you even buy a property, you should carefully inspect it and have a solid idea of the work you need to do. For more details, check out Chapter 11.

Developing an Eye for Home Improvements

A flipper is like a talent scout. She can gauge a home's potential instantly and envision it as a final, finished product on her first walk-through. She can picture the kitchen with new cabinets, countertops, sink, tile, and appliances. She can imagine the barely functional restroom converted into a luxurious new bathroom. She can close her eyes and visualize the outside of the home completely revamped to entice passersby into taking a look inside.

Some people have it, and some people don't. But if you're one who doesn't have it, don't despair — you can develop the required sensibilities by engaging in the following activities:

- **Visit open houses:** Search the classifieds for open house dates and times — they're often held on Sunday afternoons — and plan to attend two or three this weekend. Try to find open houses in your target neighborhood and in your desired price range to get a better idea of the types and styles of renovations that are optimum for your market.

  Attend several open houses and do a comparative analysis in order to gauge the hottest home fashions in your market. They vary depending on your geographical location, price range, and current styles. Become a trend spotter.

- **Attend home and garden shows:** These shows typically feature model homes, the latest in building supplies and gadgetry, and renovation ideas and demonstrations, along with plenty of catalogs and brochures you can tote home for reference.
- **Check out magazines, TV shows, and websites:** These media resources are great for getting up to speed on what's hot and what's not in home decor:
  - Better Homes and Gardens at `www.bhg.com`
  - HGTV at `www.hgtv.com`
  - DIY Network at `www.diynet.com`
  - Hometime at `www.hometime.com`
  - This Old House at `www.thisoldhouse.com`
- **Flip through home remodeling books:** Many home remodeling books feature both remodeling ideas and how-to instruction. Here are titles of a few to get you started:
  - *Bathroom Remodeling For Dummies,* by Gene Hamilton and Katie Hamilton (Wiley)

  - *Home Decorating For Dummies,* 2nd Edition, by Katharine Kaye McMillan and Patricia Hart McMillan (Wiley)
  - *Home Improvement For Dummies,* by Gene Hamilton and Katie Hamilton (Wiley)
  - *Kitchen Remodeling For Dummies,* by Donald R. Prestly (Wiley)

- **Pay attention to landscaping:** Whether you're out for a morning drive, visiting open houses, or simply taking a stroll around the neighborhood, examine the landscaping. Note the features of the landscape and try to imagine how you could landscape the front of the house to improve its curbside appeal. You may not want to chop down any 50-year-old trees, but a careful trim can freshen up a house, much as a new hairstyle can make you look years younger.

  Landscaping books, magazines, and websites are about as plentiful as plants, and most are packed with copious collections of color photos. When you need some landscaping ideas and advice, check out the following offerings:

  - *Landscaping For Dummies,* by Phillip Giroux, Bob Beckstrom, Lance Walheim, and the editors of the National Gardening Association (Wiley)
  - LandscapeOnline.com at `www.landscapeonline.com`
  - LandscapeUSA.com at `www.landscapesusa.com`

- **Recruit a renovation mentor:** If you don't have a knack or passion for remodeling, find someone who does and ask her to accompany you on your walk-throughs and offer her advice. The final decisions are still up to you, but a gifted pair of eyes can help you make superior choices.

Knowing your renovation options (and their costs) before you start looking at properties is key to buying a property you're sure can turn a profit.

Prioritizing Your Projects

Unless you have a bottomless bank account and an infinite amount of time to flip your house, you have to prioritize your renovation projects. The overall strategy for prioritizing projects is as follows:

1. **Fix any underlying structural problems and *mechanicals* (plumbing, electric, heating, and air conditioning) first.**
2. **Make any essential repairs that aren't structural or mechanical, such as dangling gutters, cracked windows, and rickety doors.**

If something is broken, repair, replace, or remove it. If it ain't broke and it doesn't look bad, don't fix it.

3. **Concentrate on renovations that promise to deliver the highest return on your investment, such as laying new carpeting, replacing the bathroom vanity, or installing a new kitchen countertop.**

   Renovate only if it makes financial sense to do so.

4. **If time allows, do anything you can do yourself for little or no money that makes the house more attractive, such as adding decorative shutters and replacing blinds.**

   Save items that won't sink your sale for last.

All home buyers want a nice, clean house in the price range they can afford, in the best neighborhood possible, with good schools for their children, and with as few mechanical problems (plumbing, gas, electric, and heating) as possible. When you buy and renovate houses, let these factors guide your decisions as you choose which renovations make sense.

In the following sections, I guide you through the process of prioritizing your renovation projects. When you're done, you should have a list of projects ranked by importance along with projects that promise the most bang for your buck. Check out "Coming Up with a Game Plan," later in this chapter, for the full scoop on making sure that you complete your projects with minimal fuss.

Start planning renovations and lining up contractors as soon as you're pretty sure you're going to buy the property, especially for larger projects — roofing, heating and cooling, foundation repairs, and the like. Don't spend any money before you close, but be prepared to start your renovations the next day. If you wait until closing, you may find that all the contractors in your area are already backed up with projects. Get things moving right away. (Check out Chapter 4 for details on hiring contractors to work for you.)

Tackling essential repairs

Making a ramshackle house look pretty is like putting lipstick on a pig — and that's not something I recommend. You want a good, solid home devoid of any problems that may crop up later during your buyer's home inspection. The best way to purge a house of problems is to go through your home inspection report and address every item on the list. (I cover home inspections in detail in Chapter 11.) Focus on the big stuff first, such as the following:

- Foundation problems
- Worn or damaged roof

- Furnace that needs to be repaired or replaced
- Electrical system that's not up to code or doesn't work
- Plumbing that's not up to code or doesn't work
- Air conditioning that's nonexistent or inoperable
- Insulation that's absent, insufficient, or ugly

After listing the major repairs required, you can address any minor problems that crop up during the inspection and are essential to fix, such as light fixtures that don't work, leaky faucets, broken doors, or peeling paint.

Gauging renovations to get the most bang for your buck

When you're planning renovations, you always want your return on investment (ROI) to exceed 100 percent. Otherwise, you become a real estate philanthropist — giving the buyer something for nothing. So when you see articles claiming that you can expect an 80 percent return on a new kitchen or a 75 percent return on a bathroom remodel, you may wonder why any flipper in his right mind would consider rehabbing the kitchen or bath. Three reasons:

- As a flipper, you already covered the cost of the renovation by purchasing the property below market value (see Chapter 12). In other words, the renovation is already paid for.
- When you look at those ROI numbers of a 75 percent or 80 percent return, keep in mind that the person punching numbers into the calculator is usually assuming that you're having a professional do all the work. By doing some or all of the work yourself, you may be able to boost the ROI well over 100 percent.
- Few buyers can afford to renovate the kitchen or bathroom after paying a boatload of money for a house. They'd rather borrow a little more and pay for a house that's finished. To avoid excluding these first-time home buyers from your market, some renovations are essential, even though on the surface they may not appear to be cost effective.

The fact that renovations boost your ROI doesn't mean that you should redo every room in the house. When you have a limited budget and timeframe, you may find that you need to make some tradeoffs. When debating which tradeoffs to make, keep your eye on the bottom line (see "Drawing Up a Tentative Budget," later in this chapter, for more about money matters) and let the following considerations guide your decisions:

- **Enhance curb appeal.** In flipping, curb appeal rules, and you usually get more bang for your buck from landscaping and exterior renovations. A fresh coat of paint coupled with some basic landscaping is often a lot less expensive than the cost of remodeling a kitchen or bath. See Chapter 16 for tips on enhancing curb appeal.
- **Add fresh paint and carpeting.** For a few thousand dollars, you can carpet most houses and add a fresh coat of paint. It's a quick, inexpensive way to make the house look new-ish. For additional ideas on quick, affordable repairs and renovations, see Chapter 15.
- **Consider the competition.** After touring comparable homes in the neighborhood, you know what your house needs to make it slightly more attractive than comparable homes. As attractive or slightly more attractive is good enough.
- **Weigh the expense.** Don't invest any more than it takes to bring your house up to neighborhood standards. If the kitchen is good enough for the neighbors, it should be good enough for you.
- **Target popular demand.** By knowing what most house hunters in your target area find attractive (see "Developing an Eye for Home Improvements," earlier in this chapter, for details), you can more effectively base your renovation decisions on what sells rather than on what you prefer.

Adding inexpensive, last-minute touches

After you've done your major remodeling and checked your bank account to see how much money remains, take a step back and see whether any final touches can further enhance the property's appearance. You may want to add decorative shutters to the windows, light up the landscaping with exterior lamps, or spring for some new throw rugs. Look for cheap, easy stuff that won't blow your budget or take more than a few hours.

WARNING!

Don't get carried away after you remodel the house with sprucing it up even more. Keep your budget in mind, or you'll end up blowing your profit on minor changes that may end up becoming major expenses.

Delegating Duties

After you have a detailed to-do list, it's time to delegate — to determine which jobs you can do yourself, which jobs you can rope your friends into doing, and which jobs you need to hire a professional to complete. In the following sections, I provide some guidance on how to pick the people on your team who are best qualified for various duties.

The first rule in house flipping is to do the job right, so as you assign duties, be honest about each person's abilities and inabilities. If you don't know a screwdriver from a scuba diver, maybe you should stick to the money end of the deal and leave the repairs to someone who's more qualified. You may save a little money by doing it yourself, but you pay later for any shoddy workmanship.

Identifying do-it-yourself projects

The most obvious way to cut costs is to do the work yourself. You may not be able to install a new furnace or hot-water heater, but most people can push a broom, mow the lawn, scrub a toilet, or tear out old carpeting. The following list points out the chores that most house flippers who are just starting out choose to do themselves:

- Scheduling
- Basic cleaning
- Yard work
- Tearing out old stuff
- Odd jobs for the weekend warrior

When considering whether to do a job yourself or hire a professional, ask yourself this question: "Can I do the job as well and as quickly as a professional?" If doing it yourself jeopardizes the quality of work or the schedule, hire a professional. The $100 per day rule (see Chapter 12) applies here. If a project takes you seven days to complete, it costs you $700. If you can hire someone to do the same project in two days for $500, you save $200 and cut five days off the schedule.

Getting a little help from your friends

Consider asking friends, family members, and neighbors to help with the cleanup and renovation and assign tasks based on your helpers' skills and experience. Of course, this means you have to pitch in when they need a hand, but you can pick up additional skills and knowledge by working alongside people with expertise in a variety of areas. You can work as a group on landscaping renovations, work alone, or team up with one other person to perform a task such as drywalling or wallpapering that's a little easier to do with four hands.

When bartering with friends, family, and neighbors, the value of what you're trading may be subject to taxes. Consult your accountant (I help you find a good one in Chapter 4).

Flagging jobs that require professional expertise

Licensed, insured contractors and subcontractors have four things that many do-it-yourselfers don't have: time, tools, know-how, and good insurance. When faced with the decision of whether to do the job yourself or hire a professional, consider these four factors:

- **Time:** Do you personally have the time to complete the job yourself, or would your time be better invested in other pursuits, such as your day job? Can you complete the job on schedule?
- **Tools:** Do you own the tools required to do the job? How much do the required tools cost to buy or rent? Do you have the means to haul large, heavy materials, such as rolls of carpet or sheets of drywall, to the worksite? How much would it cost to have materials delivered?
- **Know-how:** Do you have the expertise to do the job well? Be honest. Materials can cost a lot of dough. If you tear up fancy wood paneling in the process of installing it or ruin a roll of vinyl flooring by making the wrong cuts, these missteps add to the cost of the job.
- **Insurance:** Is the job dangerous? If you or someone who's helping you is injured in the process, will your insurance cover the doctor bills and any income lost from missed work?

Unless you have the basic qualifications to do the job right, consider hiring a professional to do the following work:

- Structural repairs, including the foundation
- Major renovations that require knocking down or building walls
- Roof replacement or repairs
- Siding or tuck pointing
- Window replacement
- Furnace and air conditioning installation or repairs
- Electrical upgrades
- Major plumbing repairs, including septic system
- Removal or treatment of toxic substances
- Installation of new carpet, tile, or vinyl flooring

For major projects, such as remodeling a kitchen or bathroom, tell the contractor, in writing, exactly what you want done, the deadline, and the budget. If you leave decisions to the contractor, you're likely to experience cost overruns, both in time and money. Chapter 4 has more information on finding and contracting contractors, subcontractors, and handymen.

Drawing Up a Tentative Budget

How much you profit from the sale of the house often hinges on the cost of repairs and renovations. Overzealous flippers get burned when their visions for improving a house exceed their ability to pay for them. Whether you have $10,000 or $100,000 budgeted for repairs and renovations, decide early on, preferably before closing, how much of that money to set aside for each project.

To establish a budget, follow these steps:

1. **List the projects you plan on hiring a professional to complete (covered earlier in this chapter).**
2. **Obtain estimates for these jobs.**

   Estimates should break out the cost of materials and labor.
3. **Jot down the projects you plan on doing yourself (covered earlier in this chapter).**
4. **For each of these projects, list the required materials.**

   If you're remodeling a bathroom, for example, you may need a new toilet, sink, cabinet, tile (for the walls), flooring, paint, and caulk. Visit your local hardware store to research the cost of materials.

   Many hardware stores display two prices for materials — an uninstalled and an installed price. Use these comparisons to determine how much you're saving by doing the work yourself.
5. **Tally all the estimated costs and add 20 percent to cover sales tax and unexpected expenses.**

   The cost of most projects exceeds estimates.

Use the renovation planner shown in Figure 14-1 to estimate costs and keep all your notes in one place. It features space for listing each project, its start and completion dates, and its costs for materials and labor. To estimate your renovation costs, head to Chapter 11.

Renovation Planner

Project	Start Date	Completion Date	Materials Cost	Labor Cost	Total Cost

Total Materials Costs		$________
Total Labor Costs	+	$________
Total Materials and Labor Costs		$________
20 Percent for Sales Tax and Unexpected Costs	x	1.2
Grand Total		$________

Figure by Wiley Composition Graphics

Figure 14-1: A renovation planner is a handy tool for estimating costs.

Don't let some sweet-talking investor charm you into taking on a project in which you assume most of the risk and the investor stands to gain most of the profit. When budgeting, make sure that you're the one making the decisions on how to spend your money. Remember, it's *your* money. It's important to keep your investor(s) happy because they're helping finance the venture, but use your own discretion in deciding what's best for *your* long-term gain.

Coming Up with a Game Plan

Without proper planning, you can literally paint yourself into a corner when you're renovating a house. If you refinish the hardwood floors first, subsequent construction traffic ruins the finish. If you install new drywall before the plumbers show up, you may find them hacking chunks out of it later to get at the pipes. Before scheduling the work, sit down with your project list and arrange your renovations in a logical sequence so that the work flows smoothly and you don't end up dribbling paint all over your new carpeting. In the following sections, I lead you through the process of drawing up an overall renovation plan.

When I schedule renovations, I try to have as much energy going into the project as possible to maximize the synergies of the workers and crews. Nobody wants to look like a slacker in the midst of fellow workers. This strategy also helps draw more attention to the house from neighbors and potential buyers.

Switching on utilities and ordering materials

Few things are more discouraging to a flipper than having workers show up at the house only to find that the electricity is turned off and they don't have the materials they need to get started. Not only does this lack of foresight undermine your schedule, but it also saps the enthusiasm of your team at a time when that enthusiasm is at its peak. In the following sections, I show you how to make sure your project launches on the scheduled date and time.

Utilities

Before you begin scheduling the work, make sure that you have the power (gas and electric), water, and materials you need to get started. Contact the utility companies as soon as possible to have them turn on the gas, electricity, and water. Otherwise, you can't work on the gas or electric furnace, repair the lights or outlets, or work on the plumbing. Call the utility companies right after closing to have the utilities switched to your name and specify a date on which you want them turned on.

If you forget to have the utilities turned on, don't use this misstep as an excuse to postpone your renovations. You can buy or rent a generator, obtain water and electricity from the neighbors, and use portable heaters to remain toasty in cold weather. Time is money! Get to work and keep working so that you can realize that profit.

When the utilities are turned on, you should be at the house to check for any leaks and be prepared to turn off the water or gas at the main shut-off if you notice any leaks. If the temperature is below freezing, turn on utilities in the following order: electricity, gas, and water. Always have the water turned off at the meter and then slowly turn it on so you can catch any leaks quickly before the pipes hit full pressure.

Materials

List all the materials you need for repairs and for your home-improvement projects, order the materials as soon as you know what you need (but not before closing on the house), and have the hardware store notify you of any items that are on back order. If you know ahead of time that a cabinet you want is not in stock, you may be able to order a similar cabinet that's in stock or locate another supplier who has it.

Some stores are willing to hold the materials for you until you're ready to start and then deliver them right to your door. If the property has a secure garage, empty out as much space as possible before delivery day rolls around.

Tackling underlying problems first

If you're scheduled for liposuction, you don't run out and buy a whole new wardrobe. You don't even know whether the new clothes will fit. The same is true when you're renovating a house. If the house isn't level, you level the house before installing a new kitchen. If pipes need to be replaced, you have that done before you paint the walls or install new flooring. For most renovations, follow the same sequence as the one used for new construction:

1. **Repair or erect the underlying structure.**

   Correct any problems with the foundation and have the carpenters rough out the walls, ceilings, and entryways first.

2. **Install new ductwork, if needed, for heating and central air conditioning.**
3. **Replace any water pipes or sewage lines that need to be replaced.**
4. **Run new electrical lines, if needed.**
5. **Drywall or plaster the walls and ceilings, install flooring and cabinets, and perform any other final renovations.**

Working from the top down

When it comes to home repairs and renovations, gravity rules, water seeks its level, and traffic runs across the floor, so schedule your work from the top down. If the roof is leaking, fix it first. Otherwise the water can damage the drywall or the new carpeting. If the house has more than one floor, consider starting at the top and working your way downstairs. In a room, paint the ceiling first, then the trim, then the walls, and then lay the carpet or flooring. If you're doing major renovations in a room, save the painting, carpeting, and installing new fixtures for last.

If you plan on living in the house during renovations, consider renovating one bathroom, one bedroom, and the kitchen (in that order) before you move in. These changes make the house livable so you can take your time with the other renovations.

Working from the outside in, or vice versa

Weather permitting, work on the outside of the house first to generate some neighborhood buzz. By working on the outside of the house first, you immediately put the wheels of your marketing machine in motion and have a much better chance of selling the house when you put it on the market.

Plan ahead to take advantage of the weather and keep in mind that house-hunting season generally starts to heat up in early spring and cool off in the late fall. You don't want to get stuck with a house over the long winter months when heating bills peak.

If the weather is super cold or super hot or you plan on spending a year or more renovating the inside, you may want to reverse your strategy. Begin inside and then complete the outside renovations when you're closer to the date on which you plan on planting the For Sale sign on the front lawn. Keep in mind, however, that if something on the outside, such as a leaky roof, is likely to cause additional damage, you need to take care of that first.

If you have to kick it up a notch to meet deadlines or get the house ready for closing, work inside and outside at the same time and consider scheduling crews in shifts, but keep in mind that the neighbors may not welcome the graveyard shift. Check with your neighbors first, invite them over to witness your progress, and ask them whether multiple shifts for a limited period of time would be acceptable. Becoming friendly with the neighbors is always (well . . . usually) a good idea.

Allotting sufficient time for your projects

At this point, you may be wondering just how long it's going to take to renovate your house and put it back on the market. The best answer I can offer is this: It depends. It depends on the condition of the house; how extensive the planned renovations are; how much work you plan to do yourself; the number of waking hours you can reasonably commit to the project; how well you plan the renovations; how much help you have; and how long you plan on holding the house, especially if you're living in the house you flip.

If you're doing a cosmetic job (as I describe in Chapter 15), you hire out the work, and you have plenty of hired hands working in unison, you can expect to complete your renovations in one to two weeks and place the house right back on the market. On the other hand, if you're completely gutting the house and doing most of the work yourself on nights and weekends, the project can easily stretch out over months and years rather than weeks.

Consult with your contractors to set reasonable dates for completing the work and, based on the information you gather, plan on placing the house on the market the day after the work and final cleanup are scheduled to be completed. Then, let everyone know the date. You can bump it out later, if needed, but having a date in place is a great motivator.

Chapter 15

Giving Your Property a Quick Makeover

In This Chapter

- Grooming the landscape around your house
- Touching up the front of the house with a little makeup
- Beautifying the interior of the house with a little elbow grease

You stumble upon a great house at a great price that's just plain ugly. The foundation is solid, the roof is only a few years old, the floor plan works, and all the big-ticket items appear to be in working condition. The house just needs a good scrubbing, a proper grooming, and a little makeup to improve its appearance and draw prospective buyers inside.

In this chapter, I show you how to do a quick flip, a *cosmetic job,* or a *makeup job,* as seasoned house flippers call it. You discover how to transform an ill-kempt home into a crowd pleaser for the cost of a few thousand dollars and several weekends. You can then quickly place the property back on the market and sell it for several thousand more than you invested in it . . . assuming you purchased it at the right price (see Chapter 12).

TIP

Home Improvement For Dummies, by Gene Hamilton and Katie Hamilton (Wiley), provides illustrated instructions on performing most of the more complicated tasks in this chapter.

Sprucing Up the Yard

Some lots are so overgrown with trees and shrubs that you can barely see the house from the street. The landscape should accent the house, not hide it. To improve the view of the home from the curbside seats, here's what you need to do:

- **Remove clutter and eyesores.** Remove the rusty carcasses of old cars or bikes, storage sheds that have outlived their usefulness, ugly lawn ornaments, old fences, piles of bricks or stones, and anything else that catches your eye . . . and not in a good way.
- **Trim tree limbs and brambles away from the house.** Overhanging limbs drop leaves and twigs in the gutters, damage the roof, and prevent light from penetrating into the house. Nicely trimmed trees and shrubs shade and accent the house without obscuring it.
- **Pull weeds.** A weedy driveway, walkway, or curb is an eyesore. Pull the weeds or spray them with weed killer and clear them out after they wither and die.
- **Fill driveway and walkway cracks.** Your local hardware store has the materials you need to patch asphalt and concrete. For asphalt drives, reseal the drive after the patch has cured. (Of course, you can always hire out this particular job — it's a nasty job, and one that you can probably get done for about the same cost as doing it yourself.)
- **Dig up any dead plants.** Dried-up, gnarly shrubs and dead flowers can make a yard look more like a cemetery. Extract the dead stuff.
- **Plant fresh shrubs and flowers.** If the weather's nice, plant fresh shrubs, decorative grasses, and flowers, especially along the front of the house and any sides visible from the curb. If the front yard doesn't have a place for flowers, you may be able to place a planter on or near the front porch or hang a basket of flowers near the front door to add color.

  TIP: Do it right. After clearing an area you want to plant, roll out landscaping fabric to keep weeds from popping up, and then cut holes in the fabric wherever you want to plant something.
- **Lay down a fresh layer of mulch.** Fresh cedar mulch or decorative stones make the greenery and other colors pop out and provide a nice trim at the base of the house.
- **Mow and edge the lawn.** Mow the lawn nice and high so it looks lush and green and chokes out the weeds. Edging improves the appearance of the walkways, giving the whole house a more manicured look. Pull any weeds that are poking up through the walkways and along the curb, and sweep up when you're done.

WARNING! Before you start digging or pulling shrubs out from around the house, call the utility companies and have them mark the locations of gas and water lines and buried electrical cables. If you don't know where the utilities are buried, you may turn up something that's quite shocking and leads to costly repairs. Hacking into a gas line or buried electrical cable can also be dangerous.

Figures 15-1 and 15-2 illustrate the selling power of a quality landscaping job. Notice the difference that adding just a few new plants and flowers can make! The homeowner also placed bricks around the planting area to create a lovely trim and removed clutter such as the garden hose near the front door.

Figure 15-1: Before landscaping, this property looks a little boring.

©Jeremy Goodell

Figure 15-2: After landscaping, this house pops out from the street.

©Jeremy Goodell

REMEMBER

Don't forget the backyard! Even though it's not visible from the street, the backyard is still an important selling point of your house and can be cleaned up in a snap. Now that you have the front yard looking like a gardener's paradise, you want the backyard to match; otherwise, the shock could sink a potential sale. Figures 15-3 and 15-4 demonstrate the difference that a little TLC can make in a backyard. Among other tasks, the homeowner removed all the ivy from the back fence and replaced it with a variety of beautiful plants.

Figure 15-3: Before landscaping, this backyard was crawling with ivy.

©Jeremy Goodell

Figure 15-4: New plants make this backyard look brand new.

©Jeremy Goodell

Freshening the Façade

When you purchase a quick-flip property, the shell of the house should be in good repair. The shell includes the roof; gutters; and brick, vinyl siding, or wood siding that covers the house. "Good repair," however, doesn't always mean "pretty." Even a house that's in good shape can use a quick power wash and some touching up. Here are some tips for shining the shell:

- **Trim the ivy . . . or not.** If the ivy is growing on brick, isn't causing damage, and looks nice, leave it be. It can add character to the house and make it more appealing. If the ivy looks bad or is tearing away the gutters or siding, trim it back.
- **Remove the window air conditioners.** A house with air conditioners hanging out of the windows looks like it belongs in a trailer court. Get rid of them.
- **Power wash the siding.** You can rent a power washer at your hardware store or a tool rental service (or buy one if you plan on flipping several houses), and do it yourself, or hire someone to do it for you. For a few hundred bucks, a power wash can make the outside shell look like new.
- **Repair or replace windows and screens.** Nothing is a better indicator of an unkempt house than broken windows and tattered screens. If the window is totaled, install a replacement window that matches the other windows in the house. See Chapter 18 for more on replacement windows.
- **Add or replace shutters.** Decorative shutters are fairly inexpensive and easy to hang, and they add dimension to an otherwise boxy, flat house.
- **Apply a fresh coat of paint.** If a power wash isn't sufficient for brightening the exterior, a fresh coat of paint can do the trick. Check out Chapter 16 for more about painting your property's exterior.
- **Paint the front door and threshold.** The first thing a buyer sees when she walks up to the house is the front door. Even if you don't paint the entire house, paint the front door or clean the stain and apply a fresh coat of shellac. Paint the trim around the door as well as the threshold.
- **Paint the garage to match.** Your house and garage should be the same color to make your property look like a complete package.
- **Replace the gutters.** Seamless gutters are relatively inexpensive to have installed and instantly add curb appeal. You can purchase gutters and hang them yourself, but they usually don't look as good as a professional, seamless gutter replacement or save you enough money to make the project worth doing yourself. If the gutters are in good shape, a quick cleaning and a fresh coat of paint should be sufficient.

- **Replace the front and rear storm doors.** Storm doors often take a beating and generally look worse than the rest of the house. Chapter 18 has details on replacing doors, including entry and sliding glass doors.
- **Replace exterior light fixtures.** Even if the exterior lights still function, if they look bad next to that fresh coat of paint, replace them with new fixtures that are in line with the neighborhood decor.
- **Paint the curbs.** Painting the curbs white or yellow is a nice touch, unless it makes the curbs clash with neighboring properties or isn't allowed by the homeowner's association. You can also paint the address on the curb. Use stencils; don't try to freehand it unless you're an artist. Use a high-quality enamel paint designed for concrete.
- **Replace the mailbox.** A new black or white mailbox with gold lettering for the address is a nice touch.

Figures 15-5 and 15-6 reveal the dramatic effects that a little tender loving care can have on the exterior of a house. The homeowner added new windows, repainted the house white, and painted the trim black. (Notice the new plants, too; see the previous section for details on updating landscaping.)

Figure 15-5: No house hunter would want to stop at this house for a closer look.

©Jeremy Goodell

Figure 15-6: After a few affordable touch-ups, the house is a real attention getter.

©Jeremy Goodell

TIP

Take a photo of your house and the neighboring houses to your local paint store and ask for recommendations on which colors to use. You want your house to stand out without clashing with neighboring homes. A medium-grade paint should be good enough. Paint the garage and fence while you're at it.

For more on making extensive repairs to a house's outside shell, see Chapter 16.

Touching Up the Interior

A home's exterior draws buyers in, but the appearance of the interior ultimately sells the home. For a quick flip, you're not doing any major remodeling. The goal here is to make the interior appear clean and properly maintained. In the following sections, I walk you through the process of preparing the interior of the house for prospective buyers. I begin with general repairs and renovations and then focus on a few key areas to ensure that you don't overlook anything that's really important.

Revitalizing the entire interior

Some repairs and renovations apply exclusively to certain rooms in the house. When you're looking at the countertops, for instance, you're in the kitchen or the bathroom. Other repairs and renovations apply to just about all the rooms in a house. Here's a quick rundown of what my crew and I typically do on a quick flip to every room in the house.

- **De-junk the house.** Every house I've flipped is like a storage shed full of junk and debris. Call a rubbish company, ask the company to deliver a roll-off dumpster, and pitch the debris. Tear out the carpet, clean out the garage and attic, and toss any trash that stands in the way of your work. You can also pitch your landscaping trimmings left over from earlier in this chapter.
- **Clean and polish.** After you eliminate the junk, gather your vacuum cleaner and cleaning supplies and scrub the house from top to bottom. Perform the following tasks:
  - Wash the windows.
  - Vacuum or sweep away any cobwebs, especially near the ceiling.
  - Wash the drapes, have them professionally cleaned, or replace them.
  - Scrub the sinks, toilets, baths, and showers.
  - Vacuum out the closets and cabinets.
  - Apply fresh contact paper to any shelves inside the closets and cabinets.
- **Apply a fresh coat of paint.** The best way to make the interior look and smell like new is to apply a fresh coat of paint. When painting, adhere to the following guidelines:
  - Remove any hooks or nails and patch holes before painting. Walls should be smooth.
  - Treat any stains with Kilz to prevent grease or mold from bleeding through the paint.
  - Use water-based paint rather than oil-based paint for the interior.
  - Paint the walls a neutral color using a flat paint — no deep purples, fire-engine reds, or lemon yellows. Flat paint hides imperfections in the walls better than semi-gloss or gloss.
  - Use white ceiling paint for the ceilings.
  - Use semi-gloss white paint for the trim. If the trim is stained wood, don't paint it. Clean the stain and then apply a fresh coat of shellac, if needed.

- **Install new window blinds.** In a high-end market, shop for quality window blinds. In a low-end market, paper blinds will do. White or cream is best. Keep the blinds closed about a quarter of the way to let in plenty of sunlight but prevent the house from appearing vacant.
- **Check and repair all doors and doorknobs.** If a prospective buyer or agent has to wrestle with a sliding glass door, fiddle with a lock, or yank on a door to shut it, his frustration becomes the focus of attention. Make sure that the doors look good and open and close effortlessly:
  - Clean and lubricate the tracks on sliding glass doors.
  - Tighten any loose hinges and lubricate them if they're creaky.
  - If locks are sticky, lubricate them with powdered graphite or WD-40.
  - If locks don't work, change them. A locksmith can common-key all locks so that the same key unlocks the front and back doors.
  - If doorknobs look crusty, polish them or swap them out.
  - If a wooden door is warped to the extent that it won't close, sand it down before painting it or have the door replaced (see Chapter 18 for more about replacing doors).
- **Update or add lighting.** Replace old light fixtures with newer models designed to better illuminate the rooms. For example, if a room has a fixture that takes a single bulb, install a new fixture that has room for two or three bulbs. Follow these three guiding principles: Make it new, make it bright, and make them match.
- **Install new light switch and outlet faceplates.** Old light switch and outlet faceplates look nasty against a freshly painted wall. Replace them with white or cream faceplates. If the switches or outlets themselves look bad or don't work properly, replace them as well.
- **Check the light bulbs.** Make sure all light fixtures have working light bulbs. If a fixture has more than one bulb, make sure all the bulbs match.
- **Swap out the register covers.** Identify all register covers in the house, measure them, and then head out to your local hardware store to purchase new ones. Some register covers, especially those that sit in the floor, lift right out. Others simply require the removal of a few screws.

  TIP

  While you have the register covers off, vacuum as far into the ductwork as the hose can reach.
- **Clean exhaust fan covers and replace the fans (if necessary).** Many kitchens and baths have exhaust fans that draw the dirty, greasy, often damp air out of the room. At the very least, clean the fan cover and fan

blades thoroughly by spraying them with a strong grease cutter and wiping off the grease and dirt. If a fan isn't working, replace it.

Before you start messing with a fan, make sure that the power is turned off. Some fans are automatic and may turn on when they sense humidity.

- **Install new smoke detectors.** Buyers, agents, and inspectors often look at and test the smoke detectors, so you can avoid problems by installing new ones. At the very least, change the batteries and test every detector to make sure it works.
- **Replace the thermostat and doorbell.** An old thermostat or doorbell can make even a new house look old. Replace them. Replacing a thermostat can be a little tricky, so consider hiring a heating and air conditioning specialist to do the job.
- **Re-carpet, refinish, or replace damaged or worn flooring.** In nearly every house I flip, I tear out the old carpeting and install new carpeting in its place (assuming those rooms don't have hardwood floors that I can refinish). Here are a few things to keep in mind:
  - Choose carpet and padding that's suitable for your market: mid- to upper-grade for the high-end market or low- to mid-grade for the low-end market.
  - Install the same carpeting throughout the house. Carpet salespeople often try to talk you into putting different colors in the bedroom so they can unload their remnants. Insist on using the same design and colors in every room. Use a neutral color (don't get creative).
  - If you plan on flipping several houses, consider buying carpet in bulk — by the roll — to save money. My carpet company allows me to buy in bulk and then stores the carpet for me in its warehouse.
  - Don't cover hardwood floors! Unless the wood is severely damaged, have the floors professionally sanded and refinished. If you don't know what you're doing, you can seriously damage a wood floor.
  - If a good scrubbing doesn't make a vinyl or tile floor look like new, install new flooring. Your choice depends on your market and your pocketbook.

    See Chapter 18 for details about redoing hardwood, vinyl, or tile flooring.

Updating the kitchen

You don't have to remodel a kitchen to make it look new. For pocket change and a moderate amount of labor, you can update the kitchen to give it a whole new look. Consider the following affordable updates:

- Install a new stainless-steel sink.
- Install a new faucet. Nothing makes a kitchen look more dated than an old faucet.
- If the countertop looks old or crusty, have it replaced.
- Short of replacing the cabinets, you can refinish them or add new hardware — knobs and handles.

New kitchen appliances can enhance the appearance of the kitchen, but now you're talking big bucks. In most cases, if your profit margin is strong enough and the house is without major kitchen appliances (dishwasher, refrigerator, and range) or the existing appliances are ugly or in disrepair, you should buy new ones. First-time home buyers often don't have enough cash to purchase these appliances after purchasing the house, so they need a house that comes fully equipped. If the house has ugly, smelly appliances or the appliances don't work, and you don't have the profit margin to cover the expense, then do without — no appliances are better than broken-down appliances.

For a more extensive discussion of kitchen renovations, see Chapter 17.

Spending quality time in the bathrooms

A bathroom can be the scene of some pretty nasty business, yet everyone expects it to look sparkling new. Fortunately, as long as the sink, tub, shower, and flooring are in pretty good shape, you can rejuvenate a bathroom with a reasonable amount of cash and in a reasonable amount of time. Following are some bathroom essentials:

- Install all new fixtures, including a faucet for the sink, a new showerhead, a new handle on the toilet, and new drain covers and plugs.
- Replace the toilet seat. For a little over twenty bucks, this small update makes the toilet look brand new.
- Replace old towel hangers.
- If the bath or shower has a curtain, at the very least, replace the curtain. If you're a little more ambitious, install glass shower doors.
- Remove old caulk and apply a fresh bead around the edges and base of the tub or shower, around the sink, and around the base of the toilet.
- You may need to replace wall tile, but if it's in fairly good shape, spraying the grout with a soap scum and mildew remover and then scrubbing it down may do the trick.
- If the bathtub looks like a breeding ground for bacteria and vermin, get it re-glazed for a few hundred dollars.

TIP

In a tiled bathroom, the grout between the tiles can begin to crack or wear away. Using a grout saw, you can grind the grout out between the tiles. You can then apply new grout and seal it when it sets to make the tile look new. Better yet, call a grout doctor in your area to do it. An affordable grout doctor can save you enough on tools and manicures to pay for the service.

See Chapter 17 for full details on redoing the bathrooms in your flip.

Modernizing the bedrooms

A bedroom is a box with lights and outlets, so if you already painted, installed new light fixtures, replaced the faceplates, cleaned or replaced the window dressings, and re-carpeted, you're pretty much done. (See the earlier section "Revitalizing the entire interior" for details on these tasks.)

The only item you may have missed is the closet. Check out the closet to make sure that it looks clean inside. If it has sliding doors, make sure that they stay on the tracks. Check the hanger bar to see whether it's sturdy, and if it's not, fix it. If the closet doors have removable handles or other hardware, you can often make them look like new by swapping out the hardware.

Now, if you want to boost the storage space in the closet without knocking out any walls, install a closet organizer. A closet organizer can nearly double the amount of clothing and shoes you can shove in a standard closet. For about $100 at your local hardware store, you can buy a kit that contains everything you need for a closet organizer, along with complete instructions.

Making the basement look livable

A finished basement can be anything from a simple, open, multi-use area to an entirely separate flat complete with a bedroom, living room, bath, and kitchen. To quickly update it, follow the instructions earlier in this chapter.

If the house has an unfinished basement, on the other hand, it can be anything from a clean, dry storage area to a dank, mud-floor cave. However, an unfinished basement doesn't have to look like a dungeon. With some deep cleaning, a little paint, and fresh insulation, it can look more like a very sanitary morgue. Consider the following affordable basement enhancements:

- Sweep the cobwebs out of the rafters. (You can paint the rafters black, as I explain in Chapter 19, to open up the ceiling.)
- Dust off any ductwork, pipes, or wiring.

- Tack up any dangling cables, but be careful if they're electrical wires.
- Seal all cracks in the walls.
- Whitewash concrete or cement-block walls with a sealing paint. Not only does this effect look clean, but it also provides a moisture barrier.
- Paint the floor using a gray or beige (depending on the color scheme of the house) enamel paint. Indoor/outdoor carpeting is another option.
- Install new glass block windows.
- Buy a roll of insulation and stuff pieces of it between the joists where the joists meet the outside wall. If these areas are already insulated, tear out the old insulation and install new.

TIP

Painting the basement not only makes it look neat and clean but also adds a fresh-painted smell to a room that may otherwise smell a little musty. Another great way to keep the basement smelling fresh is to run a dehumidifier around the clock. (Be sure to eliminate the source of the moisture first and remove the dehumidifier before showing the house.)

Attending to the furnace and hot water heater

TIP

You can't do much to make pipes or electrical wiring look more attractive, but you can enhance the appearance of two mechanicals in the home — the furnace and the hot water heater:

- **Change the furnace filters.** New filters decrease the amount of dust floating around, and if the buyer, an agent, or an inspector happens to peek inside the furnace, she sees that the house is being properly maintained. If you had the furnace recently repaired or inspected, attach the paperwork to the outside of the furnace.
- **Clean or replace the hot water tank.** If the hot water tank is relatively new and still works, clean it up so it looks like a freshly waxed car. Vacuum any dust or rust first and then wipe the hot water tank down with a household cleaning solution and dry it thoroughly. If the water tank is ugly, damaged, or more than ten years old, have it replaced.

Chapter 16

Perking Up the Curb Appeal

In This Chapter

- Pruning and preening your way to an eye-popping landscape
- Sprucing up driveways, walkways, and entryways
- Refreshing the roof, gutters, and siding
- Sprucing up the garage

When prospective buyers look at homes, they drive up to the curb and take a quick glance at the outside of the house. If the exterior looks run-down, they conclude that the interior is probably in no better shape. Many buyers simply drive away, unwilling to waste their time on a house that the owner didn't care enough about to properly maintain.

In this chapter, I show you how to enhance a property's exterior through landscaping, painting, siding, roofing, and other improvements to stimulate the interest and enthusiasm required to pack your house with prospective buyers.

If you're flipping a house in an addition that has a homeowners association, contact the homeowners association if you're planning any major renovations to the outside of the property. Homeowners associations often have covenants and bylaws that set restrictions on aluminum and vinyl siding, paint colors, fences, and a host of other features.

Revitalizing the Landscape

Most houses start out with attractive landscaping — a lush lawn, a few shrubs near the house, and maybe a couple of flower beds. After years of neglect, the landscape becomes unruly and faded. Grass and weeds creep across the borders. Shrubs obscure the house. Flowers get buried in their beds. And the surrounding lawn begins to appear a sickly green.

Because landscaping improvements often require several weeks or months to take hold, one of the first steps you should take in renovating the property is landscaping. In the following sections, I walk you through the most important tasks and provide a few tips along the way.

Doing the bare minimum

Even if you choose not to do any heavy-duty landscaping, don't overlook the bare essentials in landscaping: de-junking the yard, trimming trees and shrubs, pulling weeds, and mowing and edging the lawn. See Chapter 15 for more about refreshing the landscape.

If you're selling the house in the winter in an area where it snows, keep the walks shoveled and the driveways plowed. Consider hiring a kid from the neighborhood to shovel the walks whenever it snows, and check to make sure he does it.

Revitalizing a tired lawn

A scorched, grub-infested, or mole-infested lawn is a big turnoff in areas where lush, green lawns are the norm. The easy fix is to call a local lawn-care company, have the lawn treated professionally, and follow the company's instructions on keeping it watered. For you do-it-yourselfers, here are some tips on how to revitalize a burned-out lawn in 30 to 60 days:

- If the lawn is damaged beyond repair, and you plan on putting the house back on the market in fewer than 30 days, have it re-sodded.
- If the lawn is in terrible shape and you're not on a tight schedule, have it seeded, hydro-seeded, or over-seeded. *Hydro-seeding* consists of spraying a slurry of seed and nutrients on the ground. The slurry keeps the seeds moist, so more seeds germinate more quickly. With over-seeding, a machine cuts grooves into the ground and plants grass seed in the grooves. In either case, you need to keep the seeds moist until they germinate and take root. Don't mow until the grass is at least three inches tall.
- Patch any bare spots with a mixture of topsoil, seed, and slow-release fertilizer — about two cups of seed and one to two cups of fertilizer per 40 pounds of topsoil. Keep the mixture moist and don't mow these spots until the grass is at least three inches tall.
- Fertilize using a slow-release fertilizer if the lawn isn't weed infested or using weed-and-feed if weeds are a problem.
- Mow regularly at the highest setting to allow the grass to help choke out the weeds.

Designing an adequate landscape

Avid gardeners may be tempted to sculpt a landscape that looks like something out of *Better Homes and Gardens,* but when you're flipping a house, an adequate, affordable landscape is perfectly suitable. When designing a landscape to accent a home, you have some very simple goals:

- **Direct water away from the foundation.** To keep the foundation as dry as possible, slope the ground down away from the house.
- **Create a smooth transition from the natural surroundings to the house.** The natural surroundings must lead up to the house and anchor it without obscuring it. In other words, frame the house without hiding it. Instead of planting a tree front and center, for example, plant it off to the side and plant shrubs and other shorter plants in front.
- **Add color and variation.** A house typically has only a few color variations — the roof, siding, and trim. With landscaping, you can introduce additional variation in dimension and color. Choose complementary colors and plants of differing heights, but don't go overboard — two or three complementary colors are sufficient.

Watch your wallet. Do enough landscaping to properly accent the house, but no more than that.

Prepping areas for planting

Think of trees, shrubs, and flowers as the jewels that bedeck your landscape. The dirt and mulch create the setting for these jewels, and like any good setting, this one must hold the jewels firmly in place and provide a background against which the jewels stand out. Take the following steps to prepare a suitable bed for your plants:

1. **Clear the area.** Pull weeds and any dead or ugly plants and rake all debris from the area.

   Before digging around your house, call the utility companies to have them mark the locations of buried power, gas, and water lines. Dig slowly and carefully to avoid hacking into any power or gas lines that a previous owner may have buried.

2. **Install edging.** You can purchase affordable plastic or aluminum edging in rolls or use something more expensive, such as paving stones, bricks, or landscaping timber. Edging creates a clear division between the garden and adjacent landscaping and prevents grass and weeds from creeping into the flowerbeds.

3. **Till the soil.** Loosen the soil six to eight inches deep. If the soil is hard, add amendments, such as sand, peat moss, compost, and topsoil. You can use a shovel, but a small tiller simplifies the task.
4. **Grade the area.** Use a rake to level the ground, or if you're landscaping near the house, gently slope the earth down and away from the foundation.
5. **Lay landscaping fabric.** Apply a layer of landscaping fabric over the soil to prevent weeds from popping up in the flowerbeds. Use landscaping fabric, not plastic sheeting, so air and water can flow through to the plants.

Positioning and planting your greenery

After laying the landscaping fabric (see the previous section), set the potted plants where you think you want them planted. Take a step back to envision your new garden and then rearrange the plants until you achieve the desired look.

When you're ready to plant, cut an X through the landscaping fabric at the location of each planter, about twice the diameter of the planter. Follow the instructions that came with the plant to dig a hole and position the plant at the proper depth, and then tamp down the soil around the plant and water it.

TIP: To trim costs, landscape with small shrubs and trees, but throw in a few more mature plants, as well. Older, mature plants cost more, but they make the entire landscape appear well-established. If you have two or more properties, you may be able to dig up a plant that looks terrible next to one property and replant it at another property that needs a larger, mature plant.

Adding the final touch: Fresh mulch

Whether you plant new trees, shrubs, and flowers or simply trim back the old landscaping, you should always lay down a three-inch to four-inch layer of fresh mulch on top of the landscaping fabric. I recommend using natural cedar mulch because it's insect- and disease-resistant, it adds a nice color to the landscape, it's biodegradable, and it's easy to replace if you need to freshen it up later.

TIP: Contact your city's street and sanitation department or local electric company to see if they have any free mulch. When a city or utility company trims and cuts down trees (typically around power lines), it has a surplus of mulch to give away to anyone who's willing to haul it off. It may not be cedar, but it'll do the trick.

Don't be stingy with the mulch. You can have a truck full of topsoil and a truck full of mulch delivered to the house and dumped on the driveway. That should be sufficient to rejuvenate the entire landscape. If you have leftover topsoil, simply spread it over the lawn. You can place any extra mulch around trees and bushes or offer it to the neighbors.

After you mulch, you're done with your landscaping. Congratulations! Figures 16-1 and 16-2 reveal the power of proper landscaping. The homeowner removed old pines and shrubbery from the front of the house and then planted a variety of new trees and flowers. Notice the clear edging around the plants, the careful spacing between the plants, and the fresh mulch pulling everything together.

Figure 16-1: Before landscaping, this property looks dreary.

©Jeremy Goodell

Maintaining the landscape

After all your hard work getting the landscape into shape, you may be tempted to forget all about it and move on to the interior renovations. Don't fall into this trap! To maintain your landscaping from the time you complete it until the time the house sells, water it regularly. Read the instructions that came with the plants or ask the manager of the nursery where you purchased the plants for guidance. You can kill a plant just as easily by over-watering as you can by under-watering.

Figure 16-2: Proper landscaping makes the house appear more inviting.

©Jeremy Goodell

Tidying Up the Driveway and Walkways

Driveways and walkways, by their nature, get pretty beat up. They carry all the traffic into and out of the house; they're exposed to sun, rain, snow, and ice; and they're the favored location of the most stubborn weeds. To spruce up the driveway and walkways, trim the edges, pull any weeds or trees growing through the cracks, and then mend the pavement, as I explain in the following sections.

TIP: To significantly improve the curb appeal of a home with a rough gravel driveway, consider paving it, especially if neighboring homes have paved driveways.

Asphalt driveways

Patching and sealing an asphalt driveway is a nasty job that you can probably hire someone to do for about the same amount (or less) than it would cost you do to it yourself. However, it's also a perfect job for a do-it-yourselfer. It requires no skill or special knowledge, and the materials are cheap. You can complete the entire process in three steps:

1. Spray off the driveway with a hose, thoroughly spraying dirt out of the cracks, and let it dry.

TIP

Power washers are great for cleaning out cracks and weeds. If you don't have a power washer, use a screwdriver to get inside the cracks and then a wet/dry shop vacuum to remove all residue.

2. Squirt asphalt patch in the cracks and holes and let it dry for about a day.

3. Apply sealant with a brush, squeegee, or roller and let it dry for about a day.

WARNING!

Check the weather forecast before performing steps two and three. A good downpour washes driveway sealant right down the drain. Seal the driveway at a time when you're not expecting rain for at least 24 hours. Keep an eye on the driveway until it dries. Rope off the area with buckets (the ones that the sealant came in) and plastic "crime scene" tape (available at most hardware stores) to remind yourself and others to stay off the area.

Concrete driveways and walkways

TIP

If your driveway or walkway looks like Stonehenge, you may want to have it professionally repaved. Any deep cracks or changes in elevation that make you trip as you walk across the pavement are safety hazards that you must repair. Depending on how serious the problem is, you have several options for dealing with it:

- **Patch cracks.** You can fill in small cracks with concrete patch. If the cracks are wider than a quarter inch, stuff a rope in the crack, pour some sand over the rope, and then add a layer of flexible concrete patch. For larger cracks or areas where the pavement meets at different levels, you may need to fill the gap with concrete mix.
- **Level concrete slabs.** If portions of a sidewalk or driveway have settled, you can have entire slabs leveled off without replacing them. A contractor can drill holes through the concrete and then inject a liquid sand mixture or other substance below the slab to raise it to its original level. The service costs about half as much as having the concrete replaced, and the slab can handle traffic immediately.
- **Resurface the walkway or driveway.** If the surface of a driveway or walkway is crumbling but otherwise in good repair, you may be able to resurface it for a fraction of the cost of replacing it. Most building supply stores have epoxy materials that are perfect for resurfacing concrete.
- **Replace concrete.** Tearing out the old and pouring new concrete is the priciest option, but for walkways or driveways that are a lost cause, this choice may be your only viable solution.

Laying asphalt over a cracked and crumbling concrete driveway may seem like a brilliant, quick, and affordable repair, but it's more like a big mistake. I've tried it myself, as have many investors I know, and it never works. Anyone who works on roads for a living can tell you that a quality road is built on a stable *substrate* — large and small stones packed tightly together. Without a solid substrate, the ground beneath the driveway shifts and cracks under the weight of traffic.

Sidewalks may be the responsibility of the town or city in which the property is located, so call the streets department before taking on any expensive repairs. The city may pay all or a portion of the costs. On the other hand, if you notice a red or yellow paint mark on your sidewalk or driveway, the city may be planning to assess you for repairs. Notify the city immediately and complete your own repairs as soon as possible. If you don't have it done by the time the crew is on the street, they'll do the repairs and bill you, and they may charge five or more times as much as you would pay a contractor!

Stone or brick walkways

Stone and brick walkways can pose a problem, especially if the previous homeowner was a do-it-yourselfer and not a do-it-righter. Improperly laid bricks or stones typically settle in odd formations and turn into weed patches.

First decide whether the walkway is necessary. If it's in good shape and just needs a little TLC (weeding and maybe repositioning or replacing a stone or brick), give it the tender loving care it needs. If it's merely a decorative piece and it looks bad, remove it, lay down some new topsoil, and plant grass seed or sod (see "Revitalizing a tired lawn," earlier in this chapter, for more about sod and seeding).

Another option is to remove all the stones or bricks and redo the walkway the right way. *Landscaping For Dummies,* by Phillip Giroux, Bob Beckstrom, Lance Walheim, and the editors of the National Gardening Association (Wiley), has complete instructions on how to properly build attractive stone, brick, and concrete walkways.

Making Entryways More Inviting

Some entryways beckon visitors to step inside. Some inspire yawns. And others send visitors fleeing in disgust. An entryway should project a sense of security along with a warm greeting. In the following sections, I suggest various ways to achieve the desired look.

Refinishing the front door

As a prospective buyer approaches the house, the front door becomes the focal point. If the door is solid, you can alter its appearance through a few minor modifications, including the following:

- Paint or refinish the door in a bold color that complements the house.
- Install new hinges, doorknob, and locks.
- Install a new door knocker or doorbell, especially if the doorbell isn't working. (If the doorbell isn't working, you have three options — repair, remove, or replace.)

If the door is broken or it looks old or cheap, consider replacing the door. Most home-improvement stores have a wide selection of gorgeous, secure front doors in the range of $300 to $500.

If you install a new front door, don't hide it behind an old storm door. Replace the storm door, as well. Check out Chapter 18 for more about replacing doors.

Refurbishing the front porch

Inspect the front porch for any damage and repair it in one of the following ways:

- If you're flipping on the cheap, you can resurface concrete steps and a porch with an epoxy material designed specifically for that purpose.
- Another option is to resurface the steps and porch with ceramic or slate tile to give the porch a whole new look.
- Damaged wood is fairly easy to replace. You can patch small cracks or gaps and apply a fresh coat of paint to all the woodwork to make it match, or pry up old boards and install new ones.

If the house is in an area where people often sit out in front, you may be able to significantly increase the value of the house by expanding the porch or replacing the existing porch with something larger. If you have to pay someone to perform the work, you probably won't recoup your investment, but if you can handle the job yourself in a day or two, you can install a porch or deck for about $1,000, increasing the sale price by a few thousand dollars. For additional tips, see Chapter 19.

Adding some finishing touches

When you're done with the major repairs and renovations to the entryways, focus on a few final touches to pull the outside of the house all together. Following are a few improvements I do on all my investment properties:

- Install new light fixtures for the coach (porch) lights.
- Install a kick plate at the base of the door.
- Replace the mailbox.
- Replace the address posted on the house.
- Polish the front-door handle.
- Yank out any nails or hooks that the previous owners used to hang holiday lights.
- Add a planter or hanging plant.
- Accent the flowerbeds with a few affordable solar lights.
- Remove the pink flamingo lawn ornaments.

Refreshing the Outside Shell of the House

The shell of a house consists of its roof, gutters, siding, doors, and windows — everything that keeps the elements out and the heat or air conditioning in.

In the following sections, I show you how to refresh the exterior with improvements to the roof, gutters, and siding. Chapter 18 shows you how to improve the outside shell with some moderate makeovers, including replacement windows and new sliding-glass doors, which also enhance the appearance of the home's interior.

Laying a new roof

If the roof appears worn or stained or if the shingles are curling up at the edges, I strongly recommend that you tear off the old roofing material and install a new roof. A new roof gives the house a whole new head of hair. Inspect the roof, keeping the following important points in mind:

- The steeper the pitch, the more visible the roof is from the street, and the more important it is to make sure the roof looks great.
- If the roof has two or more layers, tear off the old roof before installing the new. This is usually required by local building codes.
- If the roof has only one layer of roofing and your budget allows for it, tear it off before installing the new roof. If the budget's tight, you can install the new shingles over one layer of old shingles.
- Don't just patch damaged areas. Blending the new shingles in with the old ones is nearly impossible.
- If the roof has any soft, spongy areas, tear off the old layers of roofing so you can inspect and repair the sub-roofing before installing the new roof.

REMEMBER

Unless you're a roofer, hire an insured roofing contractor to do the work.

To estimate the cost of a new roof, use the roofing estimator at `www.improvenet.com`. When you get to the home page, find the project calculator and select the roofing estimator.

TIP

Dimensional roofing shingles cost more than standard shingles, but they enhance the appearance of the home in excess of the added costs. Opt for a lower-quality dimensional shingle over a higher-quality standard shingle.

TIP

If the roof was damaged by strong winds or hail, the previous owner's insurance company may be willing to pay for repairs, as long as you bring up the issue before closing. If you can get the insurance company to pay, the previous owner is only out the cost of the deductible, and you can offer to split the cost or pay the deductible in full, saving on the cost of a whole new roof.

Repairing or replacing gutters

If the gutters are in great shape, you may be able to clean them out and add some gutter brackets or nails to pull the gutters flush against the house. Otherwise, call a contractor to install new, seamless gutters around the entire house and garage. This upgrade is a fairly inexpensive and quick fix, and it significantly improves the exterior appearance of the house. Pick a color (usually white or brown) that matches the trim.

Retooling the siding

When talking siding, you're in three-little-pigs territory. Is the house made of straw, sticks, or bricks? In the case of human homes, siding can consist of wood, vinyl, aluminum, brick, or stucco. Each requires its own unique upkeep:

- **Wood siding:** Power-wash the siding at the very least. If the wood is damaged, you may be able to patch or replace damaged boards, but if the damage is extensive, siding over the old wood siding with vinyl is probably best. If the wood is in good shape but the paint is peeling, repaint the house. (If you're not a professional painter, consider hiring someone who is.)
- **Vinyl siding:** When wood-sided homes are too ugly to paint or existing aluminum or vinyl siding is peeling away from the home's outer shell, consider re-siding the house with vinyl siding. However, get an estimate first. Having even a small home completely re-sided can quickly bust your budget.

  TIP: If you live in or near a major metropolitan area, locate distributors who carry seconds to see whether they have rejected materials. Sometimes a company rejects perfectly good siding from a production run simply because the color is a shade off.
- **Brick:** If the mortar between the bricks is wearing away or if settling has caused cracks in the mortar, tuck point the brick. *Tuck pointing* consists of spreading new mortar between the bricks; it's a fairly easy job, but it requires the patience of a saint.

  SANITY CHECK: Personally, I'm not a big fan of painting over brick because I like the way most brick looks, and the paint commonly peels off later, but some brick can make the house look dark and dreary. A bright paint can give some homes just the pop they need.
- **Stucco:** You can patch small cracks and holes yourself and even paint the stucco if the house is in an area with a fairly warm climate. Otherwise, hire a professional to patch and re-coat the stucco. A contractor who has the necessary equipment can spray a new layer of colored stucco over the old stuff and give the house a whole new look.

  WARNING! In a cold climate, painting stucco is a bad idea because moisture gets behind the paint and causes it to bubble and peel.

Figures 16-3 and 16-4 show the dazzling effects of a few moderate improvements to the siding of a home. The homeowner repainted the siding a slightly brighter color (with white trim as a complement) and retooled some of the brickwork.

Figure 16-3: This house, in its original state, appears ho-hum.

©Jeremy Goodell

Figure 16-4: A few enhancements to the outer shell make the house perky.

©Jeremy Goodell

Glamming Up the Garage

TIP

When you're focused on fixing up a house, overlooking the garage is easy, but when prospective buyers show up, I guarantee that they won't overlook it. Here are a few tasks you can do to breathe new life into a garage:

- Paint or re-side the garage to match the house.
- Replace the roof, if needed, to match the house.
- Replace the windows, especially if you replaced them in the house.
- Install a new automatic door with decorative glass.
- Install a new garage access door or repaint the existing door, if it's in good shape.

Prettying up the garage improves the overall appearance of the entire property, as Figures 16-5 and 16-6 demonstrate. On this project, my flipping team gave the garage a new overhead door and a new loft door on top, fixed the trim, and applied a fresh coat of paint.

Figure 16-5: This garage looks disheveled.

Figure courtesy of Ralph Roberts Realty

Figure 16-6: With some improvements, this garage is a place where you really want to park your car.

Figure courtesy of Ralph Roberts Realty

Chapter 17

Dazzling the Crowds with Updated Kitchens and Baths

In This Chapter

- Renovating a kitchen's cabinets, counters, and sinks
- Updating a kitchen with new appliances
- Revamping bathrooms for comfort and beauty

Kitchens and baths are about more than just space and functionality. People build emotional attachments to these rooms. The bathroom is a personal place where you look yourself in the mirror every day, prepare yourself for the outside world, and pamper yourself at the end of a grueling day. The kitchen is the community center where you keep the calendar and phone; where families gather to talk about their days and plan activities; and where friends and family celebrate every single holiday, birthday, and anniversary together.

As everyone in sales knows, emotional reactions trump necessities. If you can redesign or redecorate a bath or kitchen in a way that evokes a positive emotional reaction from prospective buyers, you have them hooked. In this chapter, I show you how to renovate kitchens and baths in various ways that are sure to make them more appealing to buyers.

Giving Kitchen Cabinets, Countertops, and Sinks a Facelift

Homeowners often overcook when they renovate their kitchens, spending $30,000 or more on a kitchen that boosts the property value by only about $10,000. Assuming the homeowner loves the kitchen and plans on staying in the house and using the kitchen for many years, the choice may be a good one. When you're flipping houses, however, you can significantly improve the appearance of a kitchen for just a few thousand dollars. Figures 17-1 and 17-2 illustrate the dramatic effect that a moderate renovation can have on a kitchen. Among other updates, the homeowner:

Figure 17-1: This kitchen is well-suited to curbing your appetite.

©Jeremy Goodell

Figure 17-2: The remodeled version is ready for dinner guests.

©Jeremy Goodell

- Removed some old cabinets, added some new cabinets, and replaced the doors on existing cabinets
- Added new drawer knobs and cabinet handles
- Installed new countertops, a new sink, and a new faucet
- Equipped the kitchen with several new appliances
- Laid new flooring (see Chapter 18)

In the following sections, I reveal affordable options for cabinets, countertops, and sinks that can transform a dull, dreary kitchen into one of the main selling features of the house. For more about redoing a kitchen, check out the latest edition of *Kitchen Remodeling For Dummies,* by Donald R. Prestly (Wiley).

Refinishing or replacing cabinets

I've seen investors completely gut a kitchen with solid plywood cabinets and install all new cabinets made of particle board. Sure, the new cabinets looked great, but the old ones were perfectly fine. The moral of the story is don't gut the kitchen if it doesn't need to be gutted. Not only do you risk ending up with lower-grade cabinets, but you also take on the added expense and mess of tearing out the old ones and disposing of them.

Consider the following options before replacing the cabinets:

- **Paint the cabinets white.** The safest, cheapest option is to paint the cabinets white with a high-gloss enamel. For about $50 total and a day's work, you get cabinets that are immaculately clean and shiny, which is what most buyers are looking for.
- **Strip and stain.** If the wood is good — oak, maple, hickory, cherry, mahogany — show it off. Take the doors off the cabinets, strip the stain, and re-stain everything for a fresh, new look. This option is cheap in terms of money but expensive in terms of time and mess.
- **Reface doors and drawers.** Some companies specialize in re-facing cabinets, which consists of removing the doors and the fronts of the drawers and then applying a wood or plastic laminate to all exterior surfaces. This costs much more than a standard paint job, but it's about a third less than the cost of installing new cabinets.

If the kitchen has rusting metal cabinets or wood cabinets that are falling apart, or if the kitchen layout is poorly designed, refinishing the doors and drawers won't do the trick. In such cases, new cabinets are the only choice. Affordable prefab cabinets are fine for most houses priced in the low- to mid-range. In high-end markets, consider upgrading to custom-built cabinets.

Updating hardware: A cosmetic fix

Most cabinets and drawers have hardware attached to them that's both functional and decorative. You can often improve the appearance of the cabinets simply by replacing the hardware — door and drawer handles, knobs, hinges, and latches. This improvement can cost as little as $5 per door and drawer, and you can expect to get every penny of that back when you sell the house.

TIP

Before you run out and purchase new cabinet hardware, make a list of everything you need and then take measurements so that you purchase new hardware with holes that match up with the holes already drilled in the doors and drawers. The less re-drilling you have to do, the better.

Resurfacing or replacing countertops

To gain a deeper understanding of the emotional reactions that homeowners have to kitchens, wander around the kitchen displays at the local building supply store and watch the reactions of customers to various cabinet and countertop displays. The right countertop can make homeowners swoon.

REMEMBER

Before you jump to the conclusion that you need a new countertop to make buyers swoon, consider these more-affordable solutions:

- **Polish the existing countertop.** If the countertop is made of a solid material, such as granite or a composite, you may be able to have it professionally polished for much less than the cost of a new countertop.
- **Resurface the countertop.** You can strip off the existing veneer and glue on new veneer, but when you add up the cost in terms of money, time, mess, and the dangers of using volatile solvents, you're probably better off installing a completely new countertop.
- **Replace a damaged section of the countertop.** If a section of the countertop is badly damaged, cut it out and install an attractive cutting board in its place. You can also use glass or Corian.
- **Add molding.** You can glue a molding to the leading edge of some countertops to cover damage and give the countertop a new look.

Countertops range in quality, material, and price. If you're going to install a new countertop, choose a material that's suitable for your market. In low- to mid-range markets, that means laminate. In high-end markets, look for granite, marble, Corian, stainless steel, or other custom products.

SANITY CHECK

You're not buying the countertop for yourself, so tame your personal tastes and choose colors and patterns that are conservative and neutral.

The problem with old kitchens

Old kitchens were designed for the days when moms stayed in the kitchen and cooked and people didn't have so many modern appliances cluttering the countertops. In other words, kitchens were designed to accommodate one cook, an oven/stove, and a refrigerator.

Nowadays, an entire family of four can be found doing the bump in the kitchen, and we have dozens of countertop appliances — microwave ovens, cappuccino machines, electric can openers, blenders, toasters, and sometimes even a TV or radio. Modern designs factor in all this new stuff and attempt to maximize the use of available space.

Installing a new sink and faucet

Cleaning and polishing a sink is often sufficient, but if a thorough scrubbing doesn't do the trick, install a new sink and faucet. In the low- to mid-range market, stick with stainless steel. In high-end markets, consider cast iron with a porcelain or acrylic finish or a customized sink.

TIP

While you're swapping out the sink, consider adding a garbage disposer (often called a *garbage disposal*) if the kitchen doesn't have one, or replacing the disposer if the current one looks old. A new ½ or ⅝ horsepower garbage disposer ranges in price from $50 to $100, and when the homeowner or inspector takes a peek under the sink, you've already earned that money back.

Modernizing Kitchen Appliances

When you purchased the property, the generous owner bequeathed you her 1970s refrigerator with the avocado finish. Now that you've completed your kitchen remodel with a tasteful display of muted tones, the fridge just doesn't fit. It works fine, but it doesn't work with the décor. What should you do?

You have several options. If you have rental property, move the refrigerator to one of your rental units. Otherwise, donate it to charity or call a used appliance dealer to haul it off. Whatever you do, don't keep it. The house is more valuable without a particular appliance than with one that clashes with the surrounding décor.

When you're trying to make your kitchen look its best, update any appliances you include with the property, as I discuss in the following sections.

Deciding whether to install appliances

Appliances can jack up the cost of your kitchen remodel in a hurry. You can drop anywhere from $250 to $3,500 on an electric range, $400 to $6,000 on a refrigerator, $150 to $2,000 on a microwave oven, and another $200 to $1,500 on a dishwasher. Go top of the line on every appliance and you add more than $10,000 to your kitchen remodeling budget.

Before you splurge, take a deep breath and a look around at the housing market in your area. Do most homes for sale include all those appliances? If they do, are the appliances in the low-end, medium, or nosebleed price range? Just as you assess your renovations to meet the demands of the market (see Chapter 14), gauge the amount you spend on kitchen appliances to meet the demands of most home buyers in your area without exceeding those demands:

- In low- to mid-range housing, supply the bare essentials — a dishwasher, garbage disposer, refrigerator/freezer, and freestanding range.
- In mid- to upper-end housing, consider supplying the higher-end essentials along with a cabinet with warming drawers and a built-in wine cooler. Upgrade to a built-in refrigerator with an ice maker and water dispenser, and consider upgrading the oven and cooking surfaces, as I describe in "Roaming the range, oven, and cooktop" later in this chapter.

You can trim the cost of kitchen appliances by purchasing gently used or returned merchandise at outlet stores. If you buy used or returned appliances, inspect them carefully for any damage and make sure that the doors open and close without a hitch.

Adding or replacing the dishwasher

In the not-so-distant past, a dishwasher was a luxury. Now it's a necessity. Not only does a dishwasher automate the task of washing the dishes, but it also frees up valuable counter space that may otherwise be consumed by an ugly dish drainer.

If the kitchen already has a dishwasher, inspect it inside and out. If you wouldn't take a bath in it, replace it. If you purchased a house without a dishwasher, add one, even if it involves losing a little cabinet space. Expect a first-time installation (for a kitchen that doesn't have a dishwasher) to cost another hundred bucks or more for the plumbing installation. Look for a quality unit that has a reputation for being quiet (read customer reviews).

Install the dishwasher as close to the sink as possible. This proximity makes loading the dishwasher more convenient and places the washer close to the hot-water pipe and drain pipe. If you're installing new flooring (see Chapter 18 for details on flooring), lay the flooring before installing the dishwasher.

Roaming the range, oven, and cooktop

No kitchen surface gathers as much dirt, grease, and grime as the oven, cooktop, or range. If the kitchen's cooking equipment is old, cheap-looking, or crusty beyond cleaning, look into replacing it with a new unit that's appropriate for your area's housing market. Your options are limited only by your imagination, budget, and market demands:

- **Freestanding range:** This most common cooking unit combines an oven with a cooktop and has finished sides, so the range looks good no matter where you position it.
- **Slide-in range:** Like a freestanding range, a slide-in range combines the oven and cooktop, but its sides are unfinished, so you must install it between cabinets to hide the sides.
- **Drop-in range:** Like the slide-in range, a drop-in unit has unfinished sides, but the top rests on the tops of the adjacent cabinets.
- **Wall ovens:** Unlike a range, a wall oven has no cooktop. The oven is built into a wall or the surrounding cabinets, placing it about chest high so you don't have to bend over to check your pizza.
- **Combination ovens:** A combination oven typically consists of two stacked ovens, which is great if you need to bake a pork roast and an apple pie at the same time. Some units combine microwave, conventional, and convection (hot, swirling air) energy to cook faster and more evenly.
- **Dual-fuel units:** Can't decide whether you want to cook with gas or electric? Then get a dual-fuel unit that uses both!
- **Cooktops:** A cooktop consists of burners (gas or electric) with no oven below them; they mount level with the countertop. Cooktops are great for kitchens that have wall ovens or an island on which you want to add another cooking surface.
- **Downdraft cooktops:** Downdraft cooktops are essential for those homeowners who want to grill steaks all year. A fan pulls the smoke down below the cooktop and vents it out of the house. Some downdraft cooktops include grills, griddles, rotisseries, and even woks.

TIP

You may be able to get a builder discount for ranges, cooktops, and other kitchen appliances. Tell the retailer that you flip houses on a regular basis and ask whether you qualify for the discount.

REMEMBER

Don't forget the hood. Most kitchens have a ventilation fan to pull smoke, grease, and humidity from the air and vent it outside. That's the least you should have. For a high-end kitchen, an exhaust hood over the range is a must, and an attractive hood can really jazz up a kitchen. Houses in the low- to mid-range market commonly have hoods that circulate the air through a charcoal filter, so they don't require an external vent. You can easily replace the hood without going to the trouble of venting.

Installing a space-saving microwave

The microwave oven has revolutionized the way we cook, but it also adds to the countertop clutter, unless you can move it elsewhere. One option is to go with a combination oven that has built-in microwave capabilities, as I discuss in the previous section. Another, more-affordable option is to mount the microwave over the range. Some microwave ovens double as a cooktop hood, providing ventilation for the range.

Keeping or replacing the refrigerator

I can almost guarantee that anyone looking at the house is going to open the refrigerator, so the inside of it shouldn't look like a high-school science project or smell like roadkill. The refrigerator must be immaculate, inside and out. If you have to use a bungee cord to tie the door shut, if it's beyond cleaning, if it's loud, or if it just doesn't work right, it's time for a new fridge.

Your approach to providing a new refrigerator depends on the market in which you're flipping. In the low-end market, in which you plan on selling to first-time buyers, supply an affordable *top-mount* model (freezer on the top and refrigerator on the bottom). First-time buyers are usually moving from a furnished apartment and don't want to have to spring for appliances after purchasing a house. In the mid-range market, a house without a refrigerator is the norm because most home buyers bring their old refrigerator with them. In the upper-end market, buyers expect a built-in refrigerator.

Clear all the magnets, calendars, sticky notes, and photos off the outside of the refrigerator. All that stuff contributes to the sense that the kitchen — and the owner's life — is cluttered.

Updating the Bathrooms

Modern and shiny clean — that's what most buyers want in a bathroom. Examine the bathrooms first to see what you have to work with and then head to your local home-improvement store to check out what's currently available. The latest offerings are mesmerizing — free-standing sinks, elegant fixtures, one-piece shower stalls, prefab vanities with single or double sinks, lighted medicine cabinets, and numerous collections of floor and wall tile — and they're all pretty affordable.

Don't let a substandard bathroom sink your flip. The following sections lead you through the process of exploring your many options. Figures 17-3 and 17-4 illustrate the possibilities. Among other tasks, the homeowner replaced the old linoleum floor; the shower/tub; the countertop, sink, and faucet; and the mirror and medicine cabinet.

Figure 17-3: This bathroom is a little drab.

©Jeremy Goodell

Figure 17-4: A remodeled bathroom is a sanitary sanctuary.

©Jeremy Goodell

Want more information on bathrooms? Chapter 15 has a list of affordable bathroom touch-ups; Chapter 19 has the scoop on adding a bathroom (only if necessary); and *Bathroom Remodeling For Dummies,* 1st Edition, by Gene Hamilton and Katie Hamilton (Wiley), is full of bathroom renovation ideas.

Modern isn't always better, especially in bathrooms. People spend thousands of dollars to get their hands on antique claw-foot bathtubs, so know what you have before you toss it in the roll-off dumpster. Sometimes, redesigning the bathroom around a precious antique showpiece makes more sense than trying to shoe-horn in a modern bathroom.

Repairing bathroom walls and floors

Before you get into any heavy-duty bathroom remodeling, inspect the walls and floor for any water damage. Rock the toilet to make sure that the floor below it is solid, and press on the walls, especially around the sink and the tub or shower, to test whether they're spongy. If you detect any water damage, fix any leaks and replace the walls and flooring before you do anything else. Other things to keep in mind:

- When replacing walls around a tub or shower, use cement board rather than standard drywall. Cement board is designed to repel water. Install cement board to the top of the shower stall or at least three feet above the bathtub.
- Even if the floor requires no repairs to the sub-flooring, most bathrooms can use new vinyl or tile. I recommend that you hire a professional for the job. After a quick look around, the eyes of most buyers immediately travel to the floor and check the edges around the bathtub, toilet, and baseboards, so you want the flooring done right. See Chapter 18 for details about flooring.

Refinishing or replacing tubs and showers

Bathtubs and showers are prone to becoming matted with soap scum, mildew, and other colorful collections of slime and microscopic organisms. In addition, the surfaces get scratched and eroded by years of scrubbing. When a bathtub or shower is beyond cleaning, even with that foul-smelling mildew and soap-scum remover, you have a choice to make — you can replace or refinish. In the following sections, I show you how to make the best decision for tubs, shower stalls, and tile.

Evaluating bathtubs

Bathtubs are pretty sturdy, so you rarely need to replace them unless one has severe cracks and chips. If the color is hideous or the finish is rough, you can have it professionally refinished. *Refinishing* consists of treating the old finish with a caustic substance, such as a strong acid, to roughen the surface and then applying a glaze that makes the bathtub look like new. After refinishing, replace all the old fixtures and the drain cover, and you have a whole new bathtub.

Resurfacing a bathtub is something I don't recommend for do-it-yourselfers, even though you can buy a kit at your local hardware store to do the job yourself. The chemicals are harsh, and applying the glaze properly requires the right tools and skills. If you wouldn't think of painting your own car, don't consider resurfacing a bathtub by yourself.

Whether you choose to resurface or replace the bathtub, you can't go wrong with classic white.

Surveying shower stalls

In bathrooms that have a shower stall (no tub) that is damaged or too filthy to clean, consider ripping out the shower stall and installing a brand-new one. You can purchase a new shower stall complete with a floor, walls, and glass or plastic doors. Of course, if the old shower stall is in good shape, a thorough cleaning and some fresh caulking around the edges may be enough to salvage it.

Assuming you can measure properly and cut or drill the necessary holes in the right places, installing a shower stall is within the realm of a do-it-yourselfer. Keep in mind, however, that if you're off an inch, you're going to be buying a new shower stall for a lot more than it costs to pay a qualified installer.

Taking a look at the tile

If your bath or shower walls are tiled, chances are good that they look like the inside of a Petri dish. To make them look sparkling new, you have two options — strip the tile and retile the walls or call a grout doctor. Other tips:

- Always re-tile the walls if the walls behind the tile are damaged. Don't simply try to patch the wall. Chances are good that if one section of the wall is damaged, surrounding sections are soon to follow. You should also re-tile if the existing tiles are out of style or if tiles are missing or damaged.
- If the tiles look good and are securely in place, don't waste money replacing them. Hire a grout doctor to make them look like new. A grout doctor leaves the existing tile in place and re-grouts it, typically restoring it to mint condition for a lot less than you'd have to pay to have new tile installed.

Dealing with la toilette

Toilets are built to take a lot of abuse, so a good scrubbing, a new seat, and a new handle are all that most toilets need. If the bowl or tank is cracked or beyond what a thorough cleaning can fix, however, you may need to replace it. The following sections reveal your options.

Replacing the seat and handle

The fastest, cheapest way to restore a toilet to mint condition is to replace the toilet seat and the handle, to the tune of about $25 and 15 minutes of your time. Two bolts hold the seat in place, making it a simple out-with-the-old-in-with-the-new operation. The handle is a little more complicated because you have to pop the hood on the tank, disconnect the chain, and work inside to remove the nut that secures the handle in place. Still, these fixes are easy.

TIP

When shopping for seats, make sure that you buy a round seat for a round toilet or an elongated seat for an elongated toilet. For a little extra, you can purchase a soft-closing seat and lid that doesn't slam down when a kid drops it.

Replacing the toilet

Shopping for a toilet can be more complicated than actually installing it. You can buy a basic model for less than $100, but if you're looking to upgrade in both function and appearance, check out the following features:

- **Elevated height:** Two to 4 inches higher than a standard toilet, elevated-height models make it easier for tall people to do their dismounts.
- **Elongated bowl:** An elongated bowl provides more room to relax on the throne.
- **Power flush:** To avoid having to flush twice, a power-flush toilet puts some oomph behind the water to shove it down the drain. These models can be a little on the noisy side.
- **Quiet flush:** If the bathroom is near the kitchen, hearing the toilet flush may help curb your appetite, but people generally prefer a more muted tone. A quiet-flush toilet muffles the sound.
- **One piece:** One-piece toilets combine the bowl and tank in a single unit. Although they cost extra, they give a nice, streamlined look to the bathroom, and they're easier to clean. As a bonus, most of the one-piece units include the seat.
- **Insulated tank:** Condensation often builds up on the outside of the water tank because it's colder than the surrounding air. An insulated tank reduces the condensation.
- **Two-level flush:** When a little water will suffice, pull one lever. When you need a little extra power, pull the other lever.

Here are a few tips for selecting and installing a new toilet:

- If you have a two-piece toilet (tank and bowl), you don't need to replace the entire toilet if the tank is bad. You can purchase the tank separately for about half the price of a whole new toilet.
- Match the size of the toilet to the size of the bathroom. You shouldn't have a small bathroom with a large toilet. An oversized toilet consumes precious maneuvering space, and people may mistake it for the bathtub.
- If you're a weekend warrior, a toilet should be no challenge to install, although you may need help lifting it.

Updating the sink and medicine cabinet

The first thing you see when you step into a bathroom is the sink or vanity (cabinet with a sink) and the medicine cabinet or mirror, so these items should all be in tip-top condition. If they're not in showcase condition after a good scrubbing, or if they're out of sync with the rest of your renovations, you have several options for replacements. Begin by choosing a sink:

- **Wall sink:** A low-cost wall sink is an option for a second bathroom in the basement or attic, but the pipes under the sink are visible, and this option offers no under-sink storage.
- **Pedestal sink:** Stylish pedestal sinks can add a touch of class to a bathroom and are great for small bathrooms and half baths, but again, they offer no storage below.
- **Countertop sink with vanity:** More expensive than a wall or pedestal sink, a vanity with a countertop sink features two benefits: It hides the pipes and provides additional storage.

If it ain't broke, don't fix it. You can often refinish a vanity and resurface a sink without replacing either one. You save money on both materials and labor and cut your renovation time in half.

Even if the existing sink is in excellent condition or you choose to have it resurfaced instead of replacing it, you should install a new faucet and drain. Bathroom faucets tend to corrode at the base. A new double- or single-handle faucet with a matching drain is a nice, final touch.

You also need a mirror above the sink, and in some bathrooms, that's all you have — a mirror glued or screwed to the wall. If that's what you're working with, upgrade the bathroom with a lighted medicine cabinet.

For smaller bathrooms, you can often save space by installing a corner vanity and medicine cabinet.

Adding or improving ventilation

If the bathroom you're renovating has a lot of mold and mildew, chances are good that the ventilation is insufficient. Fix the problem by adding sufficient ventilation either through a window or a ceiling or wall fan. Window ventilation isn't the best. When you're paying to heat or cool your house, the last thing you want to do is open a window in the middle of winter or summer to air out the bathroom each time you use it. A $50 exhaust fan provides a more economical solution.

If the bathroom isn't infested with mold and mildew, it probably has sufficient ventilation, in which case you don't need to worry about adding or improving the ventilation.

Make sure that you have the right size fan for the room. Fans sizes are expressed in cubic feet per minute (CFM). Multiply the area of the ceiling by 1.1 to calculate a good ballpark estimate.

You want to vent the warm, humid bathroom air to the outside of the house, not to the inside of a wall or ceiling or even into the attic. Venting the air the right way requires installing a pipe that extends through an outside wall or through the roof of the house, and that's certainly not a job for the average do-it-yourselfer.

Chapter 18

Tackling Moderate Makeovers

In This Chapter

- Swapping out windows for a whole new look
- Refining your entrances and exits
- Giving your house a new floor show

As a quick-flip artist, you search for properties that look worse than they really are with the hope that a quick makeup job is all the house really needs. But sometimes even a great property needs a more intensive facelift — maybe all new windows, a fancy new front door, or great new flooring — to bring it to life.

In this chapter, I show you how to tackle some moderate makeovers that can improve the quality of the home, increase its value and marketability, and attract buyers.

Installing Replacement Windows

When you're flipping a house with worn, aging windows in a neighborhood where most homes have updated windows, replacing the windows becomes a necessity. New windows not only look nice, but they also conserve energy and make window washing a lot easier. Figures 18-1 and 18-2 demonstrate the appeal of new windows. The bedroom looks plain with old windows, but new windows make a stylish difference.

Figure 18-1: Old windows give a room a droopy-eyed appearance.

©Jeremy Goodell

Figure 18-2: New windows make the room more perky.

©Jeremy Goodell

In the following sections, I discuss different window options and provide a few tips on cutting the costs of new windows.

TIP

When you design your marketing flyers (see Chapter 21), highlight the fact that the house has all new windows, and make sure that the MLS listing includes information about the new windows (see Chapter 7 for more about the MLS). This tactic not only advertises the new windows to potential buyers but also passes the word along to the appraiser.

Knowing your window options

REMEMBER

When shopping for new windows, call around for estimates. Every town and city in the country has plenty of window installers and building supply stores with a wide selection of windows. Building supply stores typically carry a selection of standard-size windows, or you can order custom windows if the window openings aren't standard sizes. Windows also vary based on how you install them:

- **New-construction windows:** If you're going to re-side the house (see Chapter 16), consider buying new-construction windows and having your contractor install them before hanging the new siding. New-construction windows attach to the studs on the outside of the house. If the house is stucco or brick, new construction windows aren't an option.
- **Replacement windows:** Replacement windows include a frame that fits in the old window opening. You remove the old sashes and any sliding mechanism that's in place and mount the new window in the opening. You usually have to remove some trim, but if you're careful, you can reuse the old trim. The best part of this job is that it doesn't require a ladder. Installation is an inside job.

If you're flipping a high-end house, stick with the top brands, including Andersen and Pella. For lower-end homes, middle-of-the-line vinyl or fiberglass replacement windows are sufficient.

TIP

You can add a nice touch to a kitchen or dining-room window by replacing a standard window with a garden window. A garden window is like a small bay window that juts out from the house.

Tossing your money out the replacement window

Some time ago, I called around for estimates on having replacement windows installed on a house that had 17 windows. I asked each contractor to supply me with a price to cover both the windows and installation, and I chose the least expensive window from each supplier. In terms of quality and energy savings, all the windows were comparable. Prices ranged from $5,000 to $12,000. That's about $300 to $700 per window. Quite a range.

I went down to the local building supply store to price comparable windows. They sold for about $160 apiece, not installed. The low estimate I had received from the replacement window company wasn't bad, but a couple of the high ones were astronomical. It made me think that maybe I was in the wrong business.

The moral of the story is to shop around. For realistic prices on windows, visit your local hardware store before making any final decisions.

Trimming the cost of new windows

REMEMBER

Most window companies make more money on the installation of new windows than on the windows themselves, mostly because installing windows doesn't require a great deal of expertise. The two critical tasks in window installation are measuring the existing opening and making sure that the window is square. You can significantly cut the costs of replacing windows by doing one of the following:

- **Buy locally:** The window companies that advertise on TV have the highest markups to pay for all the advertising. For more competitive prices, check your local phone book or hardware store.
- **Do it yourself:** If you're handy with a tape measure, square, and screwdriver, consider doing it yourself and saving the cost of labor.
- **Hire a subcontractor:** If you see workers installing windows in the neighborhood, pay them a visit. They're generally subcontractors working for a big window company. Ask them the best place to buy windows. If the installers are entrepreneurs, they usually offer to look at your house and provide an estimate. This enables you to cut out the middleman and directly hire professional installers for a lot less. Just be sure that the subcontractor has his own insurance or is insured under your homeowner's policy, as I explain in Chapter 4.
- **Hire a handyman:** Buy windows at your local building supply store and hire a handyman to install them. See Chapter 4 for full details on hiring subcontractors and handymen.

TIP

A good installer spends time measuring the existing window openings and ordering the right-sized windows. Measuring is the most critical step during the installation. Some installers cut corners by ordering windows that give them plenty of room for error, and then they shove a bunch of insulation around the frame and tack up the trim to hide the huge gaps. Measure the window openings yourself and compare measurements before ordering the windows. If you see discrepancies, ask the installers to explain.

Replacing Drab, Weathered Doors

Savvy buyers inspect every door in the house. When they walk through a doorway, they can't help but notice the door, and many buyers open and close the doors to make sure that they're working properly. Home inspectors follow the same routine, so you want your doors and doorways to look nice and function properly. If you have a sliding glass door that takes a gorilla to shove open, you have a problem.

In the following sections, I lead you through the process of ensuring that all the doors in your house meet market demands and steer you clear of the types of doors that can lead to problems.

Doing the quick fix with a new storm door

Storm doors are notorious problem areas. In a strong wind, a storm door acts as a sail, catching the wind broadside and nearly being ripped off its hinges. Over time, the screens rip, the metal gets dented, and the rod on the door closer gets bent.

Because the storm door or screen door is on the outside of the house, it often contributes more to curb appeal than the main entry door itself. If it looks bad, replace it. You can purchase a quality storm door for around $100 and install it yourself in an hour or two. Standard white is typically the color of choice, but check out the neighborhood to see whether another color predominates.

Replacing an entry door

You may think that entry doors never go out of style, but some of the old designs look about as appealing as a leisure suit. Walk around the neighborhood and check out the entry doors. Chances are that one or two of your neighbors have already replaced their doors with something more appealing or more secure.

Your entry door should help your house blend with the neighborhood. Installing a $500 fiberglass entry door with leaded glass in a neighborhood where solid wood doors are prevalent may make the house look gaudy instead of adding a touch of class. In most areas, a solid door with a nice stain or a fresh coat of paint that complements the exterior colors is sufficient for achieving the desired curb appeal.

TIP

Organizations like Habitat for Humanity often have stores where you can pick up scratch-and-dent doors and other building materials at bargain prices. You can purchase a quality metal door that's dented, patch it with auto body filler, sand it down, and paint it, and have a beautiful entry door for less than $100.

If the entry door opens and closes easily but just looks bad, consider refinishing it rather than replacing it. See Chapter 16 for more about jazzing up an entry door.

Repairing or replacing sliding glass doors

If you've ever seen a real estate agent or a buyer grapple with a stubborn sliding glass door, you know that these doors aren't the best when it comes to selling houses. The tracks gather dust and dirt, the rollers get gummed up, and over time you wonder what the manufacturer meant by "sliding." In the following sections, I provide tips on improving the operation of sliding glass doors and recommend some more-appropriate replacement doors.

TIP

Fixing a sliding door that's lost its slide

When your patio door loses its slide, it's time for a cleaning and lube job. Take the following steps to place the glide back in the slide:

1. **Use a toothbrush or a paintbrush with stiff bristles to loosen the dirt and grease that has gathered in the tracks, and then vacuum the debris out.**

   Clean the track both with the door open and with it closed so you cover all your tracks. If you use a toothbrush, make sure to use your spouse's and not yours!

2. **Spray a lubricant on the tracks and slide the door back and forth on the track to get it lubed up.**

3. **If you still have trouble opening and closing the door, play with the adjustment screws at the top and bottom of the door.**

   These screws raise or lower the wheels that ride on the tracks.

4. **If you can get to the wheels, spray some lubricant on them.**
5. **Lube the lock by removing it and spraying it with a lubricant.**

Replacing patio doors for a whole new look

When I install new patio doors on a house, I never install the sliding variety. Single or double French doors (the ones that open like normal doors) require much less maintenance, and you don't have to throw your back out opening them. Figures 18-3 and 18-4 demonstrate the improvement you can expect to see when you install a new patio door. Of course, several other upgrades, including hardwood flooring, a redone fireplace, and recessed lighting, also contribute to giving this particular room a whole new look.

TIP

In a house that has no clear exit to the backyard, one of the best ways to improve the marketability of the house is to add a door. See Chapter 19 for details about creating a new doorway and performing other more-extensive renovations.

Figure 18-3: This old patio door looks weathered.

©Jeremy Goodell

Figure 18-4: French doors improve both look and function.

©Jeremy Goodell

Installing new interior doors

Interior doors on bedrooms, dens, and bathrooms can take a beating, especially if the previous owners were door slammers or had neurotic pets who liked to scratch and chew doors. Make sure that the interior doors open and close easily and completely and that they look good, too. Depending on the condition of the doors, you have several options here:

- **Change the hardware:** If you have trouble opening and closing a door, you may need to change the doorknobs and install new hinges, which are fairly easy do-it-yourself repairs.
- **Refinish the doors:** If the finish is dull or scratched, remove the doors, sand them, and stain them so all the doors in the house match and look fresh.
- **Replace the doors:** If someone punched a hole through the door or it has deep scratches, consider replacing the door. An average interior door unit, complete with trim, costs around $100 and is about as easy to install as a replacement window. If your carpentry skills aren't up to snuff, consider hiring an installer or handyman.

Putting on Your Own Floor Show

New flooring is a necessity in a house that has well-trafficked, old, or damaged floors. In most rooms, new wall-to-wall carpeting is the most cost-effective option and provides you with the biggest bang for your buck (see Chapter 15 for details). In kitchens and bathrooms, however, you almost always need to lay new vinyl, linoleum, or ceramic tile, and you should sand and refinish any hardwood floors.

You may not get all your money back on the cost of refinishing floors or installing new flooring, but it's still a good investment. After you paint the house and install new light fixtures, registers, and faceplates, old flooring can make the house look like a dirt-floor hut. In the following sections, I show you several options for new flooring. For complete steps on how to lay vinyl and how to repair and refinish hardwood floors, check out *Home Improvement For Dummies,* by Gene Hamilton and Katie Hamilton (Wiley).

Laying vinyl or linoleum flooring

Next to carpeting, vinyl and linoleum are the most affordable flooring options, and because they resist water, they're perfect for kitchens, bathrooms, and laundry rooms. In addition, if the existing floor isn't warped or damaged, you can apply a new layer of vinyl or linoleum over the old. Costs are comparable for linoleum and vinyl, although linoleum tends to last about three times longer and is considered the "green" (environmentally friendly) option.

TIP

For bathrooms, laundry rooms, and other areas that get drenched, install sheet vinyl rather than the square tile vinyl or linoleum. Water tends to seep between the edges where the tiles meet and get under the tile, completely ruining the floor. Whether you install vinyl or linoleum, consider hiring an experienced flooring installer; gluing down tiles may sound easy, but installers have the right technique for making sure the tile lies flat and meets the walls just right.

Refinishing hardwood floors

In the 1970s and 1980s, sellers commonly hid their hardwood floors under a layer of cheap wall-to-wall carpeting, as if the hardwood was an ugly blemish. Now, when you stumble upon a house that has hardwood floors, it's almost like striking gold.

In Chapter 17, I mention that many do-it-yourselfers choose to sand and refinish hardwood floors themselves, something I discourage. Floor sanders have a nasty habit of taking off on you and digging deep gouges into the floor. If you don't know what you're doing, you can easily sand a hole clear through the flooring! And if you don't apply the stain just right, the finish appears splotchy. Hire a professional.

Laying new hardwood or laminate flooring

In a room that has damaged or severely worn hardwood floors and in rooms with carpeting or vinyl that are crying out for a touch of wood, consider having new hardwood or laminate flooring installed. As Figures 18-5 and 18-6 demonstrate, a new wood floor adds class and distinction to a home.

Figure 18-5: A large room with carpeting may not have the pop you're looking for.

©Jeremy Goodell

Figure 18-6: A new wood floor adds character and class.

©Jeremy Goodell

After you decide to put down new wood flooring, you have a decision to make: hardwood or laminate flooring? Most home buyers drool over hardwood floors, and they get pretty excited about laminate floors, which look like wood and cost about the same but clean up like tile. Personally, I prefer hardwood because it looks classier and lasts longer, and you can refinish it when it starts to look bad, but let your market be your guide.

TIP

Both hardwood and laminate look great, assuming they're properly installed. Hire a craftsman, not a butcher. Ask for references and then visit the homes where the installer laid the floor.

Laying ceramic tile for a touch of class

Homeowners love the look of ceramic tile flooring, but after they live in a house that has it in the kitchen or bathroom, they often change their minds. Drop a glass on a ceramic tile floor, and it shatters into a million pieces that fly everywhere. And if the tile gets a little grease and water on it, watch out! You'll be sliding right out of the kitchen.

However, you *can* install ceramic tile in the foyer — the area near the front door where visitors typically kick off their shoes. Tile not only looks nice, but it also makes this area easier to keep clean through your many house showings.

If the market demands ceramic tile floors, you need to meet those demands. If it doesn't, stick with vinyl or linoleum, which I cover earlier in this chapter.

At $10 to $15 per square foot, ceramic tile is the most expensive flooring option. Assuming the tiles don't crack or chip, they last forever, but even so, you probably won't see a big return on investment by choosing ceramic tile over vinyl. Some vinyl tile options look suspiciously like their ceramic equivalents.

Chapter 19

Reconfiguring Spaces and Other Structural Overhauls

In This Chapter

- Avoiding (or embracing) the temptation to fiddle with the floor plan
- Keeping the roof from crashing down by identifying load-bearing walls
- Expanding the living space with room modifications and additions
- Decking out the house with a deck or patio

Repairing and renovating a house is one thing. Restructuring it, converting storage space into living space, building room additions, and performing other structural overhauls is another beast entirely.

First, you need to decide whether a structural overhaul even makes sense. Misguided renovators often ruin a perfectly good floor plan by opening up too much space or chopping wide open spaces into tiny rooms. Then, you have to calculate the costs and benefits — major restructuring costs major moola. Will you get enough money back when you sell to make the restructuring worth your time and effort?

In this chapter, I guide you through the process of deciding whether you really want to monkey around with the floor plan. I reveal some techniques for identifying load-bearing walls, and I offer suggestions on restructuring and building projects that can add real value to a property.

Attending to Essential Structure and Infrastructure Repairs

Before you even think about performing major structural enhancements, attend to the structural and infrastructural repairs required to keep the house standing and the electricity and water flowing. In most cases, these repairs require building permits and the intervention of licensed contractors to ensure that the repairs adhere to local building codes:

- **Foundation:** If the basement walls are bowing in, the house is settling unevenly, or the basement or crawlspace is damp, hire a company that specializes in foundations to shore it up. Foundation repairs are costly, sometimes creeping into the tens of thousands of dollars, but you should already have budgeted for the repairs. (See Chapter 11 for more about estimating rehab costs.)
- **Electrical:** An electrical system that's not up to code not only makes the lights flicker but can also start fires. Have the electrical system checked and brought up to code by a licensed electrician.
- **Plumbing:** You may be able to perform minor plumbing repairs, but if the pipes are leaking inside the walls, water is backing up into the house, or you can't unclog the drains, call a licensed plumber. In some cases, such as with lead pipes, you may need to replace all the pipes, which may require tearing out walls and tearing up floors.
- **Furnace and air conditioning:** Whether the house needs a new furnace or air-conditioning unit or you plan to install ductwork in a house to add central air, hire a licensed HVAC (heating, ventilation, and air conditioning) technician to do the work.

Fiddling with the Floor Plan . . . or Not

When constructing a house, builders follow standard design principles and adhere to specific structural limitations. Older houses, for example, rely on load-bearing walls to support the roof and ceilings (see the next section for more about these types of walls). In newer houses, truss roofs eliminate the need for load-bearing walls, giving architects the freedom to design floor plans that allow fluid movement from one room to the next. In either case, if you begin fiddling with the floor plan and you don't know what you're doing, you risk lowering the value of the property and causing costly structural damage.

SANITY CHECK

Before you begin restructuring a house or converting unused areas into livable space, take the Hippocratic Oath and promise to "First, do no harm." Tell your agent what you're planning and consult a licensed contractor, letting them know that you want them to be brutally honest with you. They can help steer you clear of any big ideas that are likely to result in a train wreck. Then, plan your renovations carefully, as I explain in Chapter 14.

TIP

If you're living in the house you're flipping and are in no hurry to sell it, consider waiting a few weeks before you start renovating. Over time, problems in the floor plan tend to reveal themselves to you. The kitchen may seem cramped, or you may notice that you never use the breakfast nook. You can then make better decisions on how to restructure your living areas to improve flow and use.

Identifying Load-Bearing Walls

Before you take a sledgehammer to that nuisance of a wall, realize that it may store many surprises — electrical wiring, plumbing, and ductwork. In addition, that wall may be supporting the second story or the roof. Knock out that wall, and the whole house may cave in . . . with you in it. In the following sections, I define "load-bearing wall" and show you how to identify such walls.

TIP

Before tearing out a wall, strip the drywall or plaster off the studs to see what's behind it. If you find a costly surprise and change your mind, you're out only the cost of hanging new drywall. If you knock out the wall with a sledgehammer, you may find yourself paying for new plumbing, new electrical lines, and new ductwork, as well.

What is a load-bearing wall?

Load-bearing walls are the pillars of your investment. They transfer the weight of whatever is above them — the upper floor or the roof — to the foundation. Houses have three types of load-bearing walls:

- The outside walls of the house are always load-bearing walls because they support the roof.
- In a house with a conventional roof frame, interior walls that run perpendicular to the rafters support the roof. A truss roof requires no support from interior walls; it rests entirely on the outside walls of the house.
- In a house with two or more stories, interior walls or beams that are perpendicular to an upper story's floor joists bear the load of the upper story.

REMEMBER

You can remove a load-bearing wall, but never without replacing it with a support that's equally strong or stronger than what you're taking away.

How are conventional and truss roofs different?

All roofs have joists that span the distance between the front and back or side walls of a house. A house with a conventional roof frame typically has an attic and requires an interior load-bearing wall to support the joists.

Truss roof frames consist of a web of boards (typically 2 x 4s) that enable the roof to support itself by resting on only two exterior walls. Truss roof frames make removing interior walls much easier. The tradeoff is that truss roof frames provide little or no open space for an attic.

To figure out the type of roof your house has, check the attic. Search the ceilings, especially in hallways, closets, and the attached garage, for a pull-down staircase or access door. You may also be able to sneak a peek through a cubbyhole in the upper floor. If you have plenty of open space in the attic, chances are good that a load-bearing wall on the floor below is supporting the joists.

If you have a conventional roof with a lot of open space in the attic that you don't want to convert into a room (see "Creating a room in the attic," later in this chapter, for more info about converting the attic), consider using it to beef up the storage space. Add a pull-down staircase, lay sheets of plywood over the joists to create a floor, and add a couple of light sockets and a switch for turning the lights on and off.

Is this wall load-bearing?

You can't tell whether a wall is load-bearing just by looking at it. You need to know what's above the wall and what's below it:

- If the house has a basement, go downstairs and find out what's below the wall. If the wall above has a wall or beam below it, the wall above is probably the load-bearing variety.
- If the wall is below an attic, go to the attic and determine whether its floor joists are running perpendicular to the wall below. If they are, the wall is probably supporting the attic floor.
- If the floor joists are hidden by a floor above or a ceiling below, you may need to chip away some of the ceiling to determine whether the joists run perpendicular to the wall.

I've seen houses with floor joists that run one direction on part of the house and the opposite direction on another part, so don't assume that all the floor joists upstairs run in the same direction. You may have a situation in which two walls that meet at right angles are *both* supporting the roof!

If you decide to remove a load-bearing wall, an engineer can recommend options for replacing the wall with another structure that provides equal or superior support. And always obtain a building permit from your town's building inspector and ensure that your planned changes comply with building codes in your area.

Maximizing the Use of Existing Space

Dinky homes in the midst of mansions cry out for expansion. When buyers are touring the neighborhood in search of a home that can accommodate all family members comfortably, they may skip past a cramped crib. For a flipper, however, that scanty shanty may be just the bargain you've been looking for. By opening up existing space and transforming unused space into living space, you can often boost the house into a higher price bracket.

Every house has unique expansion opportunities, so I can't tell you the best solution for the property you're renovating, but the following sections offer some ideas to stimulate your creativity.

Knocking out walls

TIP

Although I provide plenty of cautionary advice to make you think twice about knocking down walls, a little demolition can often add real value to a house. Here are some ideas you may want to consider:

- By knocking out walls and perhaps raising the ceiling (see the next section), you may be able to combine the kitchen, living room, and dining room to create a *great room.*
- If combining the kitchen, living room, and dining room isn't an option, but the house has a small eating area off the kitchen, consider combining the two areas to transform them into a *country kitchen* — a kitchen that encompasses a large eating area.
- If a house has four or five bedrooms, none of which qualifies as a master suite, combining two small neighboring bedrooms into a master bedroom can often make a house more attractive and comfortable for the king and queen.
- In some cases, the previous owners may have erected a wall to create a closet, laundry room, or pantry, compromising the original floor plan. In such cases, the wall is typically not a supporting wall, and you can easily remove it to restore the original floor plan.

Figures 19-1 and 19-2 demonstrate the appeal of knocking out a wall to enhance a home's living space. In Figure 19-1, a wall awkwardly separates the kitchen and the laundry room.

Figure 19-1: This kitchen feels a little cramped.

©Jeremy Goodell

Figure 19-2: By knocking out a wall, the space becomes more airy and expansive.

©Jeremy Goodell

The homeowner knocked out the wall to increase the space of the kitchen and moved the washer and dryer into a new closet-style laundry room. You can see the result — a lighter, brighter, roomier kitchen — in Figure 19-2.

Raising the ceiling

Expanding a room by moving walls may exceed your budget, but depending on the roof structure, you may be able to remove the existing ceiling to reveal the rafters. Although raising the ceiling to the rafters doesn't open up more living space, it can make the area *feel* roomier and add a touch of character. If you're replacing the roof, as well, consider adding a skylight or two to really light up the room. (Chapter 16 has more information about laying a new roof.)

TIP: I install skylights only if I'm redoing the roof. If you install them in an old roof, they never seem to seal properly, and you end up creating a rainforest in the living room.

WARNING! Before attempting to raise the ceiling, explore the space above the ceiling to determine the type of roof structure in place. See "How are conventional and truss roofs different?" earlier in this chapter. If the house has a truss roof frame, you probably won't be able to raise the ceiling at all.

Designing a whole new kitchen

Sometimes, no matter what you do to an existing kitchen, it's not enough. The layout of the kitchen was wrong from the day it was designed, and now you have to do something about it to open it up and make it more functional. In Chapters 1 and 11, I discuss the potential investment return on kitchen renovations.

Your first step is to pick up a copy of *Kitchen Remodeling For Dummies,* by Donald R. Prestly (Wiley). That book introduces the four standard kitchen shapes — L-shaped, U-shaped, G-shaped, and I-shaped — and explores the mysteries of the work triangle to illustrate basic kitchen design principles that make a kitchen usable.

Your next step is to read the book and remodel the kitchen yourself or head down to the local home-improvement store or cabinet supplier and ask a kitchen designer for assistance. Most stores provide free consultations as long as you buy your building materials from them. (See Chapter 17 for general details on updating a kitchen.)

Adding a bathroom

A great way to add real value to a home that has only one bathroom is to convert underutilized space into a second bathroom or a *powder room.* A powder room (commonly referred to as a *half bath*) consists of the bare essentials — a toilet, a sink, and a mirror. You can cram one of these puppies under a stairwell or into a medium-sized closet. For a *three-quarter bath* (with room enough for a sink, toilet, and shower) or larger, you need a room that's at least 8 feet by 8 feet.

Unless you're a licensed plumber and electrician, hire a pro to convert underutilized space into a bathroom. No matter where you decide to locate it, a new bathroom is a mini-construction project.

If you plan on designing the bathroom and doing most of the work yourself, check out *Bathroom Remodeling For Dummies,* by Gene Hamilton and Katie Hamilton (Wiley). This handy guide leads you step by step through the tasks of designing the bathroom; installing bathtubs, showers, sinks, toilets, and vanities; and even roughing in the plumbing. (See Chapter 17 for additional information on redoing a bathroom.)

Spreading out to an attached garage

In a small house with an attached garage, converting the garage into a living room, den, or additional bedroom often adds real value to a house. You can wall off the space left by the old garage door or install a patio door in its place. If the garage has an attic, it may offer additional opportunities for growth.

Because many attached garages aren't heated or air conditioned, your renovation may require you to install additional insulation and baseboard heat, but stop short of adding a window air conditioner — it makes the house look cheap. Don't convert a garage into living space unless you can make it comfortable living space.

If you decide to convert an attached garage into living space, also consider building a new garage. I've seen homeowners transform an existing garage into living space only to have a buyer come along and ask the homeowner to convert it back into a garage. You really need to know what most home buyers want before investing a lot of money in conversion projects.

Transforming a porch into a room

Some older homes have enclosed porches that you can transform into a bedroom or home office. A porch conversion typically adds to the square footage of the house, thereby adding real value and increasing the property's salability.

Figure 19-4: Adding a deck allows the party to spill out from the kitchen to the backyard.

©Jeremy Goodell

If you have some open back-wall space, consider installing a patio door where no doorway currently exists. You may also be able to replace a large window with a patio door that lets in more light, in addition to giving the house another entryway. If the window is more narrow than a doorway, you may be able to widen the opening enough to fit a door.

You can add a patio door out to the deck for anywhere from $250 to $1,500. You may be able to pick up a good-quality patio door for much less from a Habitat for Humanity distribution center or similar organization that sells scratch-and-dent building supplies.

WARNING!

Cutting a hole through the wall in the back of the house is no job for amateurs. Some walls support the roof. Others have electrical wiring, plumbing, or heat ducts inside them.

SANITY CHECK

In some areas, sunrooms (often called *solariums*) are a popular feature. You can add a sunroom to just about any house. Most sunroom manufacturers offer kits for the do-it-yourselfer. However, unless most of the neighboring homes have sunrooms or enclosed porches, I don't recommend adding a sunroom to the house. Even if you do a classy job and the sunroom fits with the style of the existing structure, you probably won't recoup your investment.

REMEMBER

Adding or updating a deck or patio is an affordable way to transform this unused space into an outdoor sanctuary, where families and friends can gather on evenings and weekends to grill out and chill out without having to make too much of a mess in the house. Installing a patio door for easy passage between the house and deck is a nice addition that can also let in more light, making the interior appear larger.

Figures 19-3 and 19-4 illustrate how much a few affordable modifications can improve curb appeal while expanding living space. The homeowner replaced the old, cracked concrete patio with a larger concrete/brick patio. He also built a new lattice-topped wooden patio cover.

Costs for patios and decks range from about $500 to $5,000 depending on the size of the project and the costs of materials and labor. A small team of weekend warriors can slap together an average deck in a day or two.

WARNING!

I'm not a big fan of building a patio with *pavers* (stone or concrete blocks). I had a beautiful patio with pavers, but I got tired of looking at the weeds growing through, so I replaced them with a concrete patio.

Figure 19-3: This underutilized backyard has a lot of potential.

©Jeremy Goodell

- **Cash flow:** With a buy-and-hold strategy, you use the property to generate cash flow that you can use to finance future flips and build your real estate empire. The buy-and-hold strategy offers several valuable benefits:
  - By holding the property for at least one year and a day, your profit is taxed as a long-term capital gain at a rate that's significantly lower than that for short-term capital gains. See Chapter 23 for details.
  - You claim depreciation of the property as a tax deduction. This is a rare tax situation in which you claim depreciation as the property appreciates.
  - You profit in four ways — when you buy the property below market value, when the property appreciates over time, when the rent from your tenants pays down the principal on the loan, and when you perform repairs and renovations that raise the property's value.
  - You can deduct any expenses you incur for the maintenance and management of the property.
- **Both:** One option provides both cash flow and cash: selling the property on contract, usually to a buyer who doesn't qualify for traditional financing. You essentially become the bank, collecting payments (including interest) from the buyers until they pay off the loan in full, either over the course of many years or after only two or three years by refinancing with a traditional lender and paying you the balance due on the loan.

WARNING!

If you're considering a buy-and-hold approach, keep in mind that not everyone is landlord material. You have to find renters, collect the rent, maintain the property, and be able to handle calls from tenants at any time of the day or night. You may be able to hire a property-management company to take care of all this for you, but that cuts into your profits. If you're considering the leasing option, I strongly recommend *Property Management Kit For Dummies,* by Robert S. Griswold (Wiley).

Cashing Out: Selling the Property

Real estate investors who flip houses typically don't like to hold on to properties for very long. They buy properties, renovate them, and put them right back on the market, or they sell to another investor who renovates and sells

Chapter 20

Considering Your Options: Cash or Cash Flow ?

In This Chapter

- Weighing the pros and cons of cash versus cash flow
- Investigating two approaches to selling a property
- Taking a buy-and-hold approach to generate cash flow

Although this book focuses on flipping houses — the buy-fix-sell approach — you don't necessarily have to sell a property to pull your profit out of it. You have other options, including refinancing to cash out the equity, leasing the property, and selling it on contract (a lease-to-own arrangement). A couple of these options may even maximize the total profit you earn off the property.

The choice of whether to sell or pursue some other cash-out strategy hinges on whether you want cash or cash flow. Do you want to pull your profit out all at once or use the property to generate a stream of income? In the following sections, I provide guidance on how to weigh your options, and then I explain each option in greater detail.

Setting a Goal: Cash or Cash Flow

You made your money when you bought the property, but how are you going to realize that profit? Your choices hinge on whether you're wanting cash, cash flow, or both:

- **Cash:** You sell the property to a traditional buyer or to another investor, stick the money in your pocket or bank account, and move on to the next flip. Selling out is a great choice if you don't like the complexities of buying and holding a property and taking on tenants.

In this part...

- Choose a cash-out strategy: sell (to cash out right now), lease (to establish cash flow), or sell on contract (lease to own, for the best of both worlds).
- Cash out equity to finance repairs and renovations.
- Market a property with or without the assistance of a top-notch real estate agent.
- Price your property to sell quickly and for a reasonable profit.
- Stage a home inside and out to make it more appealing to prospective buyers.
- Haggle successfully with prospective buyers to get most of what you want without sinking the deal.
- Maximize your net profit with tax-saving tips.

Part V

Cashing In: Realizing Your Profit

Five Ways to Get Cash Out of Your Flip

- **Sell it.** The buy-fix-sell approach is the fastest way to cash out your entire profit from a flip.
- **Cash out the equity.** Refinance the property or take out a home-equity line of credit to help finance the costs of renovating, holding, and selling the property.
- **Lease to a renter.** Leasing a property isn't technically flipping, but it's a good alternative to selling, especially if you're looking for ways to establish cash flow.
- **Sell it on contract.** Using a lease-option agreement, you can set up a rent-to-own arrangement with an interested party — usually someone who doesn't qualify for traditional financing.
- **Sell it to another investor.** If you enjoy house hunting but don't like to get your hands dirty with renovations, consider acting as a bird-dog, finding properties and then selling them to investors for a fee that generally ranges from about $5,000 to $10,000.

web extras

Although real estate investors hope that property values continue to rise, the reality is that sometimes the housing market takes a nose dive. When that happens, you have to be more aggressive in competing against other homes for sale in the same market. Visit `www.dummies.com/extras/flippinghouses` to learn how to ramp up your efforts in a slow housing market.

Buy-sell: Selling to another investor

If you enjoy the hunt but nothing else about flipping houses appeals to you, you can still make money in the house-flipping business. The buy-sell strategy has two approaches:

- **Find the property, actually purchase it, and then turn around and sell it to an investor.** The drawback to this approach is that you have to pay at least a portion of the closing costs both when you buy and sell the property. In addition, if the investor you plan to sell the property to backs out, you're stuck with it — you have to find another investor or fix and sell the property yourself. In either case, you have holding costs to consider.
- **Flip contracts.** To flip a contract, you find a property with profit potential, negotiate the sale price and terms with the seller, and have the seller sign an agreement (a contract) to sell the property to you or to your *assigns* — anyone you want the property sold to. You then find a willing buyer and exchange the contract for a finder's fee. People who flip contracts are often referred to as "bird dogs" because they find property for the hunters (the investors who ultimately purchase the property).

  TIP: When you sign the contract, write "and/or assigns" after your name. For example, if your name is Joan Johnson, you'd sign "Joan Johnson and/or assigns." This gives anyone you decide you want the property sold to the right to buy it.

Exploring Cash-Flow Possibilities

Buying a property, fixing it up (or not), and then placing it back on the market is the most common way to profit from your real estate investment, but it's not the only way. You can instantly profit from your property by refinancing your loan to pull the equity out of it, or you can sell or lease the property back to the previous owners, or even sell the senior mortgage you bought at a foreclosure auction to another lienholder.

In the following sections, I reveal several strategies to pull the equity out of your property, along with other novel ways to profit from your real estate investment.

the property or keeps it as a rental. Either way, the house flipper rids herself of the property, cashes out her profit, and has more capital to invest in the next property.

The following sections explain two ways you can cash out by selling the property: putting the property back on the market or selling to another investor.

Buy-fix-sell: Listing the property for sale

Taking the buy-fix-sell approach consists of purchasing a property, renovating it, and holding it just long enough to make at least a 20 percent profit above the costs to buy, fix, hold, and sell the property. For more about marketing and selling the property for top dollar, see Chapter 21.

TIP

If you're going to list the property for sale, I strongly encourage you to list it with one of the top real estate agents in your area, preferably a member of the National Association of Realtors.

Sell it yourself?

Homeowners often try to sell their homes on their own to avoid paying an agent commission, but it rarely saves them enough to justify the hassle. What usually happens is that when a buyer shows up to place an offer on the house, the buyer knows that the seller is saving about 6 percent by listing the home himself. So, the buyer automatically deducts 6 percent from his offer. If the seller accepts that offer, he essentially gives the buyer as much money as he would have paid an agent, and the seller had to do all the work without the additional benefits of having professional assistance and advice. According to the National Association of Realtors, the typical FSBO home sells for $174,900, compared to $215,000 for agent-assisted home sales!

Most people choose to sell sans agent because they've had a bad experience with a real estate agent or felt that the agent didn't do enough to justify his 6 percent commission. This is a very valid point, but it simply means that the seller didn't pick the right agent.

When selling a house, don't just look at the cost of hiring an agent. Look at the cost of not hiring an agent and consider the benefits that an agent brings to the table . . . particularly the closing table.

Refinancing to cash out the equity

Homeowners commonly refinance their homes to cash out equity. To refinance, you take out a new mortgage for more than you currently owe on the property and pay off the old mortgage. Assuming you purchased the property significantly below market value and your credit is in pretty good shape, you may be able to turn right around after the purchase and refinance to cash out that equity.

I say "may" because some lenders won't refinance a mortgage until after you've owned a home for six months and a day, a year and a day, or even two years and a day. This is because a house is only worth what you actually paid for it or what it appraises for, whichever is lower. A home-equity loan to cover repairs and renovations, however, is often easier to obtain.

TIP

You don't have to cash out all the equity in a property. You can cash out a portion of it to cover the cost of repairs and renovations and cash out the rest of the equity when you sell the property.

When refinancing to cash out the equity in a home, be as careful shopping for mortgages as you were when you borrowed the money to purchase the property. Avoid high-cost loans and any loans that have prepayment penalties, especially if you're planning to place the house back on the market soon. See Chapter 5 for guidance on shopping for low-cost loans.

Reselling a foreclosure property to the previous owners . . . or their family

After you officially own a foreclosure property, it's yours to sell, and the previous homeowners have to move out . . . if they didn't move out already. Sometimes after foreclosure, however, the homeowners break the news to other family members who are in a position to bail them out by loaning or gifting them money or buying the house and letting them live in it. In such cases, you may be able to sell the property back to the original owners or their family.

In the following sections, I reveal some do's and don'ts that apply to these situations, along with some of the positive aspects of selling a foreclosure back to the previous owners.

Reselling to the previous owners

The previous owners are likely to do whatever it takes to remain in their home. If their financial situation has improved since the foreclosure or friends and family members have offered them a good chunk of cash, they may now be in a position to buy back the property. The opportunity, however, is not always available or attractive for you as an investor. Keep the following caveats in mind:

- **If the property has any liens against it that were wiped off the books by the foreclosure, those liens reattach themselves to the property if the previous homeowners buy it back.** This can often drive the homeowners back into foreclosure, which isn't something you or they really want.

  TIP: If selling the home back to the previous homeowners is not an option because of the possibility of having other liens reattach to the property, you may be able to sell to a family member who agrees to let the homeowners remain living in the house.

- **You can't strip the homeowners of all the equity they have built up in the property.** Say, for example, you purchase a property worth $300,000 for $175,000. If you sell it back to the previous homeowners for $300,000, you've taken all the equity out of the house. You have two options here — sell the house to someone else for $300,000 or sell it back to the previous owners at a discount of, say, $250,000. Whatever you do, you don't want to be an equity stripper. See the following sidebar, "Equity stripping — Don't do it!" for details.

Why would you agree to accept less than full market value for the house? Whenever I can earn a quick, tidy profit on a house and do the right thing for the homeowners, I jump at the chance. Usually, I develop a close relationship with the homeowners during the foreclosure process, and I don't want to destroy their trust by taking them to the cleaners. In addition, I don't want to ruin my reputation in the community — I'm in it for the long term. If I treat the homeowners fairly, they're likely to recommend me to others they know who find themselves in similar situations. If you can earn a fair profit while helping your fellow human beings, I strongly encourage you to do so. Otherwise, simply have them move out and sell to someone who can afford to pay the full price.

Another reason you may want to consider selling the property back to the previous owners comes down to simple economics. Say you're facing the likelihood of holding the property for six months. At an estimated $100 per day in holding costs, you're looking at a total bill of $18,000. On top of that, figure closing costs of 7 percent on $200,000 (a total of $14,000), and your bill is now up to $32,000. Now figure in your time and effort plus the costs of repairs and renovations. Sure, the homeowners get a break, but you also save yourself some money.

WARNING!

If you took out a traditional loan to purchase the property, your mortgage probably has a due-on-sale clause, which means you can't sell the property back to the previous homeowners without the lender's approval.

Equity stripping — Don't do it!

Homeowners who are facing foreclosure are often unaware of their options and of just how much equity they have built up in their property. They may have been making their monthly mortgage payments for 10 or 15 years while housing values in their neighborhood have been rising at a rate of 5 percent to 10 percent annually. They're completely unaware that the house they bought for $100,000 ten years ago is now worth $150,000, and they've paid off about $14,000 of the principal, so they now have $64,000 worth of equity. All they see are the monthly bills coming in that they can't pay.

Homeowners' ignorance of the amount of equity they have built up in their home can make them vulnerable to predatory lenders and other crooks who want to cash out that equity for themselves. These equity strippers employ a variety of schemes to bleed this money out of the homeowners, including schemes such as these:

- Mortgage brokers attempt to convince the homeowners to refinance their way out of a financial setback by taking out a loan with higher monthly mortgage payments than the homeowners can afford. The mortgage broker rakes in the payments until the homeowner runs out of money, and then the lender forecloses on the property.
- Crooked investors convince homeowners who have a substantial amount of equity built up in their property to sell the property to them for significantly less than the property is worth. The "investor" may promise the homeowners that they can continue living in the home indefinitely, and then, as soon as the homeowners sign the papers, the con artist evicts them.
- Con artists offer to save the homeowners from foreclosure. All the homeowners have to do is sign a quit-claim deed over to the con artist, and the con artist will take care of everything. What the con artist does take care of is re-conveying the property's title to his own name.
- A con artist may offer to buy the home from the homeowners and lease it back to them. The con artist collects the monthly rent and never pays off the underlying mortgage, so the homeowners lose their rent money and lose the house in foreclosure.

If you buy a property directly from a homeowner facing foreclosure or at auction for a bargain-basement price and then sell the property back to the homeowner at full market value, you're practicing yet another form of equity stripping, which the courts frown upon. Regardless of whether you get caught, it's still wrong, and if you do get caught, you can look forward to a hefty fine and perhaps some jail time or at least undoing the transaction and returning the homeowners to the position they were in before they met you.

Financing the buyback through insurance-policy proceeds and other means

Homeowners are often unaware of assets and other collateral they may have to secure financing, or they may come into some quick money after the foreclosure is a done deal. In such cases, you may be able to help the homeowners obtain the funds needed to buy back the property simply by making them aware of their options. Following are two options that may be available:

- **Life insurance policies:** If the home ended up in foreclosure because one of the homeowners passed away and the homeowner had a life insurance policy, cashing out that policy may provide sufficient funds for the surviving homeowner to repurchase the property. In some cases, a serious illness drives a couple into foreclosure, and then the spouse who was seriously ill passes away, leaving behind a life-insurance policy that can cover the purchase price.
- **Retirement savings:** You can borrow against some retirement plans for the purchase of a house. If the homeowners have sufficient retirement savings, they may be able to borrow against it to buy the house back from you.

Leasing the property to the previous owners

Families are often reluctant to move out of their home because they have kids in school. They really need to sell the house and find more affordable accommodations, but they don't want to force their kids to change schools. In such cases, you may want to consider purchasing the property and then leasing it back to the family until the kids move out or the family has more time to plan.

Don't jump into a lease agreement with the previous homeowners before you've performed some serious number crunching. If the homeowners couldn't afford the monthly house payments, don't sign them up for a lease that has them paying monthly rent they can't afford. You'll simply end up with deadbeat renters and set the family up for another failure. Before offering them the option to rent, make sure they've resolved the issues that sent them into foreclosure and that they can afford the rent.

If you decide to rent out the property to the previous homeowners, consult your real estate attorney and have her draw up a lease agreement. Keep in mind that not everyone is cut out to be a landlord.

Offering a lease-option agreement

When a buyer really wants to purchase a property but isn't currently in the financial position to do so (whether they're the previous owners or not), you may consider offering them a lease-option agreement — a rent-to-own arrangement. Perhaps the buyers need more time to secure financing or fix something on their credit report, or they're waiting for an insurance check or another influx of cash. With a lease option, the buyers agree to rent the property from you for a fixed period with the option to purchase the property at the end of that period.

Lease options are not always viable, but if the homeowners can come up with a down payment and provide some assurance that they will be receiving money or be able to qualify for financing in the specified time, a lease option enables you to establish cash flow while you're waiting to sell the property. I usually structure lease-option deals as follows:

- **Down payment:** Normally I require 5 percent to 10 percent down. You may want more money down when dealing with buyers who've just been through foreclosure. You credit them for the down payment by taking it off the purchase price, but a substantial down payment assures you that they're serious. If they can't afford it, they can't afford it — let them move on.
- **Rent:** I usually specify that rent is due on the first of the month and set the rent at about 1 percent of the purchase price or as close to that amount as is affordable. You don't want to be too flexible, but you don't want to break the bank either. I offer a bonus for paying on time and add the monthly payments to the down payment.
- **Terms and conditions:** The agreement should spell out the lease term and conditions. Your lease-option agreement should contain a forfeiture clause stating that non-payment results in the forfeiture of the option and the down payment. The agreement should also contain a statement that the option is exercisable at any time, with no prepayment penalty or anything like that. I tell the renters that if they win the lottery and want to pay it off tomorrow, that's fine by me. I want them to succeed, and I want to realize my profit — the faster the better.

Make sure the renters understand that they are renting with an option. If they don't exercise their option during the option period, they may forfeit it. If they don't pay rent, they may forfeit it. Make the terms clear. Follow up with them throughout the lease-option period, ask how their mortgage hunt is coming along, and refer them to mortgage lenders you may know.

Leveraging your position

Knowing the lienholder positions, as I discuss in Chapter 8, can often open your eyes to win-win situations with other parties who have a financial interest in the property.

I purchased a first mortgage on a property at auction. The house had a second mortgage on it — a lien held by the local police department and our county prosecutor. The owner had pled guilty to drug dealing and had to pay a fine of about $50,000, which was taken as a lien against the house. We were about a week shy of the expiration of the redemption period, and the county was going to redeem us, meaning we stood to get our money back, and that was about all.

I knew from experience that the county didn't want to pay me off and then take possession of the property and have to sell it, so I called the prosecutor in charge of drug seizures in Macomb County and explained the situation to her. I told her that if she would agree not to redeem our first mortgage, we would split our profits with the county 50/50. It took me less than an hour to work out an agreement. She came back with a counteroffer. She wanted a guaranteed minimum of $20,000, which was a smart move on her part. I agreed.

We took possession of the property and sold it for a $37,000 profit. The county received the first $20,000, and we received $17,000. We sold the house pretty quickly and got what we wanted out of it, and the county was able to acquire $20,000 without the hassle of dealing with the property. Had we not struck a deal, we would have walked away with nothing.

The take-home message here is that you have to remain constantly vigilant throughout the foreclosure process and be prepared to deal with the other lienholders. Remain flexible and constantly on the lookout for win-win opportunities . . . otherwise, you may just find yourself the big loser.

TIP

During the paper-signing stage, we get permission to make audio recordings of each conversation. I tell my client that this is a protection for all of us to make sure that we live up to our parts of the agreement. I make sure that we're thorough, that we allow them to ask questions, and that we encourage them to seek legal counsel.

Assigning your position to a junior lienholder

Say you buy the first mortgage at a foreclosure auction (see Chapter 8 for more about foreclosures). Do you have to take possession of the property to make a buck? Nope. You can sell your position to a junior lienholder and avoid the ugliness of eviction and the hassles of repairing and renovating the property. Here's how it works, assuming you're working in an area that has a redemption period:

1. **You buy the first mortgage, either at auction or by negotiating a short sale with the lender, and you pay any back taxes due.** You now have controlling interest in the property.
2. **You wait out the redemption period.** If the property has other liens against it, another investor may buy one of the junior liens. If another investor buys a junior lien on the property, the clock on that redemption period just begins to start ticking, while you're already partially through the redemption period on your investment.
3. **You approach the holder of the junior lien and say something like, "Look, if you buy my interest, I'll sign over my position to you."** Make your offer worth it for the junior lienholder; otherwise, she may be better off redeeming your lien (to gain the controlling interest in the property) and waiting a little longer. If your offer makes sense and the junior lienholder knows what she's doing, she'll find the offer attractive because she gains not only your first mortgage but also your position in the redemption period rather than having the clock reset on the redemption period.

Chapter 21

Marketing Your Home

In This Chapter

- Collaborating with your agent
- Asking the right price for a quick and tidy profit
- Staging the house to earn top dollar
- Enticing buyers with attractive financing
- Marketing your property to draw more prospective buyers

When most sellers think of marketing their properties, they envision classified ads, flyers, and maybe even an Internet listing on one of those For Sale By Owner websites, but marketing encompasses much more than that. It consists of calculating the right asking price — a price that's attractive to buyers yet profitable for you. Marketing includes listing your house on the local Multiple Listing Service (MLS) so word gets out to all the buyers' agents in the area. And no marketing strategy beats the positive word-of-mouth advertising that only your quality craftsmanship and good reputation can generate.

In this chapter, I lead you through the process of marketing your home to spark as much interest as possible and perhaps even trigger a bidding war. Here you discover how to team up with a real estate agent who's well worth his commission, price your home to sell without pricing yourself out of a profit, produce marketing materials and stage the home to dazzle prospective buyers, and provide other amenities that make the deal more attractive to first-time homeowners.

Harnessing the Power of a Real Estate Agent to Market and Sell Your House

In the following sections, I offer guidance on finding an agent who's qualified to sell your house, tell you how to increase the agent's motivation, and discuss how to take advantage of your agent's access to the MLS listings in your area. For general information about the qualities to look for when you hire any agent, whether you're selling or buying a house, head to Chapter 4.

TIP

My offer stands firm. No matter what market you're in, I can help you find the top agent in your area. E-mail me at ralphroberts@ralphroberts.com.

Knowing why you should hire a seller's agent

REMEMBER

When the time comes to sell your investment property, the temptation to sell it yourself and pocket that 6 percent or 7 percent agent commission is enticing. When you're selling a property for $100,000 or more, 6 percent to 7 percent represents a pretty good chunk of your profit. However, after looking at what a seller's agent can do for you, you may want to reconsider. A seller's agent can

- **Price your property accurately for the current market.** See "Setting an Attractive Asking Price," later in this chapter, for more information.
- **Develop an effective marketing plan.**
- **List your property in one or more area MLS listings, advertising it to all buyers' agents in the area.** I cover your agent's access to MLS listings later in this chapter.
- **Show the house to prospective buyers while you work on finding other flipping opportunities.**
- **Sell your property in half the time, on average, it would take you to sell it on your own.** Holding costs average about $100 per day. If an agent sells a house in 30 days that would take you 60 days to sell on your own, she's already earned back $3,000 of the commission you paid and saved you a lot of time and trouble.
- **Assist you in negotiating a higher price and picking the best offer.** (Chapter 22 has the full scoop on negotiating the sale of your rehabbed house.)
- **Offer the security of agent-accompanied showings to pre-qualified buyers so you know you're showing the house only to serious prospects.**
- **Present competitive market analysis to convince a buyer that your asking price is right.** A prospective buyer is more apt to listen to an experienced agent than to a seller.
- **Ensure that all the necessary paperwork is completed and the process flows smoothly from offer to closing.**

SANITY CHECK

I recommend that you sell the property yourself only if you meet the following conditions:

- **Someone walks up to you while you're rehabbing the property and is willing to sign a purchase agreement on the spot.**
- **You're in a sellers' market — an area where you have significantly more buyers than sellers.**
- **The house is on a street that already has plenty of buyer traffic, and you have the best house at the best price.** (Of course, if you follow my guidance throughout this book, you should always have the best house at the best price.)
- **You have the time and desire to show the house at any time of day or night when a buyer calls to see it.**
- **You have the computer skills required to produce slick marketing materials and advertise on the Internet.**
- **You're able to show the house without tipping your hand.**
- **You intend to hire an attorney to approve all the documentation and attend the closing.**

TIP

By listing your house with an agent and paying a fair commission, you strengthen your relationship with the agent and provide the necessary motivation — money. In the future, when your agent discovers a great investment opportunity, she's more likely to call you than some other investor who doesn't use an agent to sell his properties. In real estate, you must give to receive — the more you give, the more you get.

Negotiating with an agent during the selling process

Although agent commissions are negotiable, I discourage sellers from being too stingy on their commissions. An agent receives 6 percent or 7 percent only if he delivers a buyer who ultimately purchases your house. If the buyer's agent delivers the buyer, your agent has to split that commission with the buyer's agent — the split is typically 3 percent or 4 percent for the seller's agent and 3 percent for the buyer's agent. If you go much lower than the standard 6 percent or 7 percent, the agent is going to work harder selling other houses that offer a higher commission. In addition, agents talk, so low-balling an agent could hurt your reputation and harm future sales opportunities.

TIP

A more effective way to negotiate with an agent is to offer a higher seller's commission, especially if you're flipping in a slow market. Offer top of the scale — 4 percent. (That's the seller's cut. You pay the buyer's agent the standard 3 percent in addition to what you pay your agent.) When the agent sees that you're willing to reward performance, she's much more motivated to work for you and do an outstanding job.

Taking advantage of your agent's access to the MLS

When you hire a contractor, you indirectly hire his tools. The same is true with a real estate agent. When you hire an agent, you gain access to the most powerful tool for selling houses — the *Multiple Listing Service* (MLS). The MLS accounts for the sale of nearly 75 percent of all homes. Through the MLS, your listing goes out to virtually all the real estate agents in your area and eventually ends up in the hands of prospective buyers who are looking for homes comparable to yours. Make sure that your agent has access to all MLS listing services if your area has multiple services. Some MLS listings overlap, while others have county line borders.

WARNING!

You can find plenty of companies on the Internet or on TV who offer to list your home for a flat fee, usually ranging from $250 to $500. Avoid the temptation to list your home with them for the following reasons:

- As soon as the buyers' agents in your area see that you're listing your house with a discount broker, they don't show your property unless it's a last resort.
- Your reputation in your real estate market suffers because you're undercutting the current system that butters everyone's bread.
- You lose all the benefits (discussed in the section "Knowing why you should hire a seller's agent," earlier in this chapter) of having a full-service agent working for you.

Setting an Attractive Asking Price

Asking price is the biggest factor in how quickly a property sells. Set the price right, and the house should sell within the first 10 to 15 showings. Aim too high, and the house languishes on the market for months or even years. Aim too low, and you risk either shortchanging yourself or spooking buyers who think that the house must have something seriously wrong with it.

In the following sections, I lead you through the process of exploring the main factors to consider in order to establish a realistic asking price that doesn't sell you short.

TIP

Whenever you try to sell *anything,* you have to make sure that your price is competitive with the price of comparable products on the market. Even if you choose to sell the house yourself, meet with several agents to pick their brains for an asking price based on comparable houses in the area. Compose a one-page defense of your asking price that proves your property is worth that price. Your one-page defense should include information about the sale prices of comparable properties, along with improvements you've made and how much they're worth.

Don't be greedy

In a sizzling housing market, you may get away with padding your asking price by a few thousand dollars over comparable properties in the hopes that the market will eventually catch up. If, however, the house sits on the market for several months because you set the price too high, holding costs chip away at your profit, and you often have to lower the price anyway.

Price the house right the first time. Set a realistic asking price that's in line with or slightly below recent sale prices of comparable homes in your area. Set the price with your head, not with your heart. The amount you have invested and what the property actually sells for are two different things.

If you're debating between starting low and starting high, starting a little high is always better. List the house at the higher price for 15 days or so to test the market and see whether you get any bites. If the market shows little interest in the house at that price, then reduce the price.

Understand the current market

If you've ever invested in mutual funds, you've seen the standard disclaimer — past results do not predict future performance. What's true for the stock market applies to the housing market, as well. Housing prices fluctuate, so you need to keep your finger on the pulse of the market and set an asking price that's in line with recent sale prices of comparable homes in the same area. To assess current market prices, do the following:

- **Consult your agent.** A good agent keeps tabs on the area's housing market and can help you set an accurate asking price.
- **Visit comparable homes.** As part of your ongoing research, visit comparable homes for sale in the area to determine asking prices. See Chapter 14 for information on visiting homes in your market.
- **Research comparable sales.** Find out the prices that comparable homes have sold for within a one- to two-mile radius of your house in the last 6 to 12 months. The easiest way to obtain this information is to ask your agent, who can look it up in the MLS.

The entire time the house is on the market, keep a close watch on market conditions and be prepared to lower your asking price. The housing market can shift faster than you can say "flip."

Know the price you need to make the profit you want

One of the worst ways to establish an asking price is to base it on your desired profit, but you should know your bottom line before you put the house up for sale. Do the math to determine the lowest price you can afford to accept. You can then bump up your asking price based on the other information you gathered to bring it in line with prices of comparable properties. Chapter 12 provides guidance on how to crunch the numbers to determine how much you can afford to sell the house for and still earn a decent profit.

REMEMBER

If you can't sell the property for a profit, you have two options. You can sell at a loss (ugh!) and claim the loss against profits on other profitable flips (unfortunate, but it happens) or hold the property and lease it until market conditions improve.

Staging a Successful Showing

Products sell more quickly and for more money when they're properly showcased, or as those of us in the real estate business like to call it, *staged*. Auto dealers wax and polish a car and detail the interior before parking it on the lot. Department stores meticulously dress their mannequins to flaunt the latest fashions. Yet, when some real estate agents and homeowners put a $100,000+ home up for sale, they completely overlook the staging process, cheating themselves out of potentially thousands of dollars.

Recognizing the value of staging

A brief visit to any of the top staging company websites can convince you of the value of properly staging a home. In about ten minutes of searching the web for "staging a home," I learned that a professionally staged home sells in half the time for 7 percent to 10 percent more than a comparable un-staged home. Given those numbers, a home that would normally take two months to sell at a price of $500,000 would sell in a month for $535,000 to $550,000 with professional staging!

Making your staging checklist

You can hire a professional home stager to do the job for you, but you can probably do a great job staging the home yourself for a fraction of the cost. Staging isn't about spending a lot of money. It's about clearing the clutter and creatively rearranging the stage. Follow these basic guidelines:

- **Landscaping:** Mow and edge the lawn, pull weeds, fix any cracks in the pavement, and sweep up after yourself. Lay fresh mulch and plant fresh flowers (if in season).
- **Entryways:** Sweep the porch and stairs, lay down an attractive new doormat, fix the screens, wash the windows, polish the doorknobs, and clear the clutter out of the entryways. Make sure the doors open and close with ease.
- **Interior:** Scrub and shine the house throughout. Hide family photos, religious icons, political paraphernalia, and anything someone else may find offensive. Prospective buyers need to envision themselves living in the house, and this stuff clutters their minds.
- **Kitchen:** Clean and polish everything and clear off the counters, removing items such as knife racks, dish drainers, rags, towels, and soap. Clear out and clean the inside of the refrigerator, oven, and dishwasher; people do look inside.
- **Living room or den:** Clear the clutter and dust everything. Rearrange the furniture and place excess items in storage. If your furniture is an eyesore, you may want to rent something that's more attractive and tasteful and that makes the room look larger.
- **Bathrooms:** Empty the trash, scrub down the tub or shower (especially any mildew), keep the toilet seat down and covered, and get those toothbrushes off the vanity.
- **Bedrooms:** The master bedroom should have a good-sized bed and a small dresser. The other bedrooms should follow suit or be empty.
- **Just before showing:** Do a final walkthrough to tidy up the place, turn on all the lights, and open the windows to let the fresh air in. Most stagers recommend against using heavy air fresheners, scented candles, and potpourri. Set out a bouquet of fresh-cut flowers, instead — bring the outside in (weather permitting, of course) — or bake cookies or brew fresh coffee.

TIP

The best way to get a first-hand look at a properly staged home is to visit a builder's model home. You quickly notice that the model is impeccably clean, sparsely furnished (though not completely empty), and tastefully decorated. That's your goal. With a modest investment of time and effort and very little money, you significantly boost your chances of selling the house fast and for top dollar. Don't be a staging stooge.

Offering to Help Secure Attractive Financing

Financing is a big issue with first-time buyers, and that demographic is usually a huge chunk of your market. First-time buyers often fall in love with a house and then talk themselves out of it because they assume they can't afford it. If they really can't afford it, that's a good thing, but if they can afford it, you've just lost potential buyers simply because they made an ill-informed decision.

TIP

When marketing your home to first-time buyers, make sure that they know what their approximate monthly payment will be on a 30-year mortgage. You may also want to put together a spreadsheet that shows the average monthly utility bills. Enlist the aid of a top loan officer to help with marketing to first-time buyers and include the loan officer's contact information on your flyers and other marketing materials (see the following section). Check out Chapter 5 for a quick primer on financing. Keep in mind that all transactions must be completely transparent so no party involved in the transaction has any lingering questions or concerns.

WARNING!

Helping interested buyers secure financing to buy your house doesn't mean encouraging them to lie on their loan applications or get involved in some cash-back-at-closing scam. It means pointing them in the direction of a loan officer who works aboveboard to help the buyers decide how much house they can afford and obtain a loan based on their accurate financial portrait.

Becoming a Real Estate Marketing Maven

Marketing begins as soon as you begin renovating a property and chatting with your new neighbors, but the official kickoff for your marketing campaign doesn't really start until a couple of weeks before you put the house on the market. Then it's time to execute a marketing blitz that's guaranteed to deliver an enthusiastic herd of house hunters to your newly renovated doorstep. The day you put the house up for sale, your marketing campaign should hit high gear and flood the market with advertising.

When you sell a property through an agent, the agent takes on the role of marketing maven and consultant. He's a hired gun who handles the marketing and advertising for you and ensures that the buyers' agents in the area are in the know concerning your property.

If you choose to bypass the agent, you assume the role of marketing maven. You set the asking price, build a marketing plan, and develop the advertising media that spreads the word. In the following sections, I guide you through the process of establishing and executing an effective marketing plan. Even if you use an agent, you can assist in the marketing by suggesting or implementing additional marketing tactics. Team up with your agent to execute an effective strategy.

To effectively market any product, determine who's likely to buy it — in this case by consulting with your agent and knowing your market. When marketing a house to a first-time homeowner, for example, you may highlight the affordability of the house and provide a lead on where to go for financing. When marketing to movin'-on-up buyers, you may want to pitch the house as being spacious beyond belief. Empty-nester downsizers are often looking for something smaller that's in move-in condition and has a spare room for guests or a home office. Modify your marketing materials to appeal to your target buyers.

Choosing a method of contact

Before you start printing your full-color flyers (which I cover later in this chapter), decide how you want interested buyers and agents to contact you. Do you want them calling you at work? At home? On your cellphone? Should they send you an e-mail message? Knock on your door at midnight?

To sell your house, you need to provide an easy and reliable way for interested buyers to contact you, but you also have to preserve your own sanity and the safety of your family. After you print your phone number on a flyer and post it around town, your number is available not only to interested buyers but also to agents who want to list your house, prank callers, and telemarketers.

If you plan on flipping long-term, consider purchasing a cellphone exclusively for your flipping business, installing a separate phone line at home, or signing up for an answering service or voice mail system to field and screen your calls. If you use your home phone number, expect to receive calls at any time of day or night.

Remain available and responsive. If you've chosen to sell a house on your own, you make a commitment to customer service. If a prospective buyer calls and you don't answer or if you don't call back or send an e-mail reply within an hour a two, you risk losing a sale. The buyer may get frustrated, assume you're not interested, and move on to the next property on his list. By hiring an agent, you offload this sometimes onerous task to your agent, but some flippers like it.

Planting a For Sale sign on your lawn

The lowly For Sale sign is still the cornerstone of a solid marketing campaign. When you plant a For Sale sign on your front lawn, you automatically tap into what I like to call the Rule of 20 or the 5, 5, 10. The five neighbors on either side of you and the ten neighbors across the street immediately notice the sign and start telling their friends, neighbors, coworkers, and acquaintances about the house that's for sale on their block. You now have your own personal sales force working for you.

TIP

Don't settle for a skimpy For Sale sign that's likely to blow over in the first spring storm. Invest in something solid with an attractive design. Following are some additional For Sale sign tips:

- **Check with the local government and the neighborhood association to find out whether they have any restrictions on For Sale signs.** Some uppity neighborhoods ban them altogether.
- **Order a sign from a professional sign maker.**
- **Use a sign that you can anchor soundly into the ground.** I prefer a sign with a metal or wooden post that you have to anchor in the lawn with a posthole digger. Just be careful where you dig and how deep — you don't want to poke a hole in a gas line or sever an electrical cable.
- **Make sure that the sign is built in a way that enables you to add banners to it, such as "Basement" or "Appliances Included."** A plastic box to hold copies of flyers is also a good idea. (I cover flyers later in this chapter.)
- **Include your phone number, not your name, on the sign.** Leaving your name off the sign isn't to protect your secret identity — it just keeps the information to a minimum so passersby can quickly jot down the phone number.
- **Omit the "By Owner" part to avoid getting low-ball offers from investors and to screen out calls from agents who think that you may need a little professional assistance.** Some agents also may refuse to show FSBO properties to their buyers because they're afraid you'll try to cut them out of their commission.

Listing your home online

Several companies list homes For Sale By Owner, where buyers can search for homes without going through an agent. Before you sign up with one of these services, make sure that it's legitimate, that it lists plenty of homes in your area, and that it's used by many buyers in your area.

WARNING!

The Internet makes it easy for con artists to create a phony company that looks perfectly legitimate. Do your homework, check references, and make sure that the company has a phone number and a real mailing address before you sign up and pass along your credit-card number.

TIP

Many sellers list their homes on FSBO websites and completely miss other sales opportunities on the information superhighway. Consider beefing up your online marketing with some or all of the following techniques, regardless of whether you use an agent:

- **Post a notice on your own website or blog, if you have one.** Consider including links to neighborhood schools, parks, museums, clubs, organizations, local government agencies, and so on. You may even include a link to a loan officer who can supply information about financing (see "Offering to Help Secure Attractive Financing," earlier in this chapter).
- **E-mail notices to your friends and relatives telling them you have a home for sale.**
- **Post a classified ad on any website that provides free advertising space.**
- **Post a message in a newsgroup, assuming the newsgroup's rules and regulations allow for this.** Most newsgroups have an FAQ (frequently asked questions) page that states the rules.

Designing, printing, and distributing flashy flyers

If you have a digital camera, a computer, and a color inkjet printer, you have all the tools you need to design, lay out, and print professional-quality flyers to advertise your house. Your flyers need to include the following:

- Exterior and interior full-color photos of the house, showcasing its top features
- The address of the property
- Your asking price and terms
- Property description, preferably presented as a bulleted list
- Your name (It lends additional credibility to your flyer.)
- Your phone number and other preferred contact information

Figure 21-1 shows a sample marketing flyer.

TIP

If you're marketing the home to first-time buyers, you may also include the phone number of your loan officer, who can provide details about financing. A sample monthly payment schedule based on current interest rates can also be helpful in convincing interested buyers that they can afford the payments. See "Offering to Help Secure Attractive Financing," earlier in this chapter, for more information.

Some sellers invest hours in creating beautiful flyers and then proceed to print them on cheap paper. Buy some quality paper stock with a high brightness rating so your flyers look good in print. Because color ink and toner is so expensive, you can usually save money by having your local copy shop run off a hundred copies or so, but ask about rates before placing your order.

3284 W 56th Place

Chicago, IL 60629

$279,000

5 Beds, 3 Baths, 2 Stories +

Finished Basement w/Wet Bar

Contact: (555) 555-5555

Property Information

Beautiful brick home in pristine condition, 3 levels of living space. Main floor includes kitchen, spacious living room and dining room, 3 bedrooms, and full bath. Second floor includes large kitchen, living room, two bedrooms, full bath, two walk-in closets, and cubby holes for additional storage – perfect for rental, guests, or relatives! Finished basement with tile floor and wood paneling, laundry room, two closets, and wet bar is ideal for parties and large family gatherings. Off-street parking, brick garage, and beautiful yard with garden and built-in gas grill. Close to Orange Line, shopping, schools, and Midway Airport.

Property Features

- 2600 Square Feet
- 2 Stories + Basement
- Driveway (Off-Street Parking)
- Radiant Heat in Walls/Floors
- Cook County

- Brick Exterior
- 5 Bedrooms
- Brick Detached Garage
- Built: 1960
- West Elsdon Area

- Asphalt Shingles
- 3 Full Bathrooms
- Yard w/Garden & Gas Grill
- Lot Size: 50 x 125
- Close to Orange Line

Main Floor

- Kitchen: 12 x 11
- Master Bedroom: 14 x 11
- Bedroom 2: 11 x 12
- Bedroom 3: 11 x 12
- Living Room: 18 x 11
- Dining Room: 11 x 11
- Full Bath
- Bedrooms, Living Room, and Dining Room Carpeted

Second Floor

- Kitchen: 12 x 11
- Bedroom 1: 11 x 12
- Bedroom 2: 11 x 12
- Living Room: 18 x 12
- Full Bath
- 2 Walk-in Closets
- Cubby Holes for Extra Storage
- Separate Thermostat
- Bedrooms & Living Room Carpeted
- Like a 2nd Flat!

Basement

- 23 x 40
- Fully Finished
- Tile Floor
- Wood Paneling
- Full Bath
- 2 Closets
- Laundry Room: Large with Double Utility Sink
- Electric Faux Fireplace
- Storage cubby under stairs
- Wet Bar

Figure courtesy of Joe Kraynak

Figure 21-1: A marketing flyer contains important details for home buyers.

Now that you have those good-looking flyers, where should you put them? Here are a few ideas, subject to your agent's approval and any local regulations, of course:

- Grocery stores
- Restaurants
- Churches
- Gas stations
- Area apartment complexes

Advertising your home in the classifieds

Taking out a classified ad in your local newspaper can generate additional buzz, but don't go overboard. A small ad that provides the address and phone number along with a teaser description of the property is sufficient — something like "lakefront property," "move-in condition," "affordable living," or "convenient shopping." Your main goal is to pique the buyer's interest enough to call you on the phone.

If you're selling By Owner and an agent brings someone to purchase the property, the agent will ask you to sign a one-party listing agreement, which lists the buyers by name. Remember that everything in real estate must be in writing. The agreement is good only for the party (individual or couple) the agent brings to see your house, and it should have a price and a fee that you're willing to pay the agent if her clients buy your property.

Hosting an open house to build word-of-mouth buzz

Soon after you place your house on the market, host an open house and invite the neighbors. Sundays are the day of choice for open houses because families are together and often looking for free food and entertainment. Pretty up the house, plant some Open House signs along the major thoroughfares, lay out some tasty hors d'oeuvres and drinks, and get ready for the after-church crowd. Be sure to distribute business cards, too.

In addition to the standard Sunday afternoon open houses, consider hosting an exclusive open house by invitation only for the neighbors. This prestigious event increases the neighborhood buzz and inspires your local word-of-mouth sales force to get to work. You may also do well with staging twilight open houses on a Tuesday or Thursday evening — after work but when a little sunlight still remains.

Chapter 22

Negotiating the Sale to Maximize Your Profit

In This Chapter

- Talking to prospective buyers
- Weighing various offers as they come in
- Getting what you want with counteroffers
- Dealing with paperwork and other legal stuff at closing

You followed my advice and hired an agent to sell your house. That's an excellent decision, but it's not the last decision you need to make. Your agent can find prospective buyers, show them the house, and convince them to submit an offer, but the sale price and terms are up to you. And although your agent can help guide you through the often sensitive negotiation process, you can always benefit from a few extra techniques and strategies. You need to know for yourself how to haggle with buyers in a way that gives them what they want without giving away too much of what you need.

In this chapter, I assist you in evaluating various offers as they come in and show you how to use multiple offers to your advantage. Finally, I lead you through the process of closing the deal and introduce the paperwork you need to shuffle to make everything legal.

If you do decide, against my advice, to sell the house without using an agent, check out the latest edition of *House Selling For Dummies,* by Ray Brown and Eric Tyson, MBA (Wiley).

Think twice about flying solo when you put your house on the market. According to the National Association of Realtors (NAR), the average seller receives 16 percent more for a house when using a Realtor (a real estate agent who is a NAR member). The reason the seller gets so much less by not using an agent is that both the buyer and seller try to save the commission. When nobody comes looking at the house, the seller subtracts the commission to make the house a more attractive purchase. The buyer, who knows that the seller isn't paying a commission, also subtracts the commission when making an offer. See Chapters 4 and 21 for information on hiring an agent.

Comparing Seemingly Similar Offers

When average homeowners sell their property, they often act as auctioneers looking for the high bid, but price is only one component of an offer (or purchase agreement). In many cases, a lower offer is superior if the buyer can close quickly and doesn't demand a lot of extras, such as closing costs and repairs.

When you're flipping houses, you need to be able to evaluate offers and see beyond price to weigh all factors. In the following sections, I reveal the major factors you should consider so that you can compare offers as you receive them. Consult with your agent for specific advice on issues that concern you.

Your first offer is usually the best offer, so don't reject it outright thinking that better offers are soon to follow. If you receive an offer soon after you put the house up for sale, you may be tempted to assume that you priced the house too low and try to sabotage the deal so you can raise your asking price. This tactic is often a costly mistake. That first offer may be the only one you get. Remember, pigs get fat; hogs get slaughtered.

Does the buyer have financing?

A buyer doesn't have to be able to afford your house in order to bid on it. He can have a dollar in his pocket and ten dollars in his bank account and still submit an offer. If you accept the offer by signing the purchase agreement, he can tie up your house for several days of negotiations until you discover that he can't get financing.

When fielding offers, don't sign a purchase agreement unless the bidder provides proof of one of the following types of financing (see Chapter 5 for general information on financing):

- **Cash:** Cash offers are tops, but you should verify that the buyer has the available cash to close the deal. Verification can be in the form of a letter from the buyer's bank or credit union or from Grandma Rowland, who's putting up the money. Or, you can ask for a copy of the buyers' recent bank statements — advise the buyers to black out their account numbers so that the account numbers don't fall into the wrong hands.

If you can't get the actual statements or the buyers prefer not to provide copies of bank statements, the bank can provide an official letter stating sufficient funds are available in the buyers' accounts.

- **Preapproval:** Preapproval means that a lender has already okayed the loan. This offer is the next best thing to a cash offer, but preapproval letters are worth only as much as the paper they're printed on. Ask the buyers to talk with your mortgage person (a loan officer you trust or one your agent recommends). Don't trust the word of the buyer's loan officer, because that person may not be the most reliable source of accurate information. If the buyers balk at this suggestion, tell them that buying and financing a home is important business and they wouldn't have major surgery without getting a second opinion, so they should consider getting some additional input from your loan officer. More than likely, your mortgage specialist will be of a higher caliber then the one they may have just stumbled on.
- **Pre-qualification:** If the buyer has pre-qualification, a lender has researched the buyer's financial records and decided that the buyer is probably able to secure a loan. Pre-qualification is one rung down from preapproval.

All things being equal, a cash offer is best, but if the cash offer is more than 5 percent lower than a noncash offer, you have to weigh the benefits against the lower purchase price.

REMEMBER

Accept offers only from serious buyers who are at least pre-qualified for a loan that's sufficient for purchasing the property. Have your mortgage specialist on call to check up on a prospective buyer's qualifications before you sign the purchase agreement. Your mortgage specialist can contact the buyer's lender and perform background checks to ensure that the buyer has sufficient financing in place.

How "earnest" is the buyer?

Most offers have an earnest-money deposit attached to them that shows how committed the buyer is to purchasing the property. If the buyer backs out of the deal without due cause, he forfeits the earnest-money deposit, and you get to keep it. Needless to say, an offer with a large earnest-money deposit is less likely to fall apart at the last minute than an offer with a smaller deposit. To the seller, having that assurance carries a lot of weight.

REMEMBER

A reasonable amount to offer as an earnest-money deposit depends on the nature of the financing: 20 percent deposit on a conventional loan, 10 percent on a cash offer, and 3.5 percent on an FHA loan. Any less shows a weakness in the buyer's financing or commitment. Any more shows that the buyer is in a stronger position to purchase the property and more committed to closing the deal.

TIP

When buyers offer a low deposit, explain that by putting down more money now, they have to come up with less money at closing. You can also consider adding an incentive for putting down a higher deposit by saying something like, "I'd be much more comfortable with a deposit of $5,000 than with the $1,000 you're offering. In fact, I'd be willing to drop the price of the house by $500 in exchange for a larger deposit." If you figure that each day you hold the property costs you $100, $500 is a small investment for ensuring that the deal goes through.

WARNING!

I strongly recommend that you not hold the earnest-money deposit yourself. Ask your agent, attorney, or title company to hold onto the cash. That way, you won't be tempted to dip into the cookie jar before the deal is done.

What else is the buyer asking for?

Buyers ask for all sorts of stuff when they submit an offer. They may ask you to remove that pool you just installed thinking it would boost the value of the house. They can ask for the sports car you have stored in your garage. They can request that you pay up to 6 percent of their closing costs, pay for a home warranty, or immediately vacate the property at closing. When evaluating an offer, take all these requests into consideration. Following are suggestions on how to handle common requests:

- **Possession at closing.** Buyers often want to take immediate possession of a property. When you're flipping, this situation is ideal, assuming you don't reside in the house. If you're living in the house you flip, draw up a contingency plan and try your best to accommodate this request. It may inconvenience you, but as a flipper, you want to sell your house as quickly as possible to cut your holding costs and have cash to finance your next flip.
- **Payment of closing costs.** Many first-time homeowners request that the seller pay a portion of the closing costs so they don't have to pay these costs upfront. If buyers ask for closing costs, consider offering to pay the closing costs upfront if the buyer is willing to pay a little more for the house to cover the closing costs. Many first-time buyers would rather roll the closing costs into their mortgage than pay the fees upfront. Of course, this is only an option if the property appraises for the amount the buyers are willing to pay. If the appraisal comes in too low, you can challenge it, but if you lose that battle, you need to lower the price.
- **No tax proration.** At closing, you normally get back any taxes you paid for the months that the new owner is going to live in the house. When buyers request no tax proration, they're asking you to pay their property taxes. Ask your title company to calculate the amount you would

be getting back at closing. If the amount is small — only a few hundred bucks — you may want to agree to this request. (Chapter 4 has tips on finding a title company.) If you just paid the tax bill and the sale closes in the first month after paying, that money should be reimbursed to you. For example, if the taxes are $3,000 for the year, which equals $250 a month, you lose $2,750 at closing if you give up tax proration.

TIP

In some states, homeowners pay taxes in arrears rather than in advance. In other words, the homeowner pays this year to cover last year's property taxes. In states in which taxes are paid in arrears, the seller customarily credits the buyer at closing for as much as one year of taxes. The theory is that because the seller used the property in the previous year and those taxes are being paid this year, they are the seller's responsibility. In such cases, you're better off if the buyer doesn't ask for the taxes to be prorated. Consider offering to pay the next installment due after the closing — it can save you approximately six months in taxes versus a full year's proration. But again, if the buyer won't budge on this term and is presenting a sweet offer, you may want to give in.

WARNING!

Beware of the red herring move. Buyers often request something they know you won't agree to in an attempt to focus your attention on that one request and give in on everything else. If the buyer requests something odd, such as the Oriental rug in the living room, it should raise a red flag. Unless giving away that rug eats up your profit, giving in may be your best option.

WARNING!

Under no circumstances should you offer a buyer cash back at closing. Con artists often use cash-back-at-closing deals to gyp lenders out of money. With a cash-back-at-closing scheme, the buyer agrees to pay a little more for the house (often much more than the asking price), and the seller kicks back a portion of the extra money (or all of it) to the buyer after closing. These deals are fraudulent; if you get involved in one, you may find yourself on the wrong end of a judge's bench.

What conditions has the buyer included?

Conditional statements (weasel clauses) accompany every offer. Some are built into the offer, but the buyer can jot down additional conditions. If you're smart, you probably did the same thing when you bought the house (see Chapter 13 for details on buying a house). Following are the most common conditions buyers stipulate:

- **Financing must be approved.** Every purchase agreement has this condition, and if you're already screening out anyone who's not pre-qualified for a loan, this clause shouldn't pose a problem. (See "Does the buyer have financing?" earlier in this chapter for more information.)

- **Property must appraise at the sale price or higher.** If you've done your homework and priced your property competitively, this condition shouldn't pose a problem.
- **House must pass inspection.** You had the house inspected when you bought it, and you repaired everything, so this point is another nonissue.
- **Title must be clear.** Before you purchased the house, you researched the title and purchased title insurance, so you're safe here, too.
- **My existing home must sell first.** You don't want the sale of your house hanging in limbo because the buyers can't sell their house. If you like the offer, consider countering with an offer that gives the prospective buyers *first right of refusal*, which keeps the house on the market but provides the buyers with notice (often 72 hours) before you sell to someone else. The buyers then have that much time (72 hours, for example) to match any offer you receive. If you don't like the offer, give your other offers a higher priority.

Beware of any conditions that the buyer adds to give himself an unfair advantage or saddle you with all the financial risk. Anything that enables the buyer to easily back out of the deal with no financial loss should raise a red flag, including interest-rate contingencies (offer is removed if buyer can't get a loan at a certain interest rate), a clause saying the buyer's attorney must review and approve the offer, or a clause giving the buyer the right to back out of the deal without cause.

Avoiding the domino effect

Having the sale of your house conditional upon the sale of another house is known as a *domino effect.* I've seen this go seven deep. Each house is dependent on another one selling. If something happens anywhere along the line, your deal is dead. My advice is to sign a 72-hour contingency that allows you to keep your house on the market. This contingency gives you two opportunities to sell the house. You can sell the house to the first buyer, or if another buyer comes along, you can sign an agreement with the second buyer contingent upon the first deal not going through. You then give the first buyer notice that he can lift his 72-hour contingency or you will act on the second offer at the 73rd hour. Top-producer agents are well trained in this method, and you should be, too.

Keep in mind that each offer stands on its own terms. The first buyer is under no obligation to match a higher offer. Price has nothing to do with the contingency.

How soon does the buyer want to close?

As a flipper, you're well aware of holding costs. Every day you own your property costs you money, so the sooner you close, the less money you're out. When comparing offers, check the date on which the buyer wants to close. If one buyer who wants to close immediately is offering $2,000 less than another buyer who wants to close a month from now, the lower offer may be the better offer, assuming all other conditions are equal.

Mastering the Art of Counteroffers

Some offers are so low, all you can do is laugh and shrug them off, but in most cases, no offer is too low to reject outright. When you receive an offer that appears to be a little irrational, don't take it personally. If you're not ready to say either "yes" or "no," simply reply with your counteroffer.

REMEMBER

Take-it-or-leave-it ultimatums have no place in negotiations. Defuse your emotions. Depressurize your passions. Proceed with logic and always treat buyers with respect, even if you think they're off their rockers.

The following sections explore counteroffers in greater depth and show you some techniques for turning the tables on buyers without insulting or confronting them. For information on handling counteroffers when you're the buyer, not the seller, head to Chapter 13.

SANITY CHECK

Never counter yourself. For example, suppose you're asking $200,000 for a property, and you get an offer of $180,000, so you counter with $195,000, and the buyer hesitates. You begin thinking about it. Maybe you should have countered with $190,000. You have bills to pay. Baby needs new shoes. You want to call back with a new counteroffer. Don't do it. Your baby doesn't need new shoes that badly. Wait for the next counteroffer to come in before you decide on your next move; otherwise, you're essentially bidding against yourself.

Submitting a counteroffer

After you receive and evaluate a reasonable offer, you have two choices — you can accept the offer as is or submit a counteroffer in writing. If the buyer offers the full price and attractive terms (as I cover in the earlier section "What conditions has the buyer included?"), accept the offer immediately. Don't start to second-guess yourself or wonder whether you sold yourself short. Lady Fortune has smiled down upon you, so smile back and sign the agreement.

If the offer isn't stellar but shows some promise for negotiation, craft a counteroffer. I show you the basics in the following sections.

Coming up with a savvy counteroffer

Offering and counteroffering is like a game of chess, in which buyer and seller attempt to anticipate one another's next move. You never know what a buyer is going to request or state as a condition, so you need to tread carefully and think creatively. Following are some examples of counteroffers that have worked for me in the past:

- **Buyer offers $5,000 less than asking price and no tax proration.** Knowing that the loss of tax proration will cost you $1,000 at closing, you counter that you agree to pay the tax proration if the buyer pays the full asking price.
- **Buyer offers $10,000 less than asking price.** Knowing that your home is priced competitively with comparable homes in the area and that you're currently in a sellers' market, you counter with your original asking price but provide a comparison chart showing that your house is well worth that price.
- **Buyer makes a firm offer for less than you can accept.** Return the offer with a note that says, "Sorry, but I can't accept less than ____."
- **Buyer requests that you provide a home warranty.** The average home warranty costs around $425, so it's usually not a deal breaker. A home warranty is a reasonable request, and if it doesn't break the bank, accept it. Besides, having a home warranty may protect you from a future lawsuit if the property has some defect that went unnoticed during the inspection.

Putting your counteroffer in writing

If you decide to counter, write your counteroffer on the copy of the purchase agreement you received from the buyer or the buyer's agent, initial your changes, and either fax or hand-deliver your counteroffer to the buyer's agent or directly to the buyer if she's not working through an agent. (Some agents prefer to submit counteroffers on a separate form instead of marking up the original offer; they number the counteroffers something along the lines of Seller 1, Buyer 2, Seller 3, and so on.) If you're using an agent, have your agent present the counteroffer. Be sure to stipulate the time period in which the buyer needs to respond to your counteroffer.

WARNING!

Only what's written on an offer counts, so make sure that all offers and counteroffers are in writing. Don't make verbal agreements. They won't stand up in court.

Thinking like an agent

Agents are master negotiators, so when you're selling a house, it pays to think like an agent or work with an agent. Skilled agents know how to break down the numbers into minimums. For example, if a buyer offers $5,000 less than the asking price, the seller is out $5,000 over a single transaction. But for a buyer with a mortgage interest rate of 6.5 percent, that $5,000 represents about $30 a month or less than $1 a day! Presenting these numbers in this way to the buyer puts the offer in perspective. I've found this strategy to be highly effective in convincing buyers to up the ante when the seller won't budge.

Another strategy we use in our office is to place the buyers and sellers in separate conference rooms — we have several of them. The buyers and sellers exchange letters. They each jot down bullet points of what they like and dislike about the offer, and we eliminate their differences one by one. After everyone has agreed, we join together in one room and sign documents.

Leveraging the power of multiple offers

When you receive an outstanding offer, jump on it. If the offer falls short of outstanding, call your other prospects and let them know that you've received an offer and are going to pursue it if you don't receive an offer from them by a certain deadline (one or two days). This tactic applies pressure to all interested parties, encouraging them to get off their duffs and act quickly or lose the house for good. Keep the details about the offer you received a mystery so new bidders don't have an unfair advantage.

If additional offers arrive, you can now compare offers, as I explain earlier in this chapter, and accept the best offer or counter it. Keep a copy of those other offers on hand, however, just in case what you consider to be the best offer falls through.

TIP

If you have competing offers, get word back to both buyers that you're going to be looking at their best and final offer. If you have an agent, let the agent do the talking. After both offers come in, you can then pick the best offer and start negotiating.

WARNING!

Countering two offers with signed counteroffers is fraud. You can legally respond to more than one offer by submitting unsigned counteroffers and stipulating that none of the counteroffers is legal and binding until you sign it. However, I prefer to ask all interested parties to submit their best offer so I know who's most serious.

Shuffling Papers and Other Legal Stuff at Closing

After you and the buyers reach an agreement on price and terms, and assuming nothing happens to sabotage the deal, the sale proceeds to closing, where you receive your money and sign over the deed to the buyer. At this point, you have two goals — to make the closing proceed as smoothly as possible and to ensure that your back end is covered. In the following sections, I show you how to proceed with a closing from start to finish.

In real estate, everything must be in writing. Everything must be disclosed. You can't hide anything or make deals on the side.

Having the right folks represent you

Even if you sell the house yourself, you should never try to fly solo during the closing. Closings are complicated legal and financial transactions accompanied by mounds of paperwork. You need to make sure that your interests are protected at closing by hiring a closing agent and real estate attorney to represent you and ensure that all paperwork is properly completed. Your agent can attend the closing but usually advises you to have your attorney present; whether you choose to have your attorney present is up to you.

In most cases, your title company supplies the closing agent, but in some cases, the buyer's lender insists on handling the buyer's end of the closing. However the closing is handled, you should supply your attorney with copies of the paperwork to review before the closing date to avoid any nasty surprises at closing. See Chapter 4 for details on hiring a title company and a real estate attorney.

As soon as you and the buyer agree on price and terms, call your title company or real estate attorney and schedule a closing date. Closings typically occur 30 to 45 days from the day you sell the property, so you don't want to waste any time. As soon as you sell the property, you must order the title policy. Neither the buyer nor seller needs to worry about this — your real estate agent keeps the process moving forward and can recommend a title company or attorney to handle the paperwork.

Prepping for closing

To ensure that the closing proceeds as smoothly as possible, supply your closing agent with any documents she may need to put together the closing packets. Documents typically include the following:

- **Termite inspection report.** If the buyer is financing the purchase with a Veterans Affairs (VA) loan, immediately schedule a termite inspection, if it hasn't already been done, and send the report to the closing agent or attorney who's handling the closing. (Typically, the buyer orders the termite inspection and has it done prior to closing, and the seller pays for it at closing.)
- **Purchase agreement and any addendums.**
- **Mortgage payoff information and any second mortgages or other liens.**
- **Buyer's financial information.**

TIP: If you use the same title company at closing that you used when you purchased the property, the title company often discounts the fee it charges for title work. Even if you're using a different title company, turn in your old policy. You can usually receive a credit for it.

Sealing the deal with paperwork

At the closing, the closing agent or attorney in charge supplies you and the buyer with separate closing packages. The buyers' package is typically much thicker than yours, because they're the ones borrowing money. Your package should include the following items:

- **Settlement statement:** You and the buyer both receive a settlement statement that breaks down the charges and credits for the buyer and seller and shows the net amount each of you receives or must pay at closing.
- **Deed:** The deed is the document that transfers ownership of the property from you (the seller) to the buyer.
- **Bill of sale:** If you included any appliances in the sale of the property, your closing package may include a bill of sale that transfers ownership of these items to the buyer.

- **Mortgage payoff statement:** If you took out a loan to purchase the property, your lender supplies you with a letter indicating the full amount due on the closing date to pay off the mortgage. After the closing is final, the lender receives full payment.
- **Escrow statement:** If your monthly mortgage payments included escrow payments to cover bills, such as water and sewer, homeowner's insurance, or property taxes, some of the money held in escrow may be returned to you at closing. The escrow statement shows you how much you can expect to get back.
- **1099-S report:** The federal government requires that the 1099-S be filed to report the exact sale price of the house.
- **Estoppel certificate:** Some title companies require the buyer and seller to sign an estoppel certificate that verifies they are of legal age to enter into a legally binding agreement, that the deed has no hidden liens, and that nobody's currently disputing the title.
- **Homestead exemption update:** Some properties qualify for a homestead tax exemption. At closing, you may be asked to rescind the exemption that's in place so the buyers can claim the exemption, if they qualify for it.

A lot of times the buyers sign their closing paperwork first because they have so much more to sign. Often buyers and sellers sign together, sometimes separately, and sometimes through the mail. No way is wrong as long as it fits your circumstances.

REMEMBER

After you and the buyer sign the required documents, the deal is done. Hand over the keys and the garage door openers to the new owner along with any manuals for appliances you're leaving with the property. At this point, you should also inform the buyers of the date on which utilities will be turned off. Bring the phone numbers of the various utility companies to the closing. After closing, you and the new owners can call the companies and have the utilities transferred to the new owners. Because your name is on the utility bills, you may need to verify with the utility company that you approve the transfer. Overlooking a minor detail like switching over the utilities can inconvenience the new owners and result in your receiving unexpected bills later.

Chapter 23

Trudging Through Some Taxing Issues

In This Chapter

- Calculating the tax man's cut
- Maximizing your tax savings on a primary residence
- Discovering what you can deduct on your income-tax return
- Deferring taxes and selling property at a loss
- Handling taxes when you flip full time

You start flipping houses with the confident presumption that you're finally working for yourself. Instead of kowtowing to an overbearing supervisor and trading the best years of your life for a skimpy paycheck, you get to be your own boss and pocket the entire profit from your labors.

After you flip your first house, however, you may start to feel like you're working for the government. If you're doing quick flips, holding properties for only a year or less, your profits are subject to a short-term capital gains taxes up to a whopping 43.4 percent!

Evading taxes is always a choice, assuming you don't mind bunking with your fellow inmates at a federal prison, but I'm not about to recommend tax evasion as a viable alternative. Instead, in this chapter, I show you how to take advantage of legal tax exemptions and deductions and structure your deals to pay as little tax as required by law.

Shameless disclaimer: I'm no CPA, accountant, or tax attorney, so I'm not providing advice in this chapter. Besides, tax laws are constantly changing, and state and local taxes vary depending on where you live, so even if I could offer you some sage advice, I couldn't possibly guarantee that it would be accurate for you and where you live. The information I offer in this chapter merely provides you with a stepping-off point that can help you communicate more effectively with your CPA or tax specialist. See Chapter 4 for information on finding an accountant to add to your flipping team. For general tax information and forms, visit the Internal Revenue Service (IRS) website at www.irs.gov.

Estimating the Tax Man's Take from Your Flipping Profits

You can get yourself into a real tax jam when flipping properties if you don't know upfront how the IRS and your state and local taxing authorities classify your profits. If you go in thinking that the most you have to pay is 15 percent in capital-gains tax, you may find an unpleasant surprise in your mailbox when tax time rolls around.

To avoid any future shock, know the tax man's cut upfront and how your house-flipping strategy affects the percentage you pay in taxes:

- You owe 0 percent if you flip a home in which you lived for two of the past five years. See "Maximizing Tax Savings from the Sale of Your Principal Residence" later in this chapter for details.
- You owe anywhere from 0 to 23.8 percent of your net profit in long-term capital gains if you hold the property for at least a year and one day (See Table 23-1).
- The tax rate for capital gains varies depending on the income tax bracket you fall into based on your ordinary income (from your day job). For the two highest tax brackets, the short-term and long-term rates include a 3.8 percent Medicare surcharge.
- You owe the same percentage in tax on your net profit as you do on your ordinary income (from your day job) if you hold the property for one year or less (see Table 23-1).
- You owe standard income tax if you flip houses for a living. When profits from flipping houses are your sole income, the IRS may consider flipping to be your job and tax your profits as income, complete with an additional 15 percent in self-employment tax. (See "Paying Income Tax: When Flipping Houses Becomes Your Occupation," later in this chapter, for details.)

Table 23-1 Short-term versus long-term capital gains tax rates for 2013

Ordinary income tax rate (%)	*Short-term rate (%)*	*Long-term rate (%)*
10	10	0
15	15	0
25	25	15
28	28	15
33	33	15
35	38.8	18.8
39.6	43.4	23.8

Never postpone a sale in the hopes of improving your tax position. Take the sale when you have the sale. If the buyer backs out because of your delay, you stand to lose a lot more than you stand to save on taxes.

Maximizing Tax Savings from the Sale of Your Principal Residence

Living in the house you flip provides you with much more than a roof over your head. It qualifies you for a whopper of a tax exclusion. If you're married and you sell the house you've lived in during the past two years for a profit of $500,000 or less, you can stuff the money in your pockets and purse tax-free, at least according to the tax rules in place when I was writing this book. If you're single or married filing separately, you can deduct only $250,000, a comparatively paltry sum, but better than nothing.

Here's how it works: The profit from the sale of a house you own for more than 12 months is subject to a 15 percent capital-gains tax plus any additional taxes that your state or local taxing authorities lump on top. If you and your spouse live in the home for at least two years, however, the IRS excludes the first $500,000 of the proceeds ($250,000 if you're single) from capital-gains tax. Any amount over that is subject to tax.

To take advantage of this exclusion, your home must be your principal residence, you have to own it (duh!), and you must have lived in it for two of the past five years. The following sections help you determine whether you qualify for this most generous tax break.

Knowing the tax rules before you flip

A woman I know flipped her first house — a shabby two-bedroom job that she purchased for $120,000, renovated to the tune of $20,000, and sold for $175,000, walking away with a cool $35,000 in profit. And it took her only a little more than ten months. She was ecstatic! But when she visited her accountant to tell her the great news, ecstasy quickly turned to agony.

The woman's accountant informed her that because she had owned the home for less than a year, her profit qualified as a short-term capital gain, taxable at the rate of 35 percent (at the time), which cost her $12,250 in federal taxes alone. If she had held the home for an additional two months, the profit would have qualified as a long-term capital gain taxed at the much lower rate of 15 percent, and she could have saved $7,000!

As I say in the section "Estimating the Tax Man's Take from Your Flipping Profits," earlier in this chapter, you should never postpone a sale in order to take advantage of a tax break. The woman may have held onto her house for two more months only to find out that buyers were no longer interested in it, and she could have lost more money by having to sell the property for less later than she actually lost in having to pay higher taxes. However, this particular seller could have saved taxes by leasing the property to the new buyers until after the one year was up and then closing at that time. Know the tax laws so you can establish a well-informed plan and avoid surprises that may lead to unnecessary regret.

TIP

Consider buying two houses. Pick the one that promises the most profit and takes the longest to rehab as your principal residence, and plan on spending at least two years fixing it up. While you're taking your time slowly renovating that property, do a quick flip on the other property. When you're done flipping that one, do a quick flip on another property. Following this approach, you can take advantage of the tax exclusion on your most profitable property (the long-term flip) while generating income with lower-profit, shorter-term flips.

Proving "principal residence"

REMEMBER

Government officials like to quibble about the meanings of words. To close any loopholes in the tax law that applies to using your home as your *principal residence,* they carefully define the term "principal residence." For your home to qualify as your principal residence, you must:

- Live in the home instead of rooming with friends or renting from relatives.
- Have your mail and utility bills delivered to this address.
- File your homestead exemption for this property with your county and state.

- Use this address on your driver's license, voter registration, tax returns, car registration, and so forth.
- Bank and shop in the vicinity of your home. No, the government doesn't really care where you bank or shop, but in close calls, the auditor may want to see grocery receipts that prove you live in the neighborhood.

TIP

A good rule of thumb for determining the location of your principal residence is this: If your mom's coming to visit you, which house does she come to?

Qualifying for the two-out-of-five-years rule

The two-out-of-five-years requirement is fairly straightforward — over the course of five years, you have to use the house as your principal residence for at least two years. If you spend a year island-hopping in the Caribbean, that year doesn't count, but a year in which you're away on vacation for six weeks counts as a full year. Check with your accountant or tax specialist to determine the exact amount of time you can be away from your home and still qualify as having lived there for a full year.

REMEMBER

You can claim the exclusion only once in any two-year span. If you have two residences, both of them may qualify for the exclusion in the span of four or five years, but if you claim the exclusion on one of the properties, you have to wait two years before claiming the exclusion on the other property.

TIP

Many times people want to keep their personal residence because it has already appreciated and they think that it's going to appreciate more. That can be a costly mistake. If possible, take full advantage of this generous tax break while it's available. You could conceivably own three homes — your principal residence, a summer home, and a winter home. You could sell your principal residence, move into your summer home for two years, sell your summer home, move into your winter home for at least two years, and then sell your winter home to take advantage of the tax benefit three times in a little over six years.

Taking the ownership test

Owning a property means having your name on the deed. If your generous parents let you live in the second home they own, fix it up, and then sell it, neither you nor your bighearted parents qualify for the tax exclusion. You don't own the home, and they don't live there.

If you're married and only you or your spouse is named on the deed, as a couple you still qualify to exclude the full $500,000 from your taxes. This rule applies to your principal residence — where you live — and it doesn't necessarily matter whether both names are on the deed.

Splitting hairs: Special circumstances

What if you *have* to sell the house before the two years is up, perhaps because of a job change? Is that just tough luck? Nope. The tax code accommodates for circumstances beyond your control, including the following:

- Divorce or legal separation
- Multiple births from the same pregnancy . . . fertility drugs gone wild
- Death of the homeowner, spouse, or co-owner, making the home unaffordable
- Serious health problems that require you to move in order to obtain proper treatment
- Loss of employment that results in your receiving unemployment compensation
- Military duty that calls you away from home for an extended period
- Involuntary conversion of your home — when the government takes possession of your home by claiming eminent domain

In these and similar instances, you may qualify for a prorated exclusion. In other words, if you and your spouse live in the home for a year, you may qualify for half the exclusion or $250,000 rather than the full $500,000.

Slashing Your Capital Gains Through Careful Deductions

You buy a house for $250,000, fix it up, and flip it for $300,000 in one year or less. Now you're stuck paying short-term capital-gains tax on your $50,000 profit, right? Wrong. The $50,000 is your *gross* profit, but you pay tax only on your *net* profit — the actual profit you make after deducting all your expenses. This tax rule applies to any house you flip — the property need not be your principal residence.

Carefully log all your expenses related to the purchase of the property, holding costs, repairs and renovations, and the sale of the house, including the following:

- **Closing costs:** You can deduct the appraisal fee, title search, deed-reporting fee, and credit-reporting fee. No double dipping. If you paid discount points, deduct them as mortgage interest, not as closing costs.
- **Cleanup:** Deduct any expenses for house cleaning, landscaping, or trash removal.
- **Repairs and renovations:** All expenses for improving the property for resale are deductible.
- **Utilities:** Gas, electric, water, sewer, and trash bills for this residence for the entire time you own the property are deductible expenses.
- **Property taxes:** Property taxes you pay out of pocket or out of an escrow account are fully deductible as expenses.
- **Insurance:** Calculate the total amount of insurance you paid on the property during the time you owned it.
- **Agent fees:** Any fees you paid to a real estate agent to purchase or sell the house are expenses you can deduct from your gross profit.
- **Other expenses:** When you flip houses, you're essentially running a business out of your home, so you can deduct all expenses related to flipping — mileage, phone bills, paper, ink, and so on. If you have an office in your home, you may be eligible for the home office deduction, as well.

According to tax laws in effect during the writing of this book, you can also deduct the mortgage interest you pay on a loan of up to $1 million on your first and second homes. In effect, unless you neighbor with royalty, all or at least most of the mortgage interest on your first and second homes is deductible.

The $1 million cap on deductible borrowing applies to both married and single tax payers; if you're married filing separately, the deduction is limited to interest on a home loan up to $500,000 for each of you.

When you're flipping houses, you can deduct your mortgage interest in either of the following ways:

- On a monthly basis, so you can keep track of your profit and the taxes you owe per month.
- By property, so it appears on your books either as an interest deduction or an expense you can deduct from your gross profit.

Consult with your CPA or tax specialist on the best way to keep track of your interest payments and claim the deduction.

Deducting your expenses can make a big difference at tax time. If you flip a house for a gross profit of $50,000 but pay $20,000 fixing it up and selling it, instead of paying, say 28 percent of $50,000 — $14,000 — in taxes, you pay 28 percent of $30,000 — $8,400!

Don't be a dupe. Save all your receipts and pay taxes only on the profit you pocket.

Deferring Taxes: Rolling Your Gains into Your Next Purchase

You don't always have to pay capital-gains tax upon the sale of a house. You may be able to roll your profit into the purchase of your next investment property. Rolling the profit over doesn't eliminate the tax. It defers payment until you pocket the profit. Rollover regulations can be a little tricky, but they boil down to the following two rules:

- You can roll over the profit from the sale of your principal residence into the purchase of a pricier house. With the $500,000 exclusion I discuss earlier in the chapter, this rule won't help the average homeowner, and it won't help when you're doing a quick flip (holding the property for less than two years).
- For rental/investment properties, you can file for a 1031 exchange that enables you to roll the profit from the sale of a rental property into pricier rental property.

Selling Your Home at a Loss (Ouch!)

Paying taxes on a profit is always preferable to the alternative — saving taxes on a loss — but if you have one bad apple in your bunch, you can sell it at a loss and deduct the loss from the profits you make on other properties. As a flipper, losing money on a property isn't your goal, but if you know that the longer you hold a property, the more you're going to lose on it, sometimes cutting your losses on one property so you can focus on other, more-profitable investments is a wise move.

In addition to cutting your losses, selling at a loss may give you a tax break. Depending on how long you held the property prior to selling it, you can deduct the loss against any capital gains you've earned on other properties or other investments up to a certain limit.

Don't rush to take a loss on a property. Sure, if the property shows no signs of appreciating and it's sucking money, now may be the time to cut your losses and move on. However, if the area's in a housing slump and you think that it has potential, consider holding and renting the property until the market improves (see Chapter 3 for more about this flipping strategy). Analyze the situation and do what's best for your bottom line.

Paying Income Tax: When Flipping Houses Becomes Your Occupation

You decide to keep your day job and moonlight as a house flipper, buying and selling one or two properties a year to supplement your income. In such cases, the IRS considers your profits investment income subject to capital-gains tax. When you begin earning big bucks flipping houses and quit your day job, you suddenly become a house flipper, and your profits become self-employment income — subject to income tax and a whopping 15 percent self-employment tax.

If your annual income places you in the 28 percent tax bracket, for example, you can expect to pay about 40 percent in federal taxes alone. Why not 43 percent (28 percent tax bracket plus 15 percent self-employment tax)? Because you can deduct the 15 percent self-employment tax when figuring your income tax, which gives you a tiny break.

Because everyone's tax portrait is unique, I can't tell you whether the IRS earmarks your profits as capital gains or self-employment income, but I can provide you with a list of determining factors:

- The purpose for which you purchase the property
- The amount of time you hold the property
- The number of deals you do over the course of the tax year
- Your total sales over the course of the tax year
- The amount of income from the sales of property compared with income from your day job

No hard-and-fast rules govern the way the IRS (or your state or local taxing authority) looks at these numbers. What's most important is that you follow the rules to the best of your ability and accurately report your income and expenses. Consult your CPA or tax specialist for details to ensure that you meet the federal, state, and local tax requirements.

I hear plenty of stories about tax preparers who creatively underreport income and over-report expenses. If you bump into someone like this, turn around and start running in the opposite direction. If they're willing to do it for you, they're probably doing it for dozens of other clients already, and eventually they'll get caught.

Right after you close on the sale of a property, visit your tax expert and find out how much of your profit you owe to Uncle Sam. Remit that amount as part of your next estimated quarterly payment at the time that payment is due.

Part VI
The Part of Tens

Visit www.dummies.com/extras/flippinghouses for ten bonus tips on how to slash the costs of repairs and renovations.

In this part...

- Discover ten ways to find trash-into-cash opportunities in your local real estate market.
- Recognize the ten signs of a great real estate investment opportunity.
- Avoid the ten most common mistakes that make a flip flop.

Chapter 24

Ten Ways to Find Dontwanners

In This Chapter

- Discovering diamonds in the rough close to home
- Digging up properties on a host of websites
- Finding foreclosure, bank-owned, and probate properties
- Networking and advertising to attract opportunities

The most important step in the house-flipping process is Step 1: Find a property that you can purchase, renovate, hold, and sell for at least a 20 percent profit. Step 1 is often the hardest, especially when you're just getting started.

Where do you look for *dontwanners* — properties that the owners don't want and are willing to let go of at bargain-basement prices? In this chapter, I reveal ten ways to find dontwanners.

Cruising the Neighborhood

Drive, walk, or bicycle around your neighborhood in search of dontwanners. Some of the best properties may not be on the market or in foreclosure, so look for the following signs and symptoms of dontwanners:

- Overstuffed mailbox
- Porch littered with newspapers
- Overgrown lawn
- House looks vacant inside
- Foreclosure notice on the front door
- Cheap For Sale or For Sale By Owner (FSBO) sign

TIP: If you spot a dontwanner, try to contact the owners to see if they want to sell the house. If someone's living in the house, knock on the front door and spark up a conversation. If the house is vacant, ask the neighbors if they know who owns it.

Teaming Up with a Great Real Estate Agent

A great real estate agent, preferably a member of the National Association of Realtors, knows the market in the area you're interested in investing in and can lead you to the best deals. An excellent candidate not only has access to all of the MLS listings in your area but also knows how to explore other channels, including foreclosure, probate, and bankruptcy properties. For more about tracking down a real estate agent with the right stuff, check out Chapter 4.

TIP: Reward your real estate agent by hiring her to handle both the purchase and sale of the property so she earns a commission on both ends of the transaction. Also consider paying a commission that's 1 percent or 2 percent higher than normal. Just be sure to account for the additional cost when you're calculating how much money to pay for the property.

Checking Classified Ads and Online Listings

People sell stuff, even houses, through all sorts of interesting channels, including classified ads in newspapers, on Craigslist, and on self-listing (For Sale By Owner) services. And most real estate agents list properties for sale on their websites. Here are a few sites you may want to check out:

- `Realtor.com`
- `Homes.com`
- `ForSaleByOwner.com`
- `Hubzu.com`
- `Zillow.com`
- `Trulia.com`
- `Craigslist.com`

TIP

Visit the websites of local newspapers and check out their classified ads. Most classified listings include a section for homes for sale.

Skimming Foreclosure Notices

Whenever a bank forecloses on a property, it notifies the sheriff's department in the county in which the property is located, and the sheriff is responsible for managing the foreclosure process and evicting anyone residing in the home. The sheriff's department or, more commonly, a private company that the sheriff's department hires, publishes foreclosure notices in the local newspaper or legal news and almost always lists the foreclosures online.

One of the best ways to find foreclosure notices for a specific county is to search the web for "sheriff sale" followed by the name of your county and state, click the link for the county website or sheriff's page on the county website, and then click the link for info about sheriff sales. This is likely to take you to a site or page that lists the foreclosure properties for sale and provides valuable information, including when and where auctions are held and the rules that govern foreclosure auctions in your county. If the site has a frequently asked questions (FAQ) page, read it.

If you can't find foreclosure notices for your county on the web, contact your county sheriff's department and ask where foreclosure properties are listed online. I'd be very surprised if your county doesn't list foreclosures online somewhere.

TIP

Several third-party websites, including `RealtyTrac.com` and `foreclosure.com`, feature searchable foreclosure listings.

Monitoring Tax Sales

Unlike foreclosure sales, which are processed through the county sheriff's department, tax sales are processed through the county auditor. To find out about tax sales in your county, follow a process similar to the one I explain in the previous section regarding how to find info on foreclosure sales. Search the web for "auditor tax sale" followed by the name of your county and state, click the link for the county website or auditor's page on the county website, and then click the link for info about tax sales. This is likely to take you to a site or page where you can find more information about tax sales in your county and a listing of properties on the tax sale list. The tax sale list is commonly posted in a local newspaper or local legal newspaper, as well.

TIP: If you can't find the tax sale listings for your county on the web, contact your county auditor and ask where the tax sale notices are listed online or published in print.

Scoping Out Bank-Owned Properties

When a bank forecloses on a property, that property ends up in a foreclosure sale (a sheriff sale), but that doesn't necessarily result in an investor purchasing the property. The bank gets to set the opening bid and may even send a representative to the sale to bid up that opening price. If nobody else is willing to bid the amount the bank wants, then the bank ends up with the property. These properties are commonly referred to as real estate owned (REO) or bank-owned properties.

One of the best ways to find out about and acquire REO properties is to establish relationships with REO property managers at one or more of your local banks. If they come to know you as someone who can come up with the cash to buy REO properties and who follows through on deals, you may become their go-to guy or gal when they have properties to sell.

You can also find REO properties on various websites. Here's a short list to get you started:

- `HomePath.com` (Fannie Mae)
- `HomeSteps.com` (Freddie Mac)
- `HUDHomestore.com` (Department of Housing and Urban Development)

TIP: Many banks list REO properties on their websites. For example, you can visit foreclosures.bankofamerica.com, reo.wellsfargo.com, or servicing.chase.com/reo/property to search for REO properties at these large banks.

Probing Probate Properties

Whenever an estate ends up in probate, whoever's in charge of settling the estate usually has property she needs to sell in order to liquidate assets (turn them into cash), so she can pay any outstanding debts, taxes, and administration fees and distribute whatever's left to the beneficiaries of the estate.

To find probate properties, you first need to get your hands on a list of probate cases filed during the past six months or so. Head to your county clerk's office and ask for a list. Another great way to track down probate properties is to rub elbows with local attorneys who handle probate cases. Probate attorneys often need the services of real estate investors like you to purchase houses.

You can also find announcements of probate sales in your local newspaper. However, the earlier in the process you get involved, the better chance you have of obtaining the property because you have less competition for it. For more about finding and buying probate properties, see Chapter 9.

Digging Up Houses in Bankruptcy

Discovering bargains in bankruptcy is difficult because attorney-client privilege prohibits attorneys from sharing a client's information with anyone, let alone publishing client information. In addition, free sites don't publish personal bankruptcies except in certain cases when the bankruptcy is linked to a probate case. In other words, you're unlikely to find out about a bankruptcy unless it's linked to a celebrity or other high-profile individual or the person in bankruptcy tells you about it. However, you can find out about bankruptcies through any of the following sources:

- `Pacer.gov`, a subscription service that provides *public access to court electronic records* (PACER)
- Bankruptcy filings at the federal courthouse
- Court-appointed bankruptcy trustees
- Personal bankruptcy attorneys

Sifting through the Government's Stash

Government entities often end up with dontwanners for various reasons. Most of the properties the government owns are the result of homeowners defaulting on government-sponsored mortgage loans — those backed by the Department of Housing and Urban Development (HUD), the Department of Veterans Affairs (VA), Fannie Mae, and Freddie Mac. I explain how to search for these homes in the section "Scoping Out Bank-Owned Properties" earlier in this chapter. But the government ends up with properties for other reasons, too. For example, the Internal Revenue Service (IRS) may seize property for the non-payment of income tax.

To find government-owned properties that aren't on the "Scoping Out Bank-Owned Properties" list, check out the following websites:

- homesales.gov
- www.fdic.gov/buying/owned
- www.treasury.gov/auctions/irs
- www.resales.usda.gov
- propertydisposal.gsa.gov

Networking and Advertising for Leads

When a property is listed for sale or appears in a foreclosure notice, the information is out there, and other real estate investors in your area can find out about it as easily as you can. To reduce or eliminate the competition, try to insert yourself in the process as early as possible — before the property's availability becomes public knowledge.

The best way to get the jump on other investors is to build such a solid reputation in your area as an honest and reliable real estate investor that people bring golden opportunities to you:

- Let everyone in your neighborhood know what you do — you buy, renovate, and sell homes.
- Network with people in the real estate business, including agents, mortgage brokers, REO managers at banks, title company reps, and people who do construction. In addition to providing valuable assistance at different stages of the flipping process, all of these people can be a source for leads.
- Network with people who need to dispose of properties or who need to help their clients dispose of properties, including foreclosure and bankruptcy attorneys and trustees, divorce lawyers, and probate attorneys.
- Print and distribute business cards to everyone you meet and ask them to pass your contact information along to anyone who needs to get rid of a home in a hurry.
- Place an ad in your local newspaper that says "We Buy Homes" and include your contact information.
- Spread the word online via Craigslist, social-networking sites, local newspaper websites, and more.

Chapter 25

Ten Signs of a Great House-Flipping Opportunity

In This Chapter

- Spotting real estate hot spots
- Working with homeowners who are eager to sell
- Discovering properties that look much worse than they are

Successful house flipping demands that you execute a series of successful steps, but the most important step is the first one — locating a property at a price low enough for you to fix it up and sell it at a profit. If you trip when taking that first step, your profit is doomed to take a hit. In this chapter, I point out ten signs of a great house-flipping opportunity to help you get over that first hurdle. For more tips on finding excellent flipping candidates, check out Part II.

The Location Is an Obvious Hot Spot

In any neighborhood where housing demand exceeds supply, you have a much wider margin of error. When housing values are rising at an annual rate of 10 percent to 15 percent, you make money simply by buying and holding a property. You make even more money if you can acquire a property at a discount — a distressed property.

Observe the housing market in your area and identify the trendy areas — where people would live if they could afford to. Head to Chapter 6 for more information about targeting different neighborhoods.

Nobody's Home

In your target area, you know the sale prices of homes in various price brackets. After you identify the high-rent district, drive or walk around the neighborhood and look for the following signs of a vacant property:

- Overstuffed mailbox
- Newspapers piled on the front porch
- Weedy or overgrown lawn
- No window dressings
- No furniture inside the house

Jot down the address and head to Chapter 10 for a refresher on how to research distressed properties.

The "For Sale By Owner" Ad Is Shrinking

Sell-it-yourself homeowners often begin advertising with $50 or $100 ads. The longer the property is on the market, the less money the homeowner has available for advertising, so the ads keep getting smaller and smaller. A tiny ad is a great sign that the homeowner is getting desperate and beginning to realize that the property may not be worth the original asking price. If a homeowner places a 4-inch ad, he isn't ready to bargain yet.

Keep tabs on the classified For Sale By Owner (FSBO) ads on a weekly basis and take note of any ads that seem to be shrinking or are lingering for several weeks. Shrinking ads are the most attractive. Head to Chapter 7 for more information about FSBO properties.

The Seller Is Highly Motivated to Be Freed from the Burden of Ownership

Part of your success as a flipper hinges on your willingness to be an ambulance chaser — to capitalize on the misfortune of others. You find your best deals when homeowners are facing foreclosure, when they're getting divorced, or when a family member dies and the property ends up in probate or goes to relatives who already have a place to live. Here are some helpful tips on finding and handling these types of deals:

- Act professionally and with integrity. A homeowner's misfortune may lead to a great deal, but what they're experiencing is real pain. You can help and earn a fair profit at the same time.
- When a property is passed down to relatives, two or more relatives may own the property together and be unable to agree on what to do with it. In these situations, you may have more luck by negotiating separately with each owner. Chapter 9 has more information on finding probate properties.
- Whenever you're dealing with a divorce or probate attorney, send a letter of introduction and follow up with a face-to-face meeting explaining who you are and what you do. The relationship may produce future leads.
- Stay on top of the foreclosure notices in your target area. Remain vigilant of any signs of divorce: comments from the seller or seller's agent, only men's or only women's clothes in the closet, or any news flowing through the neighborhood grapevine. Chapter 8 delivers the full scoop on foreclosures.

The House Is Ugly Outside

To a flipper, the ugliest home on the block is the bombshell on the boardwalk. The homeowner wants to sell the property, but the exterior looks so bad that it's driving away paying customers. When you're an investor, ugly homes should have the opposite effect on you — they should grab your attention and pull you inside.

The House Is Ugly Inside

The landscaping and outer shell of the house may be attractive enough to draw visitors, but if the interior is ugly, it can push prospective buyers right out the door.

Some houses just don't show well for any of several reasons. Sometimes the owners appear to be color-blind, picking color schemes that make normal people gag. In other cases, the homeowners put no effort into staging the house. Whatever the reason, if the structure is sound and the floor plan works, the filth, clutter, and foul smells may be to your advantage. You can acquire the property at a discount, do some heavy-duty cleaning, properly stage the home, and make a good profit with a very small investment. (Chapter 15 shows you how to give a house a quick pick-me-up, and Chapter 21 features a home-staging checklist.)

The Decor Is Outdated

A house may be clean and properly maintained, but if the decor has fallen out of style with time, it can repel buyers as quickly as a herd of roaches. Of course, if you're dealing in historical homes, vintage decor may be a big plus, but if the decor is old without the accompanying elegance, you can quickly redecorate and place the property right back on the market. Such houses are a perfect opportunity for a quick flip, as I describe in Chapter 15.

The House Has Character

Some homes have panache. Something about them just has a universal appeal. Maybe the floor plan makes the human soul feel expansive. Perhaps the landscaping creates a sense that you've returned to the Garden of Eden. Or perhaps the decor pulls everything together and creates a healthy balance. Whatever it is, you know it when you see it. Don't dismiss the value of character when looking at houses. Character sells.

The House Has Undeveloped Living Space

Look for properties with unused or underutilized attic space or an enclosed porch, and modify that space to make it livable. An extra bedroom or bath typically raises the value of the home the most, but home offices are popular. If the house has an attic that's too small to use for living space and it needs a new roof anyway, calculate the costs and benefits of adding a dormer. Chapter 19 has details on reconfiguring spaces.

The Property Backs Up to Nothing

Few homeowners like to have neighbors in their backyards. They prefer having their yards back up to a wooded area, a park, or even a cemetery. If you find a property that has all the essential qualities of a good flip *and* the property backs up to nothing, you've struck gold. Just make sure, before you make your offer, that all the numbers work and that the zoning board doesn't have plans in the works to rezone the area behind the property for commercial or industrial use.

Chapter 26

Ten Common House-Flipping Blunders

In This Chapter

- Falling prey to con artists
- Playing hooky from your homework during the purchase process
- Waffling your way to a lost opportunity
- Doing too little (or too much) work on a property

Many eager, ill-informed investors become overenthusiastic about the big picture and lose sight of the critical details that can make or break a deal. They pay too much for a property, underestimate the cost of repairs and renovations, fail to inspect a property or research the title, or sign contracts that they don't fully understand. In this chapter, I present ten common house-flipping blunders to help you avoid costly mistakes and maximize your profits from the start.

Falling for a Scam

WARNING!

Money attracts entrepreneurs, but it also attracts thieves. When you flip a house, you stand to earn tens of thousands of dollars on a single transaction, but being successful requires determination, diligence, and hard work. Don't let anyone convince you otherwise. Don't be a sucker. Be on guard for the following threats:

- Get-rich-quick schemes, cash-back-at-closing schemes, no-money-down deals, and anything else that sounds too good to be true
- Partnerships, especially those that require you to take on all the risk, supply most of the money, or do most of the work
- Anyone who offers to take care of everything for you

See Chapter 1 for more warnings about house-flipping scams and illegal and unethical practices.

Speculating on the Housing Market

Like the stock market, the housing market has its ups and downs. In a hot market, investors often become infected with irrational exuberance — the belief that current appreciation rates are an accurate representation of future rates. They overpay for properties, expecting them to appreciate, and when the market flattens or takes a dive, they're stuck with a property they need to sell at a price no buyer is willing to pay. Don't bank on double-digit increases in housing values, and be prepared with plan B. Chapter 20 explains a few options for plan B, including holding a property and leasing it out to tenants until the market recovers.

Waffling on an Obviously Good Deal

Some investors experience paralysis by analysis. They overanalyze a great deal and can actually talk themselves out of it, or they waffle until another investor shows interest, and then it's often too late.

When you see a good deal, act quickly. You don't necessarily need to buy the property right away, but by making an offer on the property, you can tie it up for several days, so you can research the title and inspect the property (I cover these tasks later in this chapter).

Backing Yourself into a Contractual Corner

Very rarely do people hand you contracts to sign that protect your rights or interests. They hand you contracts that protect their rights and interests. Before you sign a contract or purchase agreement, read it carefully and make sure that it has a weasel clause — a legal back door through which you can make a graceful exit. See Chapter 11 for a complete discussion of conditional (weasel) clauses.

Failing to Inspect the Property before Closing on It

Don't rely on the seller's claims and disclosures. The real estate community has a saying: "Buyers are liars, and sellers are worse, and sellers by owner eat their young." Have the house inspected. A city inspection is best because it provides you with an inspection team consisting of a professional plumber, an electrician, a heating and air conditioning specialist, and a builder (for structural features). In some areas, however, city inspections are unavailable or are performed only on new construction.

If you're buying a house at a foreclosure sale, obtaining a thorough home inspection before handing over the cash may not be an option, but you should inspect the home yourself as thoroughly as possible. Drive by the house, inspect the outside, and do what you can to get inside to take a look around. The less you know about a property, the higher you should set your margin to cover unexpected costs. Check out Chapter 11 for additional information about house inspections.

Assuming the Title Is Clear

Anyone can sell a property. Even people who don't own a property can sell it. Some con artists wait until the owner takes an extended vacation. They move into the house, pose as the owner, print out a fake title, and sell it to an eager but clueless buyer. Sometimes, they sell the house to several buyers!

Another possibility is that a homeowner may try to sell you a house without telling you that the property has multiple liens against it. Unless you research the title and have the title company perform a title search (see Chapter 4 for details on hiring a title company), you can't be sure that the title is clear or even valid or that the person selling the house really owns it. And if you're not 100 percent certain, don't buy the property. See Chapter 10 for guidance on how to research properties and their records.

Underestimating the Cost of Repairs and Renovations

When a contractor tells a homeowner that a complete kitchen remodel costs about $30,000, the homeowner acts like one of those old geezers who grew up during the Great Depression, when you could buy a candy bar for a nickel. Beginning investors often experience that same sense of sticker shock when they hire contractors to perform repairs and renovations. Just make sure that you have your sticker shock *before* you buy a property, not after you own it — when it's too late to do anything about it. For necessary repairs and renovations, you should have an accurate estimate of all costs before you buy a property. You can jot down notes while you're inspecting a property and then consult repair and renovation services to obtain estimates. See Chapter 11 for more about inspecting a property and drawing up a budget for repairs and renovations.

Doing Shoddy Work to Save Money

Sellers have all sorts of tactics to cover defects in a home. They may carpet over a floor that has extensive water or termite damage, pump out a septic tank that's gone bad so the toilets keep flushing for a couple more months, or install wood paneling in the basement to hide defects in the foundation.

As an investor who wants to remain in business, you should treat these tactics as taboo. Don't sell your soul for a few thousand dollars.

Over-Improving a Property

Transforming a bungalow into the Taj Mahal may be a noble vision, but it ultimately lands you in the poorhouse. Know the housing market in your area and routinely visit open houses to remain abreast of current trends and market demands. Gauge repairs and renovations to meet or slightly exceed what's currently selling in your area. Your renovated home should be more appealing than comparable homes in the area, but not excessively more appealing.

Forgetting to Pay the Taxes

In the flurry of flipping, taxes are easy to overlook, especially property taxes. Forgetting to pay your taxes, however, can further complicate your flipping operation, and back taxes and penalties can take a big chunk out of your future profits.

Set aside a certain percentage of your profit from each flip in a separate account, and pay your taxes out of that account. This separate account reduces the temptation to spend the money you owe to the government. If you fall behind on taxes, catching up can be tough. Check out Chapter 23 for additional information about taxes and tips on trimming your tax bill.

Index

• Numerics •

• A •

• B •

• C •

• F •

• G •

• H •

• I •

• J •

• K •

• L •

• M •

• N •

• O •

• P •

• Q •

• R •

• S •

• T •

• U •

• V •

• W •

• Z •

About the Authors

Ralph R. Roberts's success in real estate sales is legendary. He has been profiled by the Associated Press, CNN, and *Time* magazine and has done hundreds of radio interviews. Ralph is a seasoned professional in all areas of house flipping, including buying homes, rehabbing them, and reselling them quickly and at a handsome profit. He has penned several successful titles, including *Foreclosure Investing For Dummies* (Wiley), *Financing Real Estate Investments For Dummies* (Wiley), *Foreclosure Self-Defense For Dummies* (Wiley), *Loan Modification For Dummies* (Wiley), *52 Weeks of Sales Success* (Wiley), and *Protect Yourself from Real Estate and Mortgage Fraud* (Kaplan). In *Flipping Houses For Dummies,* Ralph reveals the tips and tricks he has hammered out in his more-than-40-year career.

Joe Kraynak is a freelance author who has written and coauthored dozens of books on topics ranging from slam poetry to computer basics. Joe teamed up with Dr. Candida Fink to write his first book in the *For Dummies* series, *Bipolar Disorder For Dummies,* where he showcased his talent for translating the complexities of a topic into plain-spoken, practical advice. In *Flipping Houses For Dummies,* Joe teams up with legendary real estate pro Ralph R. Roberts to produce the ultimate guide to profitable real estate flipping — flipping the right way.

Dedications

From Ralph: This book is dedicated to the people who believed in me most. To my wife Kathleen, without whom none of my dreams would be possible. To my core supports, Ray Confer, Joe Sirianni, Frank Giannetti, Dave Wilson, Dale Hadel, Bob Van Goethem, Dave Constantine, Domenic Belcastro, Ed Stanek, Michael Huffer, Mike DiGiovanni, Norm Confer, and Hannah McCollum.

From Joe: To my brother John, who kept asking me when this book would come out, and whose eagerness and enthusiasm inspired me to do my best.

Author's Acknowledgments

Although we wrote the book, dozens of other talented individuals contributed to its conception, development, and perfection. Special thanks go to acquisitions editor Lindsay Lefevere, who chose us to author this book and guided us through the tough part of getting started. Chrissy Guthrie, our project editor, deserves a round of applause for acting as a very patient choreographer — shuffling chapters back and forth, shepherding the text and photos through production, making sure any technical issues were properly resolved, and serving as unofficial quality-control manager. Thanks also to Ashley Petry, our copy editor, who read through everything — forward and backward — to identify and obliterate our many grammatical goofs and typos.

Throughout the writing of this book, we relied heavily on a knowledgeable and dedicated support staff, who provided expert advice, tips, and research, so we could deliver the most comprehensive and useful information. For this second edition, special thanks go to Kyle Roberts, who served as point person for Team Ralph, shuffling e-mail messages back and forth, gathering information, and writing most of the new material. To Jim Maiorano, who contributed his expertise to guide the outline of the book and supply priceless insights from real-world experiences. Thanks also to the other members of Team Ralph — Jessica Rice, Heather Eliasz, and Steve Mogdis, who all contributed their experience and expertise in developing the new material on investing in probate properties and other special markets. We owe special thanks to our technical editor, accomplished real estate pro Libby Cyman, for ferreting out technical errors in the manuscript, helping guide its content, and offering her own tips and tricks.

Publisher's Acknowledgments

Executive Editor: Lindsay Sandman Lefevere

Senior Project Editor: Christina Guthrie

Copy Editor: Ashley Petry

Technical Editor: Libby Cyman

Art Coordinator: Alicia B. South

Project Coordinator: Rebekah Brownson

Photographer: Jeremy Goodell

Cover Image: ©iStockphoto.com/pavlen